West Academic Publishing's Law School Advisory Board

Bankruptcy

Bruce A. Markell
Professor of Bankruptcy Law and Practice
Northwestern University
School of Law

Lawrence Ponoroff
Samuel M. Fegtly Chair in Commercial Law
The University of Arizona
James E. Rogers College of Law

A SHORT & HAPPY GUIDE® SERIES

WEST
ACADEMIC
PUBLISHING

A Short & Happy Guide Series is a trademark registered in the U.S. Patent and Trademark Office.

© 2016 LEG, Inc. d/b/a West Academic

    444 Cedar Street, Suite 700
    St. Paul, MN 55101
    1-877-888-1330

Printed in the United States of America

ISBN: 978-1-63459-493-6

Table of Contents

Introduction

Bankruptcy is a *big* subject, but this is a short (and happy) guide. So we're not going to chase down every doctrinal nuance or try to fill you up with minutia. Rather, our main goal is to introduce you to the core concepts and major themes underlying bankruptcy law. Oh sure, we'll cover a lot of the "rules" of bankruptcy law; that's unavoidable. But the real value of this guide will be (we hope) to give you the tools you need to think about, understand, and find the answer to almost any bankruptcy problem. In other words, we want to help you become a bankruptcy *architect*, and not just a technician. In order to do this, we will approach our subject organically, focusing not just on the "what" and "how" questions, but just as importantly on the "why" questions.

It's just a fact of life that sometimes people do not or cannot pay their debts, and sometimes businesses fail. A sophisticated credit economy like ours needs a mechanism to deal with these problems. Bankruptcy is an important part of that solution, and bankruptcy cases run the gambit from cases involving individuals like all of us who fall upon hard times to cases involving Fortune 500 companies like General Motors, and everything in-between. Therefore, although their practices may be very different, you will find bankruptcy lawyers on Main Street and on Wall Street, and while their cases may have very little in common, they are all using the same statute—the Federal Bankruptcy Code.

Bankruptcy is not our legal system's only response to financial distress. Bankruptcy operates alongside, and as an alternative to state debt collection law. The two systems, however, are based on very different premises, and, for this reason, we believe an awful lot about bankruptcy can be understood right up front by contrasting the operation and goals of the bankruptcy system with the state collection law system.

First, state collection law focuses on each individual creditor's collection effort against the debtor; it is not by and large concerned with the rights of creditors as a group. Second, state collection law is what we sometimes call "grab law," meaning that the race goes to the swiftest; that is, the creditor that reaches the debtor's property first gets all the value of that property, at least until its judgment is satisfied, before later creditors get anything. If you come from a big family, think about mealtime and you probably get the idea. Third, because the race goes to the swiftest, once creditors get wind that the debtor may be experiencing financial difficulties, the feeding frenzy begins and any hope the debtor might have had of reversing its fortunes are out the door, literally and figuratively. Fourth, because the state law execution process calls for the forced sale of the debtor's property at auction, state collection law produces notoriously low values for the debtor's property; *i.e.*, much lower than would be attained if the property could be sold in an orderly, market transaction. Finally, federal bankruptcy law offers a form of debtor relief—the discharge from prepetition debts—that the states do not and, because of the "impairment of contracts" clause in Article 1 of the Constitution, cannot provide.

The last point bears emphasis, as our bankruptcy law is simultaneously about two very different interests: debtor protection and creditor rights. There is no perfect balance between these interests and, inevitably, where the fulcrum is placed by Congress at any point in time is a function of a variety of largely non-legal considerations, not the least of which are political in nature. Senator Charles Grassley (R. Iowa) thinks bankruptcy goes too far in providing debtor relief; Senator Elizabeth Warren (D. Mass.) thinks it doesn't go far enough. We suggest *you* always be thinking in the background, "does this rule go too far in favor of debtors, or too far in favor of creditors, or, like in Goldilocks, is it just about right"?

A Short & Happy Guide to Bankruptcy

Overview of Bankruptcy

A. A Little (but Still More than You Care About) History

Bankruptcy law can be traced all the way back through the medieval Italian city-states to Roman law. England adopted specific bankruptcy statutes in the sixteenth century, and amended those statutes from time to time thereafter. U.S. bankruptcy law was initially based on English law as it existed in the late eighteenth and mid-nineteenth centuries. What is most notable about early bankruptcy law is that it was not much (or really any) about debtor relief. Rather, it was seen purely as a mechanism for creditors to hold accountable debtors who were attempting to evade responsibility for their debts, and to maximize returns (payouts) for those creditors.

Probably as a reaction to the dizzying array of insolvency laws that existed during the colonial period and under the Articles of Confederation, and to promote commerce, the Framers determined to grant Congress with the authority in Article 1, § 8, clause 4 of the Constitution to establish "uniform Laws on the subject of Bankruptcies."

1

Congress exercised its authority under the Bankruptcy Clause several times during the Nineteenth Century, passing national bankruptcy legislation in 1800, 1841, and 1867. Each of these bills, however, was a short-term response to economic upheavals ("panics"), and was repealed as soon as the crisis passed. The first enduring bankruptcy law was the Bankruptcy Act of 1898, the need for which not coincidentally coincided with the latter stages of the Industrial Revolution. The 1898 Act remained in place until it was replaced by our current law of bankruptcy, which became effective in 1979.

It should be noted that until the 1841 Act, American bankruptcy law made no provision for voluntary filing by the debtor (then called "the bankrupt") or for the debtor's discharge or relief from debts, both of which are historically fairly late arrivals on the scene. That is to say, for most of its long history, bankruptcy was simply a collective remedy for assembling and then dividing the debtor's assets among the debtor's creditors.

B. The Bankruptcy Reform Act of 1978

Based on the probably accurate view that the 1898 Act had become irretrievably out-of-date, in 1973 Congress began to explore a new bankruptcy law. The result was the Bankruptcy Reform Act of 1978 (11 U.S.C. §§ 101 et seq.), which is the basis for our current bankruptcy law. The 1978 Act has been amended on numerous occasions, most dramatically with the Bankruptcy Abuse Prevention and Reform Act of 2005 (hereinafter referred to as either "the 2005 Amendments" or "BAPCPA.") Most people agree that the 2005 Amendments were a lot more about abuse prevention than they were about consumer protection. The Bankruptcy Reform 1978 Act as amended is generally referred to throughout this book as the "Bankruptcy Code" or just the "Code."

The structure underlying the Bankruptcy Code is relatively straightforward. Chapters 1 through 5 apply in all types of bankruptcy cases. Chapters 1 through 3 deal, respectively, with "definitions," "administration" and "claims and creditors."

The remaining five Chapters represent different types of debtor relief cases under which a bankruptcy petition may be filed. They include:

- Chapter 7 cases. In a Chapter 7 case, the property of the debtor is surrendered to a trustee, liquidated (that is, sold for cash), and then distributed more or less pro rata to unsecured creditors. In return, individual (that is, human) debtors receive a discharge from all but certain statutorily enumerated categories of prefiling debt. Non-humans (corporations, partnerships, limited liability companies and the like) do not receive a discharge in Chapter 7; they have to wait until Chapter 11. Numerically, the overwhelming number of bankruptcy filings today are individual Chapter 7 cases.

- Chapter 11 reorganization cases. Chapter 11 is designed primarily for businesses (human or non-human) with fixable financial problems, thus contemplating continuation rather than liquidation of the business. The goal in a Chapter 11 case is, ultimately, to confirm of a plan of reorganization that will set forth the obligations of the reorganized debtor, and to discharge those obligations not contained in the plan. That said, however, sometimes the Chapter 11 plan will call for the liquidation of the debtor's assets.

- <u>Chapter 13 debt adjustment cases.</u> These are rehabilitation proceedings for individuals (that is, humans) who, instead of surrendering their property in return for a discharge, retain that property and propose a plan for the repayment of all or some of their debts over a period of three to five years out of the debtor's future income. Chapter 13 is not available to an individual whose debts more than certain statutorily defined limits for both secured and unsecured debt.

- <u>Chapter 12 debt adjustment cases.</u> Chapter 12 proceedings are quite similar to Chapter 13 cases, but they are designed for and limited to statutorily defined "family farmers" (or "family fishermen") who, in all likelihood, are not eligible for Chapter 13 relief and cannot absorb the expense and delay associated with Chapter 11 cases. Chapter 12 bears a great deal of similarity to Chapter 13, except for higher debt limits, the ability to modify home mortgage loans, and of course who is eligible to file for relief thereunder.

- <u>Chapter 9 cases.</u> This chapter of the Code is for cases involving the reorganization of municipalities and governmental agencies—the most notable recent such case being the City of Detroit.

- <u>Chapter 15 cases.</u> Chapter 15 pertains to cross-border insolvency proceedings, and permits a trustee or other representative in a foreign proceeding to seek recognition of the case in a U.S. bankruptcy court in order to deal with assets located in the U.S.

Of the debtor relief chapters, our focus will be almost exclusively on Chapters 7, 11, and 13.

C. The Role of Nonbankruptcy Law in Bankruptcy

Although bankruptcy law is supreme federal law (just check Article VI of the Constitution), it cannot operate without other non-bankruptcy law, which most often includes state law. This is because there is no pervasive federal commercial law. Rather, commercial law and the property interests which drive it are largely created under state law. For the most part, bankruptcy law recognizes those property interests, subject to whatever attributes, limitations, and characteristics they have been assigned under state law. So, for example, whether Markell owes a debt to Ponoroff will usually be determined under state contract or tort law, as may be the case, and whether that debt is secured or unsecured and what priority it enjoys vis-à-vis other debts will also depend on state real or personal property finance law. Except where a compelling federal interest dictates otherwise, bankruptcy does not change the result.[1]

Sometime, the applicable nonbankruptcy law will be other federal law. This is often the case when the creditor is a federal governmental agency, like the IRS (think tax liens), or when the property interests are federal in nature (think copyright and patents). Again, the rights and obligations that governmental creditor brings into the bankruptcy case are determined under nonbankruptcy federal law, but, as with state law-based claims, they are then processed as provided for by the substantive law of the Bankruptcy Code and the applicable procedural rules.

D. Procedure in Bankruptcy Cases

A bankruptcy "case" under any chapter of the Code involves the administration of an *estate*—"In re Debtor"—a concept we'll

---

[1]   This principle is sometimes referred to as the Butner Rule, referring to the Supreme Court's decision in *Butner v. United States*, 440 U.S. 48 (1979).

come back to in detail later in Section B of Unit 3. Under the umbrella of the administration of that estate may be several discrete pieces of litigation over a variety of issues, such as the discharge of a debt or the confirmation of a plan. Even though bankruptcy law is federal law and bankruptcy litigation is federal litigation, the procedure within a bankruptcy case is governed not by the Federal Rules of Civil Procedure, but by the Federal Rules of Bankruptcy Procedure, what we will refer to in this book as "Bankr. R. 7001." The bankruptcy rules govern not only litigation in the case, but also the procedure governing the administration of the case, such as who gets notice of what and by when, etc. It's really not as complicated as it sounds, because most of the Federal Rules of Bankruptcy Procedure simply incorporate the Federal Rules of Civil Procedure (summary judgment in bankruptcy proceedings is essentially the same as in regular federal litigation; Bankr. R. 7056 starts by stating "Rule 56 F.R.Civ.P. applies in adversary proceedings. . . .")

Some litigation that occurs in a bankruptcy case is very similar to conventional civil litigation. These matters are referred to by the Bankruptcy Rules as "adversary proceedings" and they progress much like any ordinary piece of federal litigation. Adversary proceedings are captioned first by reference to the parties—"X v. Y"—and then by identifying the debtor's case in which they arise; e.g., "In re Debtor." So cases are reported as follows: X v. Y (In re Debtor). Sometimes the debtor is also the plaintiff or the defendant in the adversary proceeding.

Most disputes that arise in a bankruptcy case are resolved in a less formal proceeding known as a "contested matter." These disputes are usually raised by motion served by mail on the parties, rather than commenced by summons and complaint as is true for adversary proceedings. Bankr. R. 9014 governs contested matters, and any reported decision involving a contested matter is cited in the same way as the case itself is cited; i.e., "In re Debtor."

E. Bankruptcy Jurisdiction

This is a complicated, controversial, and currently very uncertain subject. Some professors don't cover it; others spend a lot of time on it. We'll just run through the basics here. First, as originally enacted in 1978, the Bankruptcy Code (1) provided that bankruptcy judges would be appointed under Article I of the Constitution, and (2) conferred jurisdiction over bankruptcy cases directly on the bankruptcy courts. The problem that concerned folks at the time was that this meant that the judicial power of the United States was being exercised by non-Article III courts (something about separation of powers ring a bell??).

The concern turned out to be warranted because in 1982 the Supreme Court, in *Northern Pipeline Constr. Co. v. Marathon Pipe Line Co.*,[2] declared the 1978 Act's entire jurisdictional scheme unconstitutional. For two years the system continued to operate under an emergency order fashioned by the Judicial Conference of the United States. Finally, after much political squabbling about whether bankruptcy judges should be reconstituted as Article III judges (the simple solution, which, of course, was rejected), in 1984 Congress passed the Bankruptcy Amendments and Federal Judgeship Act, which placed bankruptcy jurisdiction in the district courts under 28 U.S.C. § 1334. It also, however, under 28 U.S.C. § 157, allowed the district courts to "refer" most of that jurisdiction to the bankruptcy courts.

Under this system, bankruptcy courts hear matters arising in a bankruptcy case as a court of original jurisdiction and, then, depending on the nature of the proceeding, either enter final orders

---

[2]   458 U.S. 50 (1982).

subject to traditional appellate review, or make recommended findings of fact and conclusions of law that are reviewed *de novo* in the district court, which actually enters the final judgment. The distinction turned on whether the matter was deemed "core" or "non-core" under 28 U.S.C. § 157(b), with core proceedings involving matters essential to the adjustment of debtor/creditor relations, such as the dischargeability of particular debts, while non-core proceedings involving more traditional kinds of private disputes that require adjudication by an Article III judge—*Marathon*, for example, involved the debtor's common law contract suit against one of its (former) customers.

While far from perfect, the system muddled along under this arrangement until 2011, when the Supreme Court decided *Stern v. Marshall*,[3] In that case, the Court held that a bankruptcy judge appointed under Article I of the Constitution, lacking the life-tenure and protected compensation that Article III requires for other federal judges, may only enter final judgment on matters of "public right," even though the statute listed as a core proceedings certain matters of "non-public right," including the type of claim at issue in *Stern*. Thus, the distinction between core and non-core proceedings lost utility and the courts were thrown into uncertainty over (1) exactly what claims fell in the *Stern* category, and, as to such claims, (2) whether the parties could consent to the bankruptcy court's exercise of the judicial power so as to avoid the delay and expense involved with that uncertainty, and (3) what role the bankruptcy courts could play in such cases if consent was not granted or would be ineffective.

It took two more trips to the Supreme Court to answer those questions. First, in *Executive Benefits Ins. Agency v. Arkison (In re Bellingham Ins. Agency)*,[4] the Court punted on the first two

---

[3]   131 S.Ct. 2594 (2011).

[4]   134 S.Ct. 2165 (2014). Note here the structure of the citation we told you about earlier. The debtor was Bellingham Insurance Agency, and the dispute was an

questions and resolved only that *Stern* claims can be treated as non-core proceedings under 28 U.S.C. § 157(c), meaning that the bankruptcy courts can hear matters, but for their decision must submit proposed findings of fact and conclusions of law to the district court for its *de novo* review (anyone hear rubber stamps being sharpened?). Finally, in *Wellness Int'l Network, Ltd. v. Sharif*,[5] the Court held that the Constitution permits bankruptcy courts to adjudicate (that is, enter final orders subject only to traditional appellate review) *Stern* claims with the knowing and voluntary consent of the parties. The court also indicated that the consent necessary to waive adjudication by an Article III court need not be "express" and could be inferred from conduct as well as made by words. However, to the disappointment of many, the Court in *Wellness* did not clarify what claims fall under *Stern* in the first place, or what type of conduct would support an inference of consent, thus leaving considerable uncertainty still as to the scope of the bankruptcy courts' jurisdiction.

---

adversary proceeding between Executive Benefits Agency and Arkinson (the latter being the Chapter 7 trustee for the debtor)

[5]   135 S.Ct. 1932 (2015).

Initiating (and "Uninitiating") the Case

A. Voluntary Filings

Given that for most of its history bankruptcy was conceived as purely a creditors' remedy, and that voluntary bankruptcy is a relatively speaking late arrival of the scene, it's perhaps somewhat ironic that today the overwhelming (and we mean like 99 percent) of bankruptcy filings are initiated by the debtor filing a petition under section 301, or by joint (spousal) debtors filing under section 302. Bankruptcy relief is available in one form or another for virtually every debtor, but each debtor relief chapter of the Code has its own rules and limitations on who is eligible for relief under such chapter. These rules and limitations are found in Code section 109, the application of which requires frequent reference to the definitions in section 101.

When a debtor files a bankruptcy petition, that petition becomes the "order for relief" in the bankruptcy case. That means that all of the provisions of the Code now apply to the type of debtor who filed. There are no mandatory hearings on whether the debtor is insolvent or whether the debtor filed its case in good faith—although creditors might raise those issues later on, as we'll see.

Let's begin by asking under what chapters of the Code is Ponoroff (a human being, although Markell sometimes wonders about that) eligible to file? And let's take Chapters 9, 12, and 15 off the table since they are each for specialized kinds of debtors. The answer is Ponoroff is eligible to file under Chapter 7, 11, or 13, subject to one or two caveats. We know this because Ponoroff is a "person," defined in section 101(41) as including an *individual*, partnership, or corporation. Section 109(b) then says a "person" can be a debtor under Chapter 7. Section 109(d) makes a person eligible to file under Chapter 7 also eligible to file under Chapter 11. Finally, section 109(e) provides that Chapter 13 is open only to "individuals," the Code's way of referring to real living, breathing human beings. (There are, however, some limitations on the amount of secured and unsecured debt that Ponoroff, the individual, may have amassed and still be eligible under Chapter 13. We'll talk about those in a later Unit devoted to Chapter 13).

Speaking of limitations, since BAPCPA, individuals are not eligible to be a debtor under *any* chapter unless, within the 180 days preceding the date of filing, they have received a briefing from an approved nonprofit budget and credit counseling agency about opportunities for credit counseling and offered assistance in performing a budget analysis. *See* section 109(h). Exceptions to this requirement apply if the individual resides in a district where there are not enough approved agencies to serve all of the debtors in need, or in cases in which a debtor is able to show "exigent circumstances." In addition, section 109(g) imposes certain limitations on serial filings (not Kellogg's; *serial*, not *cereal*)—within 180 days of the pendency of a prior case dismissed either for willful failure to abide by a court order, or for a voluntarily dismissal after a creditor filed a motion for relief from stay (we get to those in Unit

3)—to prevent what are perceived as misuses of the bankruptcy process.

Now, how about the Markell Building and Loan Association ("MBLA")? Surely, MBLA is a "person," within the meaning of section 101(41), but section 109(b)(1) & (2) contain exclusions for railroads, insurance companies, and various kinds of bank and related entities, such as MBLA. Chapter 13 of course is not an option because MBLA is not an individual. That leaves Chapter 11, but no love there either. Other than railroads, only persons who would be eligible to file Chapter 7 may file under Chapter 11. Why do you suppose the Bankruptcy Code closes its doors to insurance companies, banks, and savings and loans? The answer lies in the fact that given the unique nature of these businesses, coupled with the special public policy considerations associated with insurance company and bank failure, we have special kinds of insolvency or receivership proceedings to handle these cases, usually at the state level. These types of procedures are not covered in introductory classes.

B. Involuntary Cases

Numerically few, but potentially important, are involuntary filings, controlled by section 303 of the Code. The filing of a petition also initiates an involuntary case, but, unlike in a voluntary filing, the petition filing does not operate as an "order for relief." Rather, it is more like a complaint in conventional civil litigation, meaning the debtor has the right to file an answer and contest the entry of an order for relief. The petitioning creditors have to show: (1) that the debtor is eligible for the relief sought (can be a debtor under the chapter indicated in the involuntary petition), (2) that the creditors have standing to file an involuntary case, and (3) that there are grounds (related to the number and amounts of debts outstanding) for the relief the creditors requested.

1. I Can't Be Put in an Involuntary Case (or at Least Not Under This Chapter)

Not every debtor who is eligible to file a voluntary petition is eligible to be an involuntary debtor. Under section 303(a), both not-for-profit corporations (think churches and charitable organizations) and farmers (including family farmers) may not be put in an involuntary case. Moreover, an involuntary case may only be filed under Chapter 7 or 11, meaning that there are no involuntary Chapter 13's. The reason for this exclusion is that, in addition to concerns that a "compulsory Chapter 13" might violate the Thirteenth Amendment, Congress correctly believed it was probably futile to allow an involuntary Chapter 13 case, since a debtor that did not want to work in order to make payments under a Chapter 13 plan would just not do so.

2. You Don't Have Standing to Put Me in an Involuntary Case

Section 303 also governs who has standing to bring an involuntary case. Section 303(b) has both a number and an amount test. Specifically, as to number, it requires at least three *qualifying* petitioning creditors, unless the debtor has less than 12 creditors, not counting certain creditors excluded by section 303(b)(2), such as employees or insiders of the debtor. As for the amount test, the petitioning creditor(s) must, in the aggregate, hold *qualifying* claims equal to (currently) $15,325.[6]

To qualify as a petitioning creditor, an entity must be the holder of a claim against the debtor that is (1) not contingent as to

---

[6] We say "currently" in the parenthetical before the amount—as we do in a number of other places throughout the book—because this is one of several dollar amount numbers in the Bankruptcy Code that adjusts every three years based on the Consumer Price Index. *See* section 104(a). The last adjustment became effective on April 1, 2013, and those are the numbers used in this book. Adjustments made under section 104(a) do not apply to cases filed before the date of each date.

liability (that is, it is not dependent on someone else's action; an example would be a guaranty of a debt for which the principal debtor was current), and (2) not subject to bona fide dispute as to liability or amount. Also, to count toward the $15,325 amount, at least that much of the noncontingent, undisputed claim must be *unsecured*. Although some courts treat a claim that has not been reduced to judgment as "contingent," the better view is that a contingent claim is one as to which liability depends on the happening or nonhappening of a future event not certain to occur—such as default by the principal debtor in the guaranty example.

Claims not reduced to judgment are at most unliquidated, which does not itself bar standing. This was particularly important before BAPCPA, when the "not subject to bona fide dispute" requirement was limited to "liability." Now a petitioning creditor's standing can be contested even if the alleged debtor acknowledges the debt, but claims a setoff in a lesser amount or simply disputes the amount of the debt.

3. You Don't Have Grounds to Put Me in an Involuntary Case

The grounds for involuntary relief [i.e., what the petitioning creditors must establish to obtain an order of relief from the court] are in section 303(h). They are either that (a) the debtor is insolvent in an equity sense; i.e., generally not paying current obligations as they come due, or (b) that a custodian was appointed in the 120 days preceding the filing to take possession of all or substantially all of the debtor's assets. The later ground gives creditors the right to have any nonbankruptcy collectivized debt collection proceeding, such as a state law assignment for the benefit of creditors, preempted in favor of a bankruptcy proceeding. The first ground, failure to pay current obligations as they come due, is by far the most common; indeed, the appointment of a custodian under nonbankruptcy law is usually a consequence of the debtor's failure to keep up with current debts.

As with the limitations on standing in section 303(b), the analysis of whether the debtor is generally not paying its debts excludes debts that are subject to bona fide dispute as to liability or amount. In many cases, the determination of whether grounds for relief exists based on the general failure to pay debts will turn on an interpretation of the meaning of "generally" for purposes of section 303(h)(1). Many factors can go into this analysis including the percentage of unpaid debts in both number and amount, as well as the length of the delinquency and the debtor's overall conduct of its financial affairs. Not much to do here on an exam other than recognize the issue and discuss the factors bearing on its resolution.

4. A Couple of Other Things About Involuntary Cases

Because of the potentially devastating effect that an involuntary filing can have on a business debtor, even if the petition is later determined to be unfounded, section 303(i) provides that, upon dismissal, the court may award costs and attorney's fees to the debtor. In addition, if the court finds the petition was filed in bad faith (such as in order to gain a competitive advantage over a business rival), the debtor may also recover actual or punitive damages. Lastly, while the case is pending, the court may, on request of the debtor and for cause, order the petitioners to post a bond to indemnify the debtor for amounts later awarded under section 303(i). *See* section 303(e).

C. Dismissal and Conversion

1. In General

The rules relating to dismissal (the case goes away) and conversion (the case remains but is heard under the rules of a different chapter) under somewhat different under each chapter of the Code. You're also not likely to spend a lot of time on them in class, so there just a few points we need to make here. First, a request for dismissal or conversion may come from either the debtor or another party in interest.[7] Often, the standard for granting the request also differs depending on who is making the request. For instance, under sections 1307(a) and (b), a Chapter 13 debtor has an unqualified, non-waivable right to convert to Chapter 7 or dismiss. Other parties seeking the same relief must establish cause. *See* section 1307(c).

Second, while a Chapter 7 debtor has fairly broad latitude under section 706(a)to convert to another chapter, the right to dismiss is much more constrained, requiring a showing of cause. *See* section 707(a). This is intended to prevent abuse of the system, as, for example, by a debtor who files to obtain the benefit of the stay and then, when the immediate threat is past, dismisses. In addition, the requirement of cause prevents a debtor from manipulating the filing date to extend the discharge. Suppose, for example, Markell files under Chapter 7 on February 1. The next day, running late for work, in his haste Markell runs over Ponoroff. Realizing he's now facing a big tort debt that is not dischargeable (because it was incurred *after* the filing), Markell would like to dismiss his February 1 filing and then immediately refile so that Ponoroff's debt is

---

[7]   A party who has standing to be heard by the court in a matter to be decided in the bankruptcy case is a "party in interest." For most matters, parties in interest will include the debtor, the U.S. trustee or bankruptcy administrator, the case trustee, creditors, equity security holders, and various committees. The term is sort of defined in section 1109 for Chapter 11 cases.

dischargeable. Chances are this won't work; Markell must live with his filing date unless he can convince the court that no creditor would be legally prejudiced by the dismissal of his case—a very high standard.

Third, even though a Chapter 7 debtor's right to convert appears to be absolute under section 706(a), there are some limits. First, section 706(d) requires that the debtor be eligible for relief under the chapter of the Code to which the debtor seeks to convert. Second, a judicial "bad faith" exception to section 706(a) has been recognized in situations where the debtor initially files Chapter 7 and is not forthcoming about all of her assets. When and if the trustee catches on and goes after those assets, the debtor then tries to protect them by seeking conversion to Chapter 13 (or 11). In this situation, the Supreme Court has approved of the bankruptcy court's authority to deny conversion in such cases. *See Marrama v. Citizens Bank of Mass.*.[8]

Section 349 governs the effect of dismissal, and the rules here are fairly straightforward. Creditors get to treat the debtor as if the case had not been filed; actions taken during the case are reversed. The effects of conversion, which are governed by section 348, can be far more complicated and also differ depending on the chapter of Code involved. Perhaps the most important issues to be decided are how to treat (1) claims that arose after the original filing but prior to the conversion (for purposes of participation in the case and discharge), and (2) how to treat property acquired in the same period (i.e., whether it's subject to administration in the case). Generally speaking, but with lots of tricky exceptions, section 348(b) treats these claims as if they were prepetition, but conversion will not change the date for determining property of the estate. More on both "claims" and "property of the estate" in Unit 3 below.

---

[8] 549 U.S. 365 (2007)

Another issue that plagued the courts for nearly 30 years was who (the debtor or her creditors), under section 348(f), should receive funds paid into the debtor's Chapter 13 plan, but not yet distributed at the time of conversion. The Supreme Court finally settled the issue in *Harris v. Viegelahn*,[9] a unanimous decision holding that, in the event of a good faith conversion to Chapter 7, section 348(f)(1)(A) requires that the funds be returned to the debtor in order to facilitate the fresh start.

2. *Bad Faith Filings*

Section 1325(a)(7) imposes an express good faith filing requirement to confirm a Chapter 13 plan. Both Chapter 11 and Chapter 13 also require that the debtor's plan be proposed in good faith, but Chapter 11 does not contain a statutory good faith filing requirement. Nevertheless, there is some case law suggesting that there is an implied good faith filing requirement in Chapter 11, either as "cause" for dismissal under section 1112(b) or pursuant to the inherent authority of bankruptcy judges to police abuses of their jurisdiction. However, it was established over 30 years ago, in *In re Johns-Manville Corp*,[10] that the mere fact that the Chapter 11 debtor is not insolvent or otherwise suffering traditional indicia of financial distress does not alone establish bad faith. In that case, the debtor was using Chapter 11 to manage tens of thousands of product liability lawsuits that had been filed against it (with many more expected) by individuals who had been exposed to asbestos-containing products that had been manufactured by Johns-Manville.

In Chapter 7 cases, an individual consumer debtor's filing could, prior to 2005, be dismissed if the bankruptcy judge found that granting relief would constitute a "substantial abuse." Most typically, this provision would be employed when the court found

---

[9] 135 S.Ct. 1829 (2015).
[10] 36 B.R. 727 (Bankr. S.D.N.Y. 1984).

that the debtor had the ability to pay some portion of her debts under Chapter 13. Based on the belief that abuse of Chapter 7 by so-called "can pay" debtors was rampant, and that bankruptcy judges were not being sufficiently vigilant in policing these abuses, Congress amended section 707(b) to add a formulaic "means test" for determining if abuse should be presumed for purposes of section 707(b)(1). This means test in section 707(b)(2) is complicated and controversial. We will wait until Unit 6 to take it up in greater detail. In addition, even where the presumption of abuse does not arise under the means test, the bankruptcy courts retain the authority under section 707(b)(3) to dismiss if the debtor is found to have filed her case in bad faith.

Core Concepts of Federal Bankruptcy Law

There are four basic concepts you need to know to analyze any bankruptcy problem. They are *claims, property of the estate*, the *automatic stay*, and the *discharge*. In short, *claims* are what creditors have against the debtor and what the debtor wishes to get rid of. They come in all flavors and types, but bankruptcy law categorizes them broadly to afford the debtor the greatest possible relief. Property of the estate is what the debtor has before filing that will pay or provide for the claims after the bankruptcy. The automatic stay protects property of the estate (and some other property) after filing and before the bankruptcy case is over. The automatic stay also and incorporates the important bankruptcy concept of adequate protection of third party rights. Finally, the discharge is the mechanism by that the debtor obtains financial relief and which limits his or her creditors' ability to collect on any pre-petition debt.

A. Claims

1. Overview

The concept of "claim" is critical in bankruptcy cases. It is claims that are subject to the automatic stay; claims that participate in distributions; and claims that are discharged. One of the foundational policy objectives of the Bankruptcy Reform Act of 1978 was to provide the most comprehensive relief possible for both debtors and creditors. The idea is to permit a complete settlement of the debtor's affairs and, thus, a complete discharge and fresh start.

Accomplishing this end requires that all legal obligations of the debtor, no matter how remote, will be dealt with in the bankruptcy case. For this reason the definition of "claim" in section 101(5) is expansive, including any right to payment, whether or not reduced to judgment, "liquidated, unliquidated, fixed, contingent, matured, unmatured, disputed, undisputed, legal, equitable, secured, or unsecured."

We talked about the meaning of "contingent" earlier. The term "liquidated" means that, while the claim is not dependent on the occurrence of some future event, the *amount* of the claim is presently uncertain. So if Ponoroff guarantees Markell's obligation to Bank, that's a contingent claim unless and until Markell defaults and Bank calls on Ponoroff for payment. Contrast that with the situation where Markell slips and falls in Ponoroff's deli because Ponoroff negligently left a banana peel on the floor. Here the obligation exists, but the exact amount owed isn't known and won't be until there a judgment or settlement on the claim.

So, if Markell batters Ponoroff (assaults him, not turn him into a human corn dog) and then files bankruptcy before Ponoroff can sue for his injuries, Ponoroff's unliquidated tort cause of action is a claim in Markell's bankruptcy case. Likewise, if Ponoroff had guaranteed Markell's debt to Harry's Adult Videos, LLC, Ponoroff would have a claim in Markell's bankruptcy case, even though the obligation was contingent—would only arise should Markell default to Harry's. Finally, if Markell owes Ponoroff $1,000 under a promissory note due in two years, Ponoroff has a claim now against Markell's bankruptcy estate for that debt. The point is that all claims relating to Markell's prefiling life will be dealt with in his bankruptcy case.

The definition of "claim" includes not just a "right to payment," but also an equitable remedy, such as an injunction, if the creditor has an alternative right to payment in the event performance under the injunction does not occur. *See* section 101(5)(B). The ability to shed the constraints of an injunction or other equitable decree can be a significant advantage to a debtor, although determining when there is an alternative right to payment can be tricky—as we'll discuss in Section 3 below concerning the automatic stay.

The question of *when* a claim arises can also cause problems. If Markell batters Ponoroff, the claim arises as soon as Markell has finished his pummeling. But potential problems arise if there is a temporal gap between the conduct giving rise to the claim and the time the injury becomes manifest or the claimholder discovers the injury.

In product liability and environmental cases, for example, years and even decades might elapse between, respectively, the exposure to the dangerous product or the discharge of the pollutant and the time the harm becomes apparent or known. Even though the claim may not arise under state law until the discovery of the damage or injury, the events giving rise to the claim occurred in the debtor's prepetition past. Because of the core bankruptcy policy of providing a complete settlement of all affairs, most courts have taken the position that a claim is deemed to arise once there is some relationship, such as conduct, exposure, impact, or privity, prior to the commencement of the bankruptcy case. This is what's known as the "prepetition relationship" test for determining when a claim arises.

Here are some of the other important questions/issues concerning claims, which we'll look at in this Unit:

- What is the process for "allowing" claims?

- What is the difference between unsecured and secured claims?

- How are unsecured claims paid (or not)?

- What types of unsecured claims are entitled to priority?

- What types of unsecured claims are subject to subordination?

- How are secured claims paid (or not) in Chapter 7?

- How are secured claims treated in Chapter 11 and 13?

2. Claims Allowance (and Disallowance)

To participate in a bankruptcy case, that is, to vote in a Chapter 11 case or to receive a dividend or distribution in any case, a claim must be deemed "allowed." The first step in the claims allowance process is the filing of what's called a "proof of claim." If you want to see what a proof of claim looks like, review Official Form 19 in your statute book assigned with the course. There are a couple of situations where a proof of claim form does not need to be filed, but in most situations a creditor of the debtor will take advantage of the invitation in section 501(a) to file a proof of claim.

Note that under section 501(b) an entity that is liable with the debtor on a debt (like a co-signer on a loan) may file a proof of claim against the creditor if the creditor fails to do so. The reason to do so is that whatever distribution the creditor receives from the bankruptcy estate will reduce the balance for which the jointly liable party remains responsible. So, assume Markell and Ponoroff are jointly and severally liable on a promissory note to Bank for $50,000. Markell files bankruptcy, but Bank doesn't bother filing a proof of claim in the case because it figures it will just collect from Ponoroff. Assuming there will be at least some distribution to unsecured creditors in Markell's bankruptcy, Ponoroff should file a proof of claim on Bank's behalf, since every dollar Bank receives from Markell's bankruptcy estate is a dollar less that Ponoroff will have to pay.

Finally, under section 501(c), the debtor may file a proof of claim on behalf of a creditor that fails to do so itself. That's right, the person who owes the debt can file a claim for the person who is owed the money. The situation where the debtor will want to do this is in a case where the debt will not be discharged by the bankruptcy case. From the debtor's point of view her pre-filing assets are gone, so whatever is applied to the nondischargeable debt reduces the balance that the debtor will have to satisfy with postpetition assets.

Once filed a proof of claim is *deemed allowed* by section 502(a). This means it's good unless an objection to the claim is filed and upheld by the court. In Chapter 7, it is most often the trustee who will file the objection, as the trustee has the duty under section 704(5) to examine filed proofs of claim to be sure they are proper. The time for objecting to a filed claim is handled differently by chapter, and is covered generally by Bankr. Rules 3002 & 3003. Failure to file a proof of claim in a timely fashion is grounds for disallowance of the claim. *See* section 502(b)(9).

The grounds for objection to a claim, nine in total, are set forth in section 502(b). Most important among these are: (a) for claims that would not have been enforceable under applicable nonbankruptcy law (section 502(b)(1)), (b) claims for unmatured interest (section 502(b)(2)), and (c) certain claims for future rent under real property leases (section 502(b)(6)). With respect to the first ground for objection, the bankruptcy estate may assert any defense to a claim that could have been raised by the debtor. *See* section 558. Thus, for example, a claim for breach of contract incurred by means of fraud will be disallowed if an objection based on fraudulent inducement is raised and would be a good defense to the claim under state law.

As for unmatured interest, with the important exception of oversecured claims, bankruptcy freezes all claims at their value as of the date of filing. So no interest accrues from and after the filing for unsecured claims. The exception for oversecured claims (collateral is worth more than the debt) is in section 506(b), and it covers fees, costs, and other charges provided for by the parties' agreement or (in the case of a statutory lien) state law. So, assume Markell owes Ponoroff $10,000 under the terms of a promissory note providing for interest-only payments at five percent per annum and entitling Ponoroff to attorney's fees involved in collecting the debt. Assume further the obligation is secured by property owned by Markell worth $12,000. If, at the time of Markell's filing he is current on the debt(all of the required interest payments have been made), Ponoroff's claim will be $10,000. However, six months later, Ponoroff's claim will be $10,250, plus any attorney's fees he incurs. Ponoroff's claim will continue to grow until it equals the value of the collateral. Of course, the collateral might be declining in value just as the claim is growing. We'll talk about what that means later when we take up the concept of "adequate protection" in Section C.5.b of this Unit.

Section 502(b)(6) establishes a "cap" on a lessor's recovery of rent under long-term leases. It is predicated on the concern that, without such a limit, these claims could consume a disproportionate amount of the estate. The determination of the cap is a bit complicated. It entails first calculating fifteen percent of the unexpired term of the lease. If that results in less than one year, then the cap will be one year's rent under the lease. Note, however, this is a *cap*, meaning that if the actual claim is less than one-year's rent because, for example, of the opportunity to re-let the premises, then the claim will be the actual damages. In either case, however, accrued but unpaid prepetition rent will be part of the claim. If fifteen percent of the remaining lease term is *more* than one year (which is to say that the remaining term exceeds 80 months), then the cap will be the rent due for that fifteen percent period, but not to exceed three years.

So, to illustrate, suppose Ponoroff files bankruptcy with ten years left on his lease of Markell's premises. The lease calls for a monthly rental of $1,000 ($12,000 per year) and, as of the date of filing, Ponoroff owes $5,000 in back rent. Markell's rent claim will be capped at $23,000 (18 months future rent—15 percent of the remaining term—and the unpaid prepetition rent.[11] Again, note this is a cap, meaning that if Markell is able immediately to re-let the space for $990 per month, then his claim will be $17,000 ($12,000 ($1,200 per year times 10) for future rent and the $5,000 past due rent). Simple, eh? Actually, once you work with it a bit, it kind of is. So let's keep going.

Now, in the above example, if there were five rather than ten years remaining on the lease, what is the cap on Ponoroff's rent

---

[11]   There is some disagreement in the case law as to whether the cap should apply to claims other than those based on lost rent and the tenant's failure to complete the lease term, such as collateral damage to the premises. *See, e.g., Kupfer v. Salma (In re Kupfer)*, 526 B.R. 812 (N.D. Cal. 2014) (discussing Saddleback Valley Community Church v. *El Toro Materials Co. (In re El Toro Materials Co.)*, 504 F.3d 978 (9th Cir 2007), *Cert. denied*, 552 U.S. 1311 (2008)).

claim? Correct—$17,000! One year's rent ($12,000) plus the past due prepetition rent ($5,000). Ok, you're getting the hang of it.

3. *Claims Estimation*

If an allowed claim against the estate is unliquidated, contingent, or disputed, it is incumbent on the court to fix the amount of the claim so the creditor can participate in the bankruptcy case. To allow this to occur without unduly delaying the case, section 502(c)(1) gives the court the power "estimate" the claim, using, at its discretion, a summary proceeding. This will be particularly important where there are lots of future and unknown claimants; usually mass tort cases.

Though the language of the statute would seem to allow it, courts have generally not used this estimation power to permanently fix the amount of the claim, but only to set a number for purposes of, typically, voting on a plan of reorganization in Chapter 11, with the actual amount established by subsequent adjudication. For example, in the A.H. Robins case, the court estimated all the product liability claims after a week's trial.[12] Very fast.

4. *Unsecured and Secured Claims*

The definition of "claim" includes both secured and unsecured debts, but the meaning of "secured claim" is different in bankruptcy than under state law. Under state law, a creditor with a security interest in the debtor's property is a secured creditor without regard to the value of the collateral. In bankruptcy there are no "secured creditors" *per se*, only creditors with secured claims and creditors with unsecured claims. In allocating a claim between

---

[12] A.H. Robins was the manufacturer of the Dalkon Shield. Within a few years of the products initial distribution, the company was facing over 15,000 personal injury claims, including lawsuits in every state of the country. With countless thousands more to come.

secured and unsecured portions, 506(a)(1) is pivotal. In somewhat stultified language, it says that a claim is secured only to the extent of the value of the underlying collateral. This means that the holder of an undersecured claim—i.e., the debt is more than the value of the collateral—really has two claims, a secured claim to the extent of the collateral's value, and an unsecured claim for the balance (sometimes called the "deficiency").

To illustrate, suppose Markell owes Ponoroff $10,000 and has granted Ponoroff a security interest in Markell's Prius as security for the debt. If, at the time of Markell's bankruptcy filing the Prius is worth $7,500, Ponoroff's $10,000 claim will be bifurcated into two claims: a $7,500 secured claim and a $2,500 unsecured claim. On the other hand, if Markell only owed $5,000, Ponoroff's claim would be fully secured. Let's consider both types of claims in more depth, beginning with:

a.   Unsecured Claims

Unsecured claimholders are the beneficiaries of the residual estate. That is to say, (1) after lienholders have been paid from encumbered property, (2) after the exempt property is removed from the estate, and (3) after the costs of the bankruptcy administration (like the trustee's fees) have been paid, what remains is available for distribution among the holders of allowed unsecured claims. As noted above, unsecured claims will include will include the undersecured portion of claims by creditors whose collateral is worth less than the amount they are owed.

Generally speaking, distributions to unsecured claimholders are made pro rata, or *pari passu* (don't you love it when we talk French? Whoops, wait, it's *Latin*—oh well). This means that, theoretically, if Markell's unsecured claim of $1,000 represents five percent of all unsecured claims ($20,000) against Ponoroff's estate, then Markell will receive a distribution equal to five percent of the residual estate. So if the net distributable estate is $10,000, Markell receives $500, or, as it's sometime put, a fifty percent dividend.

But, that is *in theory*. The reality is a bit more complex. You see, despite bankruptcy's emphasis on the policy of equality among similarly situated creditors, some unsecured creditors are actually *more equal* than others. These are unsecured creditors that enjoy a *priority* over their less privileged counterparts due to competing policy interests. Later we'll see that other unsecured creditors may be *less equal*.

i.   Priority Claims

First, don't confuse the Bankruptcy Code's use of the term priority with the general usage of the term "priority" outside of bankruptcy. In the latter situation, lawyers use the term "priority" to refer the order in which liens are to be satisfied out of particular property. Section 507 of the Code uses the term "priority" to refer to those allowed unsecured claims that are to be satisfied ahead of all other allowed unsecured claims. In a Chapter 7 case, distribution of estate property is made in accordance with section 726, which provides first for payment of claims of the kind specified in section 507. *See* section 726(a)(1). In Chapter 11, a plan may not be confirmed unless priority claims are, in some cases, paid in full in cash on confirmation, and, in other cases, paid in full in deferred payments over the life of the plan. *See* section 1129(a)(9). In Chapter 13, priority claims must also be paid in full, although this may occur in deferred cash payments over the life of the plan. *See* section 1322(a)(2).

Second, in Chapter 7, the ten categories of priority claims set forth in section 507(a) are paid in the order listed. Thus, all section 507(a)(1) claims must be satisfied in full before any payment is made to claims at the next (or any other) priority level. If it turns out that within a particular category of priority claims there are not sufficient assets to pay all such claims, then claims within that category are paid pro rata. To illustrate, assume there are three levels of priority claims, and $1,000 of claims at each level. If the assets available for distribution to priority claimants are $1,500, the holders of first priority claims will be paid in full; the holders of second priority claims will receive 50 cents on the dollar; and the holder of third priority claims, along with nonpriority (general) unsecured creditors and equity interest holders, will receive diddlysquat.

aa. Domestic Support Claims

Probably the most significant "consumer protection" contained in BAPCPA was a series of provisions to elevate protection for domestic support claims based on obligations like alimony, maintenance, and child support. Of course, some debtors responsible for these obligations probably don't see these provisions as providing much "consumer protection." In any case, among these provisions was an amendment to the Code designed to give domestic support claimants a first (the highest) priority among unsecured claimholders. Within the re-designated section 507(a)(1) there are three internal priority levels, although they are frustratingly not listed in order. Pursuant to section 507(a)(1)(C), the "administrative expenses" of a trustee under section 503(b)(1)(A), (2) & (6) come before any other claim based on a domestic support obligation ("DSO"). We discuss administrative expenses below. This priority ensures that, when a DSO will consume the entire value of the estate, the trustee will still have incentive to liquidate estate assets for the benefit of the DSO claimant.

Subsections (a)(1)(A) and (B) of section 507 then distinguish situations where, respectively, the claimant is the direct beneficiary of the obligation, such as a former spouse or a dependent child, from cases where the claimant is a governmental unit that took the claim by assignment. The former is given priority over the latter. This means that if Ponoroff defaulted on an alimony obligation to his former spouse and a support obligation to a child, but the county provided the promised support to the child and took an assignment of the claim, Ponoroff's former spouse's claim would have priority over the county's claim.

Another important distinction to be aware of under this section is that "domestic support obligation" is a defined term in section 101(14A). It includes, as would be expected, debts in the nature of alimony, maintenance or support. What it does *not* include are obligations that arise out of a property settlement or division order in connection with a dissolution proceeding. Section 523(a)(5), regarding the nondischargeability of domestic support obligations, makes the same distinction and there is a healthy body of case law under that provision that should be precedential as well under section 507(a)(1).

The fact that the priority for DSOs largely mirrors the description of domestic support obligation under section 523(a), which we discuss in Unit 6 below, is of value to the debtor since it is obviously in the debtor's interest to see as much of a nondischargeable debt as possible paid-off with prebankruptcy dollars. A similar pairing of priority and nondischargeability exists with respect to tax claims under, respectively, sections 507(a)(8) and 523(a)(1). More on that later.

bb. Administrative Expense Claims

You will probably spend most of your class time devoted to priorities on the   section 507(a)(2) priority for administrative expenses allowed under section 503(b). Until 2005, these claims enjoyed the top priority, and they are still very important, since this is where the trustee gets paid as well as the professionals in the case, such as lawyers, accountants and investment bankers, whose employment has been approved by the court under section 327(a). *See* sections 503(b)(2)–(6).

There are nine categories of administrative expense covered in section 503(b), two of which merit further discussion here. The first is section 503(b)(1)(A) relating to "actual, necessary costs and expenses of preserving the estate. . . ." This language refers, except as noted below, to postpetition debts arising out of a transaction between the creditor and the trustee (or debtor in possession). The purpose for this priority is mostly to facilitate reorganization by encouraging third parties to continue to transact business with the debtor, although administrative expenses may also be incurred by the trustee in Chapter 7, such as for obligations incurred in connection with arranging for the sale of estate property.

Note that the priority in section 503(b)(1)(a) attaches not simply because the right to payment arises postpetition. It must also have been induced by a representative of the estate after the bankruptcy filing and not based on a prepetition contract or consideration supplied prepetition. Thus, Markell's claim for legal services based work done after Ponoroff's Chapter 11 filing on a case in which Markell was retained prior to that filing is not entitled to administrative priority. Rather, Markell must be "re-hired" by Ponoroff, as debtor in possession, and that hiring approved by the court, neither of which will occur unless Markell's continued representation has or has the potential to provide value to the estate.

Another possible requirement of section 503(b)(1)(A) is that the consideration supporting the claimant's right to payment must be *beneficial* to the estate. Specifically, some courts interpret the language of the statute referring to "preserving the estate" to exclude priority for costs incurred in the operation of the business that do not benefit the estate—such as debts attributable to post-filing torts., Other courts, however continue to apply the Supreme Court's holding in a Bankruptcy Act case, *Reading Co. v. Brown*,[13] finding that the "costs of preserving the estate" may include costs normally incident to operation of a business when other policies, such as compensation of a tort victim, are implicated. In addition, 28 U.S.C § 959(b) requires that operating debtors comply state law. This might mean that even a civil penalty, if assessed based on postpetition bankruptcy activities, could enjoy administrative expense priority. *See In re N.P. Mining.*[14]

The remaining category of administrative expense to mention is section 503(b)(9), added to the Code by BAPCPA. It represents an exception to what had been the traditional understanding that administrative expenses could only arise out of postpetition transactions. This provision provides vendors an administrative expense for the value of all goods received by the debtor within 20 day *prior* to the petition date so long as that the goods were sold in the ordinary course of the debtor's business. The exact purpose for this priority, and the preferential treatment it allows sellers of goods to enjoy over other unsecured creditors, is a bit obscure. One theory is that it is to encourage vendors to continue to do business with a financially troubled debtor. However, particularly in the case of a reorganization of a large retail debtor, like Radio Shack, these claims can run into the hundreds of millions of dollars. Moreover, unless they agree to a different treatment, because these claimants must be paid in cash on confirmation of a reorganization plan, section 503(b)(9) may give these creditors as a group enormous leverage in certain Chapter 11 cases.

---

[13] 391 U.S. 471 (1968).

[14] *Alabama Surface Mining Comm'n v. N.P. Mining Co.*, 963 F.2d 1449 (11th Cir. 1989).

cc. Employee Wage and Wage-Related Claims

Sections 507(a)(4)(A) & (5) operate in tandem. Together, they provide employees with a priority for prepetition wages and associated fringe benefits (such as health insurance and sick pay), subject to the limitations set forth below. The policy reason for this priority supposedly is to prevent employees from abandoning ship when the debtor encounters rough financial waters, although it's not clear that most employees are that in tune with the financial condition of their employer. It also presumes that there are other jobs out there just waiting for these employees.

In any case, claims arising under these priorities may not, in combination, exceed (currently) $12,475. This figure, like several other dollar figures in the Bankruptcy Code, adjusts every three years based on the Consumer Price Index. *See* section 104(b). The next adjustment will occur on April 1, 2016. In actual operation, the priority for contributions to an employee benefit plan under section 507(a)(5) is limited to the *unused portion* of the $12,475 claimed under the section 507(a)(4) priority.

In addition to the dollar limitation, these priorities only apply to wage and benefit claims relating to services provided within 180 days prior to the earlier of the debtor's bankruptcy filing or cessation of business. This is not much of a limitation: after all, how many people do you know who would keep working for up to six months without getting paid? Not us!

To illustrate the operation of these two limitations, assume Markell has a claim against the bankrupt Ponoroff for $10,000 in wages, all earned in the three months prior to filing. Assume Markell also has a claim of $3,000 for contributions that Ponoroff was supposed to make to various employee benefit plans on Markell's behalf during that same period of time. Markell's maximum priority claim for the unpaid employee benefits can be no more than (currently) $12,475, less the amount of his priority wage claim, or $2,475. The balance of $525 (the difference between Markell's aggregate $13,000 claim and the priority cap of $12,475) will just be a general unsecured claim. Also, the actual amount allocable to section 507(a)(5) priority could actually be less, as the language of the statute provides that the $12,475 cap must be reduced by (1) the aggregate amount actually paid to employees under section 507(a)(4), *and* (2) the aggregate amount paid by the estate on behalf of those employees to any other benefit plan.

In *Howard Deliv. Serv., Inc. v. Zurich Am. Ins. Co.*,[15] the Supreme court decided that unpaid premiums for workers' compensation insurance did not fall under the section 507(a)(5) priority, as such contributions are not "wage substitutes" in same the sense of health insurance, retirement plans, etc. Lastly, in 1994, a disagreement in the case law was resolved when what is now section 507(a)(4)(B) was added to the Code to provide a priority for sales commissions earned by a non-employee independent contractor. The priority only attains, however, if the contractor received 75 percent or more of her commissions in the prior year from the debtor.

dd. Tax Claims

It's no surprise that the folks who enacted the bankruptcy law would make taxes a priority, although, in the government's defense, tax claims enjoy only an eighth priority. Again, as in the case of priority DSOs, this priority benefits the debtor since priority tax claims are, as we will see, also nondischargeable under section 523(a)(1). The entirety of section 507(a)(8) is intricate and complex. However, the part that you are likely to be responsible for in a basic bankruptcy case is income taxes, which is what we will focus on

---

[15]   547 U.S. 651 (2006).

here. Don't forget, however, that the priority for taxes extends to payroll taxes, property taxes, excise taxes, etc.

The basic rule for income taxes is found in section 507(a)(8)(A)(i). It provides priority for unpaid income taxes for any taxable year that ended on or before the date of the bankruptcy, and for which a return "is last due, including extensions, after three years before the date" of bankruptcy. The cumbersome "after three years before language" is actually appropriate since it sets, as it's intended to do, a time bar in the past, but not necessarily after the date of filing. The explanation cries for an example.

So, let's suppose Ponoroff files for Chapter 7 bankruptcy on April 1, 2016. He's not paid his federal income taxes for the last four calendar years—2011-2015. Which of the government's tax claims are entitled to priority. Well, if we assume Ponoroff never received any filing extensions, the return for 2011 was last due on April 15, 2012. This is *more* than three year before the date of filing, so that claim is not entitled to priority. The return for Ponoroff's 2012 taxes was due on April 15, 2013, so it is "after three years before the filing'' and entitled to priority. Likewise, the taxes for 2014. Note had Ponoroff waited an additional 16 days to file, the 2012 taxes would also have fallen outside the three-year period.

Now, what about the taxes for 2015, for which the return was not due until after Ponoroff's bankruptcy filing, and 2016, for which a return will not be due for over a year? This is where the after/before language comes into play. A return for taxes for the year ended 2015 is due on April 15, 2016, which is *not* within the three years preceding the bankruptcy filing. It is, however, *after* three years before the date of the bankruptcy. Indeed, 2020 taxes would also be due *after* three years before the date of the bankruptcy. The point being that the awkward language about "after three years before" only imposes a cutoff in the past, but not in the future. The same applies for 2016, or at least for the first three months of the year. In case this wasn't enough, postpetition taxes incurred by the estate are administrative expenses under section 503(b)(2)(1)(B), entitled to a second priority under section 507(a)(2).

ii.   Subordination of Claims

Just as some unsecured claims are superior to general unsecured claims, other unsecured claims may be not as good. This is because they are subordinated, either (a) because the creditor contractually agreed to that treatment, or (b) by operation of the law on equitable grounds.

aa.   Contractual Subordination

Under Code section 510(a), an agreement of subordination between or among creditors is enforceable in bankruptcy to the same extent as under applicable nonbankruptcy law. Why would a creditor willingly agree to subordinate its priority status? There could be many reasons, but not uncommonly the subordination is undertaken to induce an extension of credit to a common debtor. Many publicly-issued bonds are contractually subordinated to bank debt for just this reason.

As another example, suppose Markell Finance has advanced $100,000 to Ponoroff, Inc., secured by all of Ponoroff's inventory and receivables. Assume that several months later, Ponoroff, Inc. has become financially wobbly and the only hope of turning things around is more credit. Markell knows it's likely to take a big loss if it calls its loan, but it's also leery of increasing the amount of its debt from Ponoroff. However, First National Bank of Bruce is prepared to extend credit to Ponoroff, *but* only if it receives 1) a security interest in Ponoroff's inventory and receivables, *and* 2) Markell Finance agrees to subordinate the priority that its lien on the same collateral would otherwise enjoy under U.C.C. Article 9. Such an agreement is recognized under U.C.C. § 9-339 and, hence, would also be enforced under section 510(a) if, notwithstanding the new funding, Ponoroff ends up in bankruptcy anyway.

bb. Equitable Subordination

The Bankruptcy Reform Act of 1978, for the first time, incorporated into the substantive law governing bankruptcy cases an express provision (section 510(c)) recognizing the courts' power to subordinate particular claims on equitable as well as contractual grounds. The roots of court-ordered subordination, however, are found much earlier in bankruptcy jurisprudence. The doctrine was first articulated and developed in series of Supreme Court cases in the 1930's and 1940's arising under the former Bankruptcy Act, and recognizing the inherent power of the bankruptcy courts to subordinate a claim when equity demanded.

Note that the authority of the bankruptcy court under section 510(c) is to *alter* the legal priority of a claim, ordinarily based on misconduct by the claimholder. In other words, the court can lower the priority of the claim, but it cannot disallow it *in toto* as a result of the misconduct. The Code does not set out the standards that the courts should apply in the exercise of their power under section 510(c). Rather, the legislative history simply says the courts should follow pre-Code case law, and that the codification of the doctrine was not intended to limit the courts' powers in any way.

Nonetheless, courts have been circumspect in invoking this power, most frequently citing the Fifth Circuit's statement in *In re Mobile Steel*[16] of the three conditions that must be satisfied to establish equitable subordination: First, the holder of the claim to be subordinated had to engage in inequitable conduct; next, that misconduct must have resulted in injury to other creditors or conferred an unfair advantage for the claimholder; and, finally, subordination of the claim must not violate other provisions of the

---

[16]   563 F.2d 692, 700 (2000).

Bankruptcy Code. Although the *Mobile Steel* test does not distinguish between insider and noninsider creditors, the reality has become that a close relationship to the debtor will trigger greater scrutiny, although exploitation of that relationship to the detriment of other creditors is required to trigger equitable subordination.

In addition to equitable subordination, in most circuits, the courts have recognized the bankruptcy court's authority to *recharacterize* a creditor's claim debt to equity, even in the absence of inequitable conduct, when, under applicable law, the advance was in substance an infusion of risk capital and not a loan. There is, however, a split in the circuits as to whether the "applicable law" is state or federal law. Undercapitalization can also be a factor in an equitable subordination analysis, leaving some confusion over the two doctrines, but, at least conceptually, the recharacterization decision rests on an assessment of the actual *substance of the transaction* giving rise to the claimant's demand, whereas the equitable subordination decision rests on the court's assessment of the *creditor's behavior*.

b.   Secured Claims

The benefit of having a secured claim is that the creditor holding the lien has special rights in the property subject to its lien and in the proceeds from any disposition of the property. Specifically, the secured claim, if properly perfected, must be satisfied from the property securing the claim, or its proceeds, before the trustee, the other creditors, and even the debtor receive anything. Indeed, it is probably not an exaggeration to say that a security interest is a hedge against bankruptcy since an important principle of our bankruptcy law is that a property interest created under nonbankruptcy law carries forward and will be generally recognized in bankruptcy.

As we've seen, a creditor only has a secured claim up to the value of the creditor's collateral. If the debt exceeds the value of the collateral, the creditor's claim is bifurcated under section 506(a)(1). In a certain of key areas, however, the Code departs from this principle by requiring payments to secured claim holders measured by the full value of their debt, regardless of the value of the underlying collateral. More on those situations later. For now, the point to be made is that, except where expressly displaced, the definition of "secured claim" in section 506(a)(1) pertains throughout the Code.

A secured claim is one secured by a "lien," defined in section 101(37) as "charge against, or interest in property." Thus, secured claims can arise out of consensual liens, like Article 9 security interests or real estate mortgages, or out of nonconsensual liens, such as statutory liens and judicial liens (like the liens creditors can obtain outside of bankruptcy to enforce their judgments). Like any other claimholder, in order to participate in the case, the secured claimholder must file a proof of claim under section 501, and have her claim "allowed" under section 502. However, unlike unsecured claims that, by and large are discharged, a secured claim will remain enforceable against the collateral (but not the debtor) even if the creditor does not participate in the case. This rule is sometimes expressed in the not entirely accurate adage that "liens pass through bankruptcy unaffected."

i.   **Treatment of Secured Claims in Chapter 7**

Generally speaking, if property of the estate is subject to a lien, the trustee will either abandon it to the secured creditor, if there is no value over and above the lien, or sell it to realize that excess value. In the latter case, after reimbursement for the costs of sale, the proceeds must go first to the secured creditor to pay off the lien. Thus, the secured creditor may find itself delayed somewhat in realizing on its collateral, but will eventually be able to enforce its *in rem* claim against the property. If the secured creditor believes the delay is too long, it can seek relief from the stay (a topic discussed below in Section C.4 of this Unit) while the case is pending, but most Chapter 7 cases move fast enough that there's usually not much need to do anything.

Section 506(d) says that: "To the extent that a lien secures a claim against the debtor that is not an allowed secured claim, such lien is void." Under section 506(a)(1), of course, an allowed secured claim is limited to the lesser of the underlying debt or the value of the collateral. So, the argument went that if Ponoroff owned a piece of property worth $50,000, subject to a lien in favor of Markell securing a debt of $75,000, Ponoroff should be able to void the lien to the extent of $25,000 and, if he can come up with the cash, thus purchase the property from the estate for $50,000.

But, not so fast. In *Dewsnup v, Timm*,[17] the Supreme Court said "no" to strip down of an undersecured lien in Chapter 7 in an opinion that has come in for considerable criticism in both lower court decisions and the academic commentary. In principal, the Court based its decision on the unusual proposition that the phrase "allowed secured claim" in section 506(d) did not mean the same thing as the exact same phrase section 506(a). Instead, the court read the phrase in section 506(d) to mean a claim that is *not* an allowed or a secured claim. In short, the "allowed" aspect only modified claim, and thus the only relevant considerations were those in section 502(b), not the bifurcation provided for in section 506(a). Since Markell's claim was both allowed and secured, it could not be voided under subsection (d).

Dewsup involved the strip down (reduction) of a partially secured lien to the amount of the allowed secured claim. In *Bank of America v. Caulkett*,[18] the Supreme Court addressed the related

---

[17]   502 U.S. 410 (1991).

[18]   135 S. Ct. 1995 (2015).

question of whether section 506(d) allowed *strip off* a junior mortgage lien in its entirety when the outstanding debt owed to a senior lienholder exceeded the current value of the collateral, i.e., where the lien is completely underwater. Concluding that its decision in *Dewsnup* contained no such distinction, the Court held that the answer was, again, "no." Some courts have limited the rules on strip off and strip down in,[19] respectively, *Dewsnup* and *Caulkett*, but we're not so sure the Supreme Court would agree if presented with the question.

ii. Treatment of Secured Claims in Chapters 11 and 13

Because there is explicit statutory authority for stripping down liens in rehabilitation proceedings, the impact of *Dewsnup* has been limited to Chapter 7. Thus, with certain important exceptions that we will address in the Units specifically covering Chapter 11 and 13 cases, one of the important advantages of Chapters 11 and 13 is the ability to modify secured debts. To confirm a Chapter 11 or 13 plan, the plan proponent must, unless the secured creditor agrees otherwise, either surrender the collateral or, most importantly, retain the collateral and "cram down" the secured creditor's clam. In order to cram down a secured claim, the plan must provide for the creditor to receive payments under the plan with a value, as of the date of confirmation, at least equal to the allowed amount of the claim. *See* sections 1129(b)(2)(A) and 1325(a)(5)(B).

This means that if Markell has a lien on Ponoroff's property securing a $100,000 debt bearing an interest rate of 10 percent, but the property is only worth $75,000, then Ponoroff can confirm his Chapter 13 plan, whether Markell likes it or not, if the plan provides that the sum of the payments under the plan will not only total the amount of the allowed secured claim ($75,000), but also have a present value equal to the amount of that claim. How do you get to

---

[19] *See, e.g., In re Mayer*, 2015 WL 7424327 (Bankr. E.D. La. 2015).

present value? We'll go into that later when we talk about Chapter 11 and Chapter 13 plans, but for now you can take on faith that a promissory note in the amount of $75,000 that has a market rate of interest has a present value of $75,000. So if Ponoroff's plan proposes to give Markell a $75,000 note, secured by the property originally subject to the lien, with a market rate of interest of 5 percent, Ponoroff can confirm the plan over Markell's pitiful cries of complaint.

For this analysis, it does not matter when Markell's debt came due under the original credit contract, or whether or not the debt currently in default. It also doesn't matter that the debt originally had a much higher interest rate than current market rates, as illustrated in the above example. Rather, Ponoroff is creating a new loan with a new principal amount, a new rate of interest, and a new term. So, if it is determined that the appropriate rate of interest to properly present value the payment stream is five percent, and the term of the plan is 60 months, then Ponoroff's plan must provide for monthly payments of $1,312.50 ($75,000 divided by 60 ($1,250) plus five percent).

Obviously, there are two key determinations that must be made in this process: (1) how to value the collateral, and (2) how to calculate the interest (or discount) rate. As for the first question, in *Associates Commercial Corp. v. Rash*,[20] the Supreme Court determined that a "replacement-value" (rather than a foreclosure-value) standard should apply. However, in a footnote, the Court also suggested that in calculating replacement value the bankruptcy courts should deduct from the valuation items that a consumer pays for when buying the property in a typical retail transaction (such as warranties, inventory storage, reconditioning, and the like), and that the debtor does not enjoy when she retains (as opposed to purchases) the collateral. As a reaction to *Rash*, BAPCPA adopted

---

[20] 520 U.S. 953 (1997).

section 506(a)(2), providing that, for personal property in individual Chapter 7 and 13 cases, replacement value, without deduction for costs of sale or marketing, must be used. *Rash*, however, continues to control in Chapter 11 cases and valuations concerning real property.

As to the appropriate rate of interest, the debate has been whether to use the contract rate, a current market rate, or something else entirely. The Supreme Court got into the act here, too, in *Till v. SCS Credit Corp.*,[21] involving in a Chapter 13 case. In a plurality opinion, the court endorsed a "formula" approach, which starts with prime rate (a rate that banks supposedly give to their best customers),[22] and then allows for the creditor to prove that an adjustment upward for the added risk of default is in order. Using a formula approach, the bankruptcy court had applied a rate of 9.5 percent (the then-national prime rate of 8 percent plus a 1.5 percent adjustment) even though the contract rate had been 21 percent. It's not clear the extent to which *Till* should govern in an Chapter 11 case, since, unlike in Chapter 13, there is a real market for cram down loans from which an actual rate might be determined with precision. Still, most courts give *Till* at least some weight in Chapter 11.[23]

In 2005, the confirmation standards for secured claims in Chapter 13 was amended to include two additional requirements. First, that if the plan calls for periodic payments (as it usually will), such payments must be in equal monthly installments. Second, the amount of the payment may not be less than the amount necessary to assure that the holder's claim is adequately protected during the plan period. *See* section 1325(a)(5)(B)(iii). This means that if the

---

[21] 541 U.S. 465 (2004).

[22] You can look up the current prime rate at:. http://wsj.com/mdc/public/page/2_3020-moneyrate.html.

[23] See, e.g., Wells Fargo Bank N.A. v. Texas Grand Prairie Hotel Realty, L.L.C. (In re Texas Grand Prairie Hotel Realty, L.L.C.), 710 F.3d 324 (5th Cir. 2013).

collateral is declining rapidly in value, plan payments may have to exceed the amount necessary to assure the holder the present value as of the date of confirmation of the allowed amount of its secured claim. Plan confirmation standards in Chapter 13 are discussed in more detail in Unit 7.

B. Property of the Estate

1. The Importance of Property of the Estate and Who Decides

"Property of the estate" is another key concept you need to know. Property of the estate is what is protected in bankruptcy, and what forms the basis of any bankruptcy dividend. Creditors cannot unilaterally seize property of the estate during the case, and will only get paid their bankruptcy dividends from property of the estate.

So what is it? Easy, sort of. Section 541(a)(1) defines the estate as "all legal or equitable interests of the debtor in property as of the commencement of the case." As before, we have the issue of what law defines property rights. Clearly, anything that the debtor holds or owns and which is recognized as property under state law will be property of the bankruptcy estate.

But there is more. Just as the question of what constitutes a claim for bankruptcy purposes does not depend on state law, it follows that the determination of the property of the estate cannot be made by *solely* by reference to state law and without regard to the balance that Congress has struck between the competing interests of debtors and creditors under the bankruptcy law. Central to accomplishing that balance is the necessity to cleave a wide chasm between the debtor's pre and postpetition lives, such that in return for the fresh start that the debtor receives in the latter, creditors receive all of the debtor's property attributable to the former. Put another way, claims and property interests belonging to the debtor's prepetition life must be matched in the same fashion that an auditor will match revenues and expenses to the particular accounting period to which they relate.

It would be manifestly inequitable, on the one hand, to limit a creditor to its ratable share of the assets of the bankruptcy estate without, on the other hand, including within that estate all of the assets that existed as of the commencement of the case. Hence, the Code's far-reaching approach in defining property of the estate. The primary inclusive provision is section 541(a)(1), which, as we stated above, defines the estate as "all legal or equitable interests of the debtor in property as of the commencement of the case." The Supreme Court has also routinely found that, to fulfill the purposes of bankruptcy law, the definition of property of the debtor's estate must be broadly interpreted to include all legally cognizable interests extant as of the time of filing, even if contingent or not subject to possession until a future time. *See, e.g., United States v. Whiting Pools,* 462 U.S. 198, 204-205 (1983).

2. So What's Included in the Estate?

It is well settled that the issue of what constitutes property of the estate within the meaning of section 541 is a federal question, and it is irrelevant that state law might not call the same interest "property." *Board of Trade of City of Chicago v. Johnson.*[24] That said, however, of necessity the nature and attributes of a debtor's interest in that property is often determined by reference to nonbankruptcy law, most frequently state law. This principle was established by the Supreme Court in *Butner v. United States,*[25] holding that unless some federal interest requires a different result,

---

[24] 264 U.S. 1 (1924).
[25] 440 U.S. 48 (1979).

property interests should be analyzed no differently in bankruptcy than under state law.

The sweeping language of section 541(a)(1) includes all forms of property, real and personal, tangible and intangible, and wherever located and by whomever held. So any land the debtor owns. Any cars. Any cash. Any rights to receive money from someone else. Any rights to use something or to exclude someone from using something (think patents or copyrights).

There are, however, two important limitations that warrant mention, both of which derive from the fact that it is the *interests of the debtor* in property that becomes part of the estate. Thus, first, if Ponoroff and Markell jointly own a car wash that they use to launder money earned from their illegal trafficking in crystal meth, and Ponoroff files for bankruptcy, it is only his partial ownership interest in the car wash, and not Markell's, that becomes property of the estate. Second, if Ponoroff, even as the sole owner of the car wash, had granted a lien to Markell Finance to secure a loan that Ponoroff needed in order to purchase certain "cooking" equipment, it is only Ponoroff's interest in the car wash, and not the interest in favor of Markell Finance created by its lien, that becomes estate property.

Once established, property of the estate may subsequently be added to (as, for example, when the trustee recovers property by exercise of her avoiding powers, which we'll discuss in Unit 4) or taken away from (as, for example, when the debtor claims his exemptions, as discussed in Unit 6). Property acquired by the debtor in a Chapter 7 case after filing is not property of the estate—it is part of the debtor's fresh start—but this statement is subject to some important qualifications. First, under section 541(a)(5) certain property interests—inheritances, property settlements from a divorce, and life insurance proceeds—acquired or to which the debtor becomes entitled within 180 days of filing are included in the estate. The purpose for these exceptions is to prevent strategic filings, such as, Markell, knowing that he is the principal beneficiary of Ponoroff's estate, quickly filing after learning that Ponoroff is terminally ill with two weeks to live at most.

Second, while section 541(a)(1) limits the estate property to the debtor's interests as of the commencement of the case, section 541(a)(6) adds "proceeds, products, offspring, rents of or from property of the estate," excluding only postpetiton earnings of an individual, which the debtor retains as part of her fresh start. This means, effectively, that in all other cases, including those involving corporations, partnerships, LLCs, etc., the estate includes property acquired by the debtor after the filing. Moreover, In a Chapter 13 case, section 1306 includes the postpetition earnings of a the debtor as property of the estate, and, since 2005, the same is true under section 1115(a)(2) for *individual* debtors in Chapter 11.

3. What's Excluded from the Estate?

For a long time, a big question was whether or not a debtor's ERISA-qualified retirement assets were excluded from the estate under the language of section 541(c)(2), which was originally adopted to recognize so-called "spendthrift clauses" in non-self-settled trusts.[26] ERISA is the 1974 law that established tax-favored treatment for certain retirement vehicles like pension and employer-sponsored 401(k) plans, but to qualify the plan has to contain a provision prohibiting the transfer or assignment of benefits. Because section 541(c)(2) recognizes a restriction on transfer that is enforceable under *applicable nonbankruptcy law*, and not just state law, in *Patterson v. Shumate*,[27] the Supreme

---

[26] A spendthrift clause places the trust assets beyond the reach of creditors of the beneficiary of the trust.

[27] 504 U.S. 753 (1992).

Court resolved the matter in favor of exclusion of the assets in ERISA-qualified plans from the estate.

This still left an issue regarding non-ERISA qualified assets, including IRAs, but, at least with respect to employee contributions to such plans, BAPCPA added section 541(b)(7) to the Code to provide statutory protection. As for employer contributions to these plans, *Patterson* remains controlling. As we will see, as to those retirement assets that fall through the crack and do become estate property, a debtor will usually be able to find an exemption under section 522, which we'll discuss in Unit 6.

Section 541(b) contains a number of other fairly specific exclusions from property of the estate, but none of them as potentially important as the exclusion for retirement assets. Section 541(d) reaffirms that it is property *of the debtor* that comprises the estate by excluding the beneficial interest of any party in assets in which the debtor holds bare legal title only. Thus, if before filing Ponoroff, as agent, purchased property in his own name but on behalf of and for the benefit of Markell, Ponoroff's bankruptcy estate would assume legal title to the property, but not Markell's underlying equitable interest. Presumably, the trustee would quickly see that this property—Ponoroff's naked legal title—was of no value to the estate and abandon it.

4. *Turnover*

Upon filing, property of the estate will ordinarily be in the possession of the debtor. However, property of the estate for purposes of section 541(a) is not limited to property in the debtor's hands. "Interests of the debtor in property" include property "wherever located and by whomever held." "Turnover" of property of the estate in the possession of a third party is governed by Code sections 542 and 543.

a. Turnover Generally

The basic requirement that any entity (a defined term that includes a natural and non-natural person) in possession of property of the estate (other than a custodian) turn that property over to the trustee are set forth in section 542(a) and (b) governing, respectively, tangible property and debts or other amounts owed to the debtor. Think about a dress at the dry cleaners when the debtor files or the debtor's lawnmower in her neighbor's garage. They are still the debtor's property, but in the possession of another. Section 542(a) is limited either to property that the trustee may use under section 363 or that the debtor may exempt under section 522.

The rationale for the latter is obvious—permit the debtor to claim and enjoy her exemption in the property. If the dress or lawnmower is exempt, the debtor ought to be able to reclaim it. The former simply assures that the property will be of some use or value to the estate. If it will, then there must be turnover, even if another may also have an interest in the property. This principle was established in *United States v. Whiting Pools, Inc.*,[28] a case in which the Supreme Court affirmed the obligation of a secured party lawfully in possession of repossessed collateral to return that collateral to the debtor in possession. This is a good demonstration of how bankruptcy can be used to accomplish an objective that could not be accomplished under state law.

Because section 542 mentions section 363, and because section 363(e) conditions the sale or use of property in which a third party has an interest on that party being provided with "adequate protection," the argument has been raised that a secured creditor that lawfully repossessed collateral prior to the bankruptcy filing, and still has the property in its possession, should not be required to turn it over to the trustee unless first provided with adequate

---

[28] 462 U.S. 198 (1983).

protection. While hardly a spurious argument, it has been rejected by a majority of the cases to address the issue.

Section 542(c) provides protection for a third party that, ignorant of the bankruptcy case, transfers property of the estate, or pays a debt to the debtor, in good faith to a party other than the trustee. That protection does not, however, extend to the transferee who, as discussed in Unit 4, may have to return the property to the estate under section 549(a)(2)(A). Lastly, section 542(e) requires professionals, such as attorneys, to turn over any records or documents relating to the debtor's property or financial affairs, but does limit the obligation in the case of any privileged materials.

b.   Turnover by Custodian

Section 543 governs the turnover of property in possession of a "custodian," which might include a receiver appointed under state law (*see* section 101(11)) to take possession of the debtor's property. In general, upon the filing of a bankruptcy case, section 543(b) requires turnover of all property to the trustee and constrains further action by the custodian. In effect, the bankruptcy case largely preempts the state law proceeding. There are, however, a few wrinkles that don't exist under section 542. First, the court may award reasonable compensation to the custodian and order reimbursement of expenses. Second, section 543(d) provides that, upon a showing that the interests of creditors and equity security interest holders would be better served, the court may permit the custodian to remain in possession of and continue to deal with the property.

C. The Automatic Stay

1. Overview

The automatic stay is central to the core bankruptcy objectives of equality among similarly positioned creditors, fresh start for the Chapter 7 debtor, and rehabilitation of the Chapter 11 or 13 debtor. Section 362(a) accomplishes this feat by imposing a kind of commercial demilitarized zone the moment the petition, voluntary or involuntary, is filed. Under its subdivisions, section 362(a) stays all actions against the debtor, the debtor's property, or the property of the estate to enforce or collect on a prepetition debt.

The stay is self-executing and does not depend on the offending creditor's knowledge either that a bankruptcy case has been filed or of the stay's existence. Some courts say actions taken in violation of the stay "void," others say they are "voidable"; we don't think it matters; in either case they are ineffective and must be undone. This means that all claims against the debtor are essentially frozen in time, such that relationships between each creditor and the debtor, and among creditors *inter se*, are fixed as of filing, pending their resolution in the bankruptcy case. **Note:** the stay does not extinguish any claims against the debtor, it simply delays their enforcement

Here are the questions we want to examine in relation to the automatic stay and section 362:

- What acts are covered by the stay?

- What acts are excepted from the stay?

- When does the stay end?

- How can a creditor get relief from the stay before it ends?

- What are the consequences of violating the stay?

2. Scope of the Stay (What Acts Are Covered)

Section 362(a) is broken into eight paragraphs. Paragraphs (a)(1), (2), and (5)-(8) relate to actions against the debtor or the debtor's property. Paragraphs (a)(2)-(4) preclude actions against property of the estate. If any act does not come within one or more paragraphs, it is not stayed, but do not underestimate the broad scope of section 362(a). It includes, among other things, initiation of formal proceedings, enforcements of liens, seizure of property, enforcement of judgments, and setoff.

Assume, for instance, that Markell owes money to Ponoroff secured by a lien on Markell's boat. After Markell files for bankruptcy, Ponoroff realizes he can't sue Markell for the debt and he knows he can't repossess the boat. Would it be ok if Ponoroff sent Markell a really nice e-mail, complimenting him on his wardrobe, wishing good luck next semester, and suggesting it would "be great if you were also to see your way fit to pay me back." Afraid not. In addition to everything else a creditor can't do to try to get his claim paid, under the catchall provision in 362(a)(6), he also may not undertake "any act . . . to collect a debt that arose before the commencement of the case. . . ." This would include any act or omission done with the objective of coercing (even gently) payment of a debt. So, if Ponoroff simply intimates that Markell is unlikely to get invited to Ponoroff's "must be seen at" Super Bowl party unless Markell ponies up, Ponoroff may also find himself in front of the bankruptcy judge for violating the stay.

While the stay is obviously intended to be, and in fact is, very far-ranging, note what is *not* covered by the stay. First, actions against third parties (nondebtors), including persons who may be liable with the debtor, are not stayed. That means if Markell's Mom guaranteed his debt, Ponoroff can file suit against his Mrs. Markell. Can Mrs. Markell tell her son he better pay or he's facing a "whuppin?" Or that he can't come to her famous Thanksgiving feast (she makes some mean banana and pumpkin bread) unless he makes good his debt? Afraid not on both counts, since Mrs. Markell, as a guarantor of her son's debt, has a contingent claim against him, she's subject to the stay as well!

That said, on rare occasions, courts will exercise their general equitable authority under section 105(a) to extend the stay in Chapter 11 cases to nondebtor third parties where the action against such parties is likely to have a materially adverse effect on the estate. Examples include staying third party actions that threaten to exhaust insurance proceeds critical to reorganization, or diverting the attention of key officers of the company from the reorganization effort. There is some uncertainty as to whether the Supreme Court's decision in *Law v. Siegel*,[29] holding that a bankruptcy court may not use its authority under Code section 105(a) to contradict the clear command of the statute, has limited the authority of bankruptcy judges to extend the stay beyond its statutory reach, but we think the better view is not.

In Chapter 12 and 13 cases there are specific statutory provisions that extend the stay to co-debtors with regard to consumer debts. They are intended to prevent creditors from exerting undue influence over a debtor by threatening to pursue a guarantor who is usually a close relative or friend. Thus, Mrs. Markell would have been protected had her wayward son been thoughtful enough to file under Chapter 13 rather than Chapter 7. *See* section 1301(a)

Second, actions that do not involve an attempt to "recover on a claim" are not barred by the automatic stay. Suppose, for instance, Markell agreed to do 40 hours of community service as part of a plea bargain in an earlier action for driving under the influence. If Markell files bankruptcy before finishing his community service

---

[29]   134 S.Ct. 1188 (2014).

and refuses to continue, can the prosecutor's office haul him back to court to explain himself. The answers if "probably yes," since the state is not seeking on recover on a *claim*.

The reason for the "probably" qualification is that the term "claim," as defined in section 101(a)(5), as we discussed above, includes not only a right to payment against the debtor, but also an equitable remedy if there is an alternative right to payment. Thus, if Markell is responsible, for example, to pay a civil fine in the event he fails to complete his community service, an action against him to compel his compliance might be stayed.

As we saw when we were discussing "claims" at the beginning of this Unit, the distinction not infrequently comes up in connection with environmental cases where the debtor is subject to a "clean-up" order; something that, on its face, does not entail a right to payment. If, however, the governmental authority has, upon the debtor's failure to effect the clean-up, a right to payment for the costs it incurs in remediating the property, that has been held to constitute a "claim," which would then be subject to the stay. The issue also affects whether the (1) obligation is subject to discharge (as only "claims are discharged), and (2) enforcement of the obligation is permitted under the police powers exception to the stay, discussed in Section 3.b below.

3. *Acts Excepted from the Stay (What Acts Are Not Covered)*

The exceptions to the automatic stay are collected in section 362(b) and there are currently no less than 28 of them! By far, however, most of the reported cases involve the exceptions for (1) criminal proceedings against the debtor, and (2) actions by governmental units involving exercise of their police or regulatory power. It is also worth just noting that almost any action to enforce a domestic support obligation is now pretty much insulated from the stay. *See* section 362(b)(2)(B)-(C). Also, actions concerning the withholding, suspension, or restricting of a driver's license or an occupational (professional license), if done in connection with the nonpayment of a child support obligation, are permitted to proceed free from the stay. *See* section 362(b)(2)(D).

a. Criminal Prosecutions

The justification for the exception in 362(b)(1) is obvious. Although some people think you get away with murder just by filing bankruptcy, you shouldn't literally be able to get away with murder—or arson, robbery, etc. The only difficult question involving this exception is in circumstances where the prosecution is being used essentially as a disguised collection device. Suppose the casino where Ponoroff has run up big debts and passed some rubber checks has referred the matter to the county district attorney for prosecution under the state's deposit account fraud statute. After the indictment, the Assistant D.A. handling the case advises Ponoroff's lawyer that the charges will be dropped if Ponoroff makes restitution. At least arguably, these facts suggest that the criminal law has been invoked for debt collection purposes. Thus, some courts have not applied the exception to the stay in section 362(d)(1) where it is determined that the "principal motivation" for the prosecution was to secure repayment of a debt, not vindicate the people's interest in punishing individuals who write checks against insufficient funds.

The more difficult question is whether the bankruptcy court may *enjoin* the state court proceeding if it determines that collection is the primary motive. The consensus that has emerged in the appellate courts is that the bankruptcy courts should not interfere with the state criminal proceeding, except in the case of an imminent threat to a federally-protected right, a standard that federal fresh start policy does not meet. This is consistent with the principle of deference to state court proceedings that the Supreme Court expressed in its decision in *Younger v. Harris*.[30]

b.   Police Powers by a Governmental Unit

Section 362(b)(4) is intended to protect the "health, safety, and welfare" of the public. Thus, it allows a governmental unit to take action free from the stay to prevent or cease violations of the laws regulating things like fraud, consumer protection, safety, environmental protection, etc., including enforcement of any injunctive-type relief obtained in such action. The theory is that, in cases like this, the governmental unit is simply carrying out its regulatory duties and not acting in its capacity as a creditor, even though its action against the debtor may establish money damages due for violation of the law. Much of the case law involving this exception focuses on what's known as the "exception to the exception" in section 362(b)(4); namely, the provision that reads, "including the enforcement of a judgment *other than* a money judgment."

While this distinction makes perfect sense in the abstract, ascertaining in practice when the governmental unit is operating as a creditor, rather than in a regulatory capacity, can be a perplexing undertaking. As previously discussed, environmental cases present a particular challenge in this regards because actions to prevent or remediate violations of the environmental laws fall squarely within the goals intended to be covered by the police powers exception. On the other hand, since the effect of enforcing a clean-up order is to spare the governmental unit from incurring the cost of same, which then would undoubtedly be a claim for money damages, the argument can also be made that enforcement is tantamount to enforcement of a money judgment. In any case, as one commentator has put it, the environmental cases are a mess!

---

[30]   401 U.S. 37 (1971).

The two somewhat overlapping tests that courts have developed in making this determination of whether the governmental entity may be found to be acting as a creditor or in its regulatory capacity—the pecuniary purpose test and the public policy test—are decidedly unhelpful. This means that in most instances the determination will hinge critically on the facts and circumstances of each case. *See In re Nortel Networks, Inc.*[31] wherein the court found that in attempting to enforce liability for underfunded pension plan the governmental entity's motive was to protect its pecuniary interest and not to protect public safety and health.

4. *Termination of the Stay*

The automatic stay is not intended to be permanent. In a manner of speaking, the stay terminates when the purpose for its imposition no longer exists. Up until 2005, there were only two Code provisions addressing termination of the stay. First, with regard to property of the estate, the stay terminates, appropriately enough, when such property is *no longer* property of the estate. *See* section 362(c)(1). So if the property is abandoned, or sold to a third party, the stay terminates. Second, as to any other act covered by section 362(a), the stay terminates upon the earliest of when the case is closed, dismissed, or the debtor's discharge is either granted or denied. *See* section 362(c)(1).

BAPCPA added two more subparagraphs to section 362(c), both intended to address the perceived abuse of the stay by debtors who engaged in serial or bad faith filings. Section 362(c)(3) provides that if an individual debtor (including a joint filer) files a case under Chapter 7, 11, or 13 within one year of the dismissal of an earlier case, then the automatic stay in the new case will terminate 30 days

---

[31]   669 F.3d 128 (3d Cir. 2011).

after the filing, unless the court specifically finds that the case was filed in good faith.

Section 362(c)(4) applies when there was more than one earlier case dismissed in the year prior to the new filing. In these circumstances, there's no messing around with a 30-day grace period before the stay expires. Instead, in the two (or more)— dismissal scenario, the stay simply does not arise on filing and will never arise unless someone (presumably the debtor) convinces the court that the new case has been filed in good faith. Even then, the stay will not apply retroactively, so the damage may already be done.

Both sections 362(c)(3) and (4) operate to augment section 109(g), which limits eligibility of an individual to file a bankruptcy case when the debtor had a bankruptcy case pending in the preceding 180-day period that was dismissed for (a) failure to prosecute or abide by an order of the court, or (b) at the behest of the debtor after a motion for relief from the stay had been lodged. In addition, each of these new paragraphs of section 362(c) contains a lengthy list of circumstances that create a presumption of lack of good faith to assist courts in situations where the debtor seeks to have the stay continued (or imposed) on the ground that her petition was filed in good faith. Finally, they are both blanket in application, except for the exception in section 362(c)(3) for an earlier case dismissed under section 707(b)—a provision governing dismissal of "abusive" Chapter 7 filings (that we take up in Unit 6 below)—and re-filed under Chapter 13, since the whole point of section 707(b) is to re-direct the case to Chapter 13.

Yet another circumstance that can result in the termination of the stay is found in section 362(h)(1), added by the 2005 Amendments. That section terminates the stay in individual Chapter 7 cases with respect to personal property securing a claim as to which the debtor fails to state her intentions, and then perform in accordance with that statement, per section 521(a)(2).[32] BAPCPA also added a provision (section 521(a)(6)) providing that an individual Chapter 7 debtor may not retain personal property subject to a purchase money security interest unless the debtor, within 45 days of the first meeting of creditors, redeems such property or executes a reaffirmation agreement. While section 362(h)(1) refers only to section 521(a)(2) and not section 521(a)(6), the last paragraph in subsection (a)(6) provides that: [i]f the debtor fails to so act within the 45-day period . . ., the stay under section 362(a) is terminated . . . [and], such property shall no longer be property of the estate, and the creditor may take whatever action as to such property as is permitted by applicable nonbankruptcy law, . . .

5. *Relief from Stay*

A creditor who cannot find an exception for its claim, and who is not inclined to wait until the stay terminates, may seek relief from stay, which is principally governed by section 362(d). Relief under section 362(d) is not limited tp termination of the stay with respect to the moving creditor's claim, it could also come in the form of modifying or conditioning continuation of the stay, as we'll see. While any "party in interest" may move for relief from the stay, most often it will be a creditor who does so, and, just as often, a secured creditor To be successful, the moving creditor must establish cause under section 362(d)(1) or, pursuant to 362(d)(2), prove that there is no equity in the property encumbered by the lien *and* that it is not necessary for an effective reorganization. In our usual backassward way, we'll look at the second ground first, and then the first ground second.

---

[32] An individual debtor's obligations with respect to Section 521(a)(2) are discussed in Section C.2 & 3 of Unit 6.

a.   Relief Based on Section 362(d)(2)

In a Chapter 7 case, if there's no equity in property (meaning that the amount of valid liens against a property exceed its lien-free value), then there's nothing in it for general unsecured creditors and really no reason for the trustee to retain the property. Therefore, relief will be granted so that the creditor can repossess and foreclose. Sometimes in these circumstances, as we mentioned earlier, the trustee will recognize this and just "abandon" the property under section 554. If the property is abandoned to the debtor, to whom the stay applies as well, the creditor either still needs relief from stay to seize the property from the debtor. However, section 554 does not specify to whom property is abandoned, and its generally agreed this could be any party with a possessory interest in the property, including include a secured creditor.

In Chapter 7 the absence of equity, once established, pretty much ends the inquiry. In Chapter 11, and even Chapter 13, however, section 362(d)(2) requires examination of another issue, namely whether the property is necessary for an effective reorganization. Under section 362(g), the creditor bears the burden of proving the absence of equity, and the party opposing relief has the burden of proof on all other issues. Thus, the debtor and debtor in possession will have to show necessity; i.e., Ponoroff needs his car to get to work and it is the income from his job that will fund his Chapter 13 plan, or Markell, Inc., a widget manufacturer, cannot possibly hope to reorganize if it loses its widget stamping machinery. Even when necessity is established, the inquiry is not at an end. Particularly in Chapter 11, the debtor in possession must show that it has a "reasonable possibility" of confirming a plan in "a reasonable time." While, early on in a case, courts are inclined to give the debtor in possession some latitude, if the financial problems vexing the debtor are patently unfixable—say the debtor is in the business of manufacturing floppy disks and can't retool to manufacture something else, relief from the stay will be granted in spite of necessity.

b.   Relief for "Cause" Under Section 362(d)(1) (Herein of Adequate Protection)

Even if there is a reason to continue the stay in the interests of the bankruptcy case under section 362(d)(2), relief may also be granted if the moving party can show that its interests are somehow at risk. This entails establishing "cause." Section 362(d)(1) states that cause "includes" lack of adequate protection of an interest in property of the movant. Note that when the Code uses the term "includes" and "including," it is *not limiting*. *See* section 102(2). Thus, lack of adequate protection is only one example of cause, although it's the big one. Before examining that concept, consider what else might constitute cause. If the encumbered property is somehow in jeopardy, such as not properly insured or not being properly maintained, this might constitute cause for the court to condition continuation of the stay on the estate promptly remedying whatever it is putting the creditor's interest at risk. Cause might also include that a state court action is sufficiently far along that it makes sense to reduce the claim to judgment in that setting. Thus, Ponoroff might assert, "Judge, my battery claim against Markell (the debtor) was just a couple of days away from trial when that scoundrel filed bankruptcy. Let me go ahead and have my claim determined in that forum." This is an example when the court might modify the stay to permit the state court action to proceed to judgment (that is, to allow the claim to be liquidated in state court), but of course not allow any action to collect on that judgment.

Lack of "adequate protection," a concept that comes up a lot under the Code, is most often the basis on which stay relief is sought under section 362(d)(1). Because Chapter 7, and even Chapter 13, cases move along fairly quickly, adequate protection issues in relation to the stay most often come up in Chapter 11 cases, which can go on for months and even years.

Two questions must be answered in relation to the allegation of lack of adequate protection: (1) what is the interest in property entitled to adequate protection, and (2) what is the method for providing adequate protection. In the case of secured debt, adequate protection is concerned with the *value of the interest in property*, and not necessarily the amount of the debt. Section 361 offers a nonexclusive list of the methods for providing adequate protection of that interest, including periodic payments, additional collateral, or such other relief as will provide the moving party with the "indubitable equivalent" of its interest in the debtor's property.

What this all means can be illustrated by the following example. Let's assume Markell's Awesome Videos, Inc. ("MAV") files Chapter 11. Ponoroff has a security interest in all of MAV's photographic equipment securing a debt of $500,000. If the equipment is only worth $400,000, Ponoroff might seek relief under section 362(d)(2) based on lack of equity, but MAV has a pretty good argument that this equipment is necessary for an effective reorganization. Whether or not Ponoroff can then seek relief under section 362(d)(1) on the grounds that his interest is not adequately protected will depend on whether the *value* of the equipment is stable. If so, or if it is actually increasing in value, then Ponoroff's interest in property is adequately protected. If it is declining in value, however, then Ponoroff is entitled to adequate protection, unless that decline is not due to the delay experienced by Ponoroff in realizing on his collateral on account of the stay. Adequate protection might take the form of periodic payments equal to the rate of depreciation in the value of the equipment. The idea is that Ponoroff's $400,000 secured claim must be protected. If MAV cannot come up with those payments, or some equivalent form of protection, then Ponoroff gets relief from stay.

Now, let's change the facts so that the equipment is worth $600,000. Clearly no relief under section 362(d)(2). What about, however, under section 362(d)(1) if Ponoroff can show the equipment is declining in value at the rate of $500 per month. Sorry, Charlie, no dice. Ponoroff is adequately protected by the "equity cushion"—that is, the positive difference between the value of the equipment and the amount of the debt—and will remain so unless and until the equipment reaches and falls below the amount of Ponoroff's secured claim. As noted, "cause" under section 362(d)(1) is not limited to lack of adequate protection, so Ponoroff might still prevail if he can show, for instance, that MAV had allowed its insurance coverage on the equipment to lapse

For a time, there was a question in the scenario immediately above as to whether Ponoroff's "interest in property" for purposes of section 362(d)(1) included the opportunity to reinvest the value of the property; that is the "lost opportunity cost" associated with the stay and the inability to sell the collateral; i.e., the time value of money. That is a right with real economic value that is part of the creditor's state law bargain with the debtor, and payment of postpetition interest as adequate protection would rectify the loss.

The issue came to a head in *United Savs. Assocs. Of Texas v. Timbers of Inwood Forest Assocs., Ltd.*,[33] a case in which the Supreme Court rejected the argument that adequate protection entitled an undersecured creditor to compensation for lost opportunity cost. The conclusion that an undersecured creditor is not entitled to compensation for delay due to the stay is, in other words, a holding that the undersecured creditor is not entitled to postpetition interest on its secured claim. Once more, a creditor's

---

[33]   484 U.S. 365 (1987).

entitlement to adequate protection focuses only on preservation of the value of the *collateral* throughout the case (depreciation), not losses due to delay in payment. Except as provided in section 506(b) (with respect to oversecured claims as we discussed above), *Timbers*, together with section 502(b)(2) (disallowing claims for unmatured interest), establishes an important point about bankruptcy. That is, the filing of a bankruptcy case stops the clock insofar as interest is concerned. This "free money" can be particularly important—and valuable to the debtor—in a Chapter 11 case.

Now, suppose, in the example above, that the court determines that equipment is worth $500,000 (the amount of the claim), but that Ponoroff is entitled to adequate protection payments of $500 per month because that's the rate of depreciation on the equipment. Then, six months later, when the debtor converts to a Chapter 7 case and the equipment is actually sold, it yields only $475,000, instead of the $494,000 as predicted by the $500 depreciation estimation. Is Ponoroff just out of luck because the court goofed in either its valuation of the collateral or the rate of depreciation? Certainly not. In these circumstances section 507(b) comes to Ponoroff's rescue and provides him with an administrative expense priority for, in this scenario, $22,000 (the excess depreciation over the $500 per month). Moreover, it is a kind of superpriority, in that it ranks above all of the other section 503(b) administrative expenses entitled to second priority under section 507(a)(2).

6. *Violations of the Stay*

Although operating as an injunction against collection, the automatic stay is effective without notice to claimholders and any action, even unknowing innocent actions, taken in contravention of the stay must be undone—and fast. Actions taken in violation of the estate are without legal effect. So, if a foreclosure occurs one second after a bankruptcy filing (and bankruptcy courts clock in documents with precision to the second), then the foreclosure can and will be unwound, even if the foreclosing creditor did not know about the bankruptcy filing, and despite the fact that the debtor has no defense whatsoever under state law to the foreclosure.

The principal question, then, in this area is under what circumstances a creditor who knowingly violates the stay, or fails to undo a stay violation after being made aware of the bankruptcy case, can be held liable for damages. To begin with, the operative statutory provision is section 362(k)(1), which provides for actual damages, including costs and attorneys' fee, for *willful* violations of the stay, as well as, if the circumstances warrant, punitive damages. What does it take to constitute a willful violation? Suppose Markell, a local butcher, has a security interest in Ponoroff's car, which was taken as collateral for a personal loan from Markell that Ponoroff needed in order to pay for a hair transplant. Ponoroff is in default in his payments, and, even though he received a notice yesterday from the bankruptcy court advising him of Ponoroff's filing, Markell sends one of his meat cutters to pick up the car. In response to Ponoroff's action to recover damages and attorneys' fees under section 362(k)(1), Markell argues: "Hey, I'm a butcher, what do I know about bankruptcy and this automatic stay thing." Will the argument prevail? Probably not, Markell intentionally engaged in the violation after receiving notification of the bankruptcy. The fact he wasn't aware of the legal consequences of that filing is irrelevant; it was incumbent on him once he learned of the case to consult with a lawyer to determine what was and what was not kosher.

Now suppose in this last problem the borrower was Ponoroff Finance, Inc. ("PFI"), rather than Ponoroff the elegant but unhirsute individual. Does Markell now have a defense to an action under section 362(k)(1)? Read the statute carefully; it says that an *individual* injured by a willful violation is entitled to damages thereunder. PFI is a corporation. So, is Markell out of the woods? Probably not. First, some courts have not limited application of section 362(k)(1) to natural persons, but this is dubious when measured against the clear language of the statute. A second approach, which avoids doing violence to statutory text, is predicated on the fact that because the stay is in the nature of an injunction, it can be enforced under the court's power to punish for civil contempt. Thus, the contempt sanction is available to remedy Markell's stay violation. It should be noted, however, that the decision to impose sanctions for contempt is discretionary with the court, whereas section 362(k)(1) states that a human being injured by a willful stay violation *shall* recover damages, including possibly punitive damages. Additionally, contempt must be proved by clear and convincing evidence (and not just a mere preponderance). So, perhaps, if Markell could convince the court that it was "all just a big mistake," he might escape punishment for contempt.

Section 362(k)(2), added to the Code in 2005, also insulates some stay violations from liability for punitive damages. Specifically, if the violation was undertaken with the "good faith" belief that the stay had been lifted under section 362(h)(1), when it hadn't, liability is limited to actual damages. It will be recalled, section 362(h)(1) terminates the stay in the case of an individual debtor who fails to state his or her intentions with respect to personal property that is collateral for a loan within 30 days of the filing of the bankruptcy case.

D. Discharge

1. Limitations on the Discharge

Perhaps no aspect of the system is more commonly associated with term "bankruptcy" in the public mind than the discharge from debts. The discharge *is* a big deal, but there are a few limitations that need to be kept in mind.

First, *who* is entitled to discharge and *when* the discharge is granted varies based on the chapter of the Code under which the case is pending. For example, corporations can't receive a discharge in Chapter 7. Because we have separate Units in this book examining some of the unique aspects of Chapters 7, 13 and 11 cases, we will reserve discussion of the differences in application of the discharge in each type of case until we get around to those Units (if you can't wait, we can't stop you of course from jumping ahead).

Second, the discharge doesn't *eliminate* any debts, it only relieves the debtor from personal (*in personam*) liability on his or her obligations. Accordingly, if Ponoroff's debt to Bank is guaranteed by Markell, Ponoroff's discharge does not affect Markell's liability on his guaranty. Bank can sue Markell on the guaranty and just ignore Ponoroff's discharge. By the same token, if Ponoroff's debt to is secured by a lien on his property, Ponoroff's discharge will not affect the Bank's rights as a lienholder to satisfy its claim out of its collateral. A secured creditor's *in rem* claim against property is not discharged in the bankruptcy case. Bank could foreclose and sell or take the collateral, but of course it could not pursue Ponoroff for any deficiency.

Third, not all debts are dischargeable; though which debts survive again depends on who is the debtor and under what chapter of the Code the case is filed. Once more, we will take these matters up in the individual Units relating to Chapters 7, 13, and 11. For now, it is sufficient to recall the oft-repeated (and not quite accurate) point made by the Supreme Court in *Local Loan Co. v. Hunt*,[34] that the discharge "gives the honest but unfortunate debtor . . . a new opportunity in life and a clear field for future effort, unhampered by the pressure and discouragement of preexisting debt."

Fourth, in Chapter 7, only debts arising prior to the filing of the case are discharged. If the debtor runs over a pedestrian on his way to the courthouse, that claim is subject to discharge. If the debtor runs over that same person on her way *back* from the courthouse, the resulting tort claim will *not* be subject to the discharge. In Chapter 13, the discharge, when entered, relates only to claims provided for in the plan or disallowed under section 502. Finally, in Chapter 11, the discharge relates to all claims arising prior to confirmation of the debtor's plan of reorganization, although, as we'll see, that rule may be subject to qualification in individual Chapter 11 cases.

2.   *The Discharge Injunction*

Section 524(a) bars any attempt to collect a prepetition debt "as a personal liability of the debtor." Like section 362(a), section 524(a) operates as an injunction, the violation of which can be sanctioned under the court's contempt power. Indeed, in a manner of speaking, section 524(a) permanently continues the stay with respect to discharged debts. Any action in violation of the discharge injunction is void. Again, bear in mind that the discharge injunction does *not* prevent the holder of a lien from enforcing its claim against the property subject to the lien, or from pursuing collection against any other party also liable on the debt, such as a guarantor.

---

[34]   292 U.S. 234, 244 (1934).

While even a polite request by a creditor to the debtor to pay a discharged debt will violate section 524(a)(2), nothing prevents the debtor from voluntarily paying the debt if she chooses. *See* section 524(f). That is, the money does not have to be returned by the creditor. In addition, courts have recognized an exception to section 524(a)(2)'s prohibition in circumstances when the debtor is ordered by a court in a criminal case to make restitution on a discharged debt. As discussed above in connection with the stay exception for criminal actions, the federal courts are generally disinclined to interfere with criminal proceedings in the state courts.

3. *Protection Against Discriminatory Treatment*

The fresh start that the discharge from debts is intended to facilitate could be weakened considerably if various parties were allowed to retaliate against a debtor for having filed bankruptcy. Section 525 is designed to prohibit such conduct, but this provision definitely has its limitations. It is broken into three parts, so let's take a look at each.

First, section 525(a) applies to governmental units and proscribes discrimination based on the filing of the bankruptcy case or the discharge of any unpaid debt in connection with (1) license/permit grants and renewals, and (2) employment. So, California can't refuse Markell's annual application for renewal of his bar registration because Markell discharged last year's registration fee in a bankruptcy case.

Second, section 525(b) restricts discrimination by private employers based on bankruptcy. Just like governmental units, a private employer may not fire an employee or discriminate with respect to employment because of her bankruptcy filing. *But* unlike section 525(a), section 525(b) does *not* preclude private employers from engaging in discrimination with respect to *hiring*. So the district attorney's office can't reject Ponoroff's employment application because he filed bankruptcy last year, but Carvass, Swaim, and Moorg, which pays ten times as much as the DA's office, can tell Ponoroff to get lost when, as part of the hiring background check, the firm's HR department learns of his prior bankruptcy.

Lastly, section 525(c) is a latter (1994) addition to the statute which, you'll be pleased to hear, prohibits discrimination in connection with student loans. It applies to both governmental units and private persons engaged in the business of making student loans, although the government has largely now taken over that business *in toto.* Under this provision, lenders are proscribed from denying a student loan because the borrower is or was in a bankruptcy proceeding, or failed to pay a dischargeable debt.

It is important to recognize that both sections 525(a) and (b) prohibit discrimination based *solely* on bankruptcy. Section 525(c) is not so limited. It's easy to see how that language can cause some mischief. Specifically, the language suggests that if the discrimination with respect, for example, to the debtor's employment was motivated by factors *in addition to* the debtor's bankruptcy, the statute is not violated. But how do you prove that? Suppose on learning that Markell filed bankruptcy last year, Ponoroff terminates him from his job parking cars at the country club based on concern that members will feel uncomfortable trusting their expensive cars to a deadbeat like Markell. Tough one, huh? The courts think so too, and haven't given us any clear answerz.

In relation to the revocation of a license under section 525(a) the Supreme Court has shed a little light on the issue. In *FCC v. NextWave Personal Communications,*[35] the debtor had acquired certain broadcast licenses in an FCC auction, paying partly in cash

---

[35]   537 U.S. 293 (2003).

and partly by executing a promissory note secured by a security interest in the licenses. While still current on it payments under the note, the debtor later filed under Chapter 11. After the filing, the debtor defaulted on its payments and the FCC cancelled the licenses based on an "automatic cancellation of default" provision in the loan documents. The debtor challenged the FCC's action under section 525(a), and the FCC defended claiming that its actions were based at least in part on advancing its regulatory mission with respect to the broadband spectrum. The Court rejected this argument on the ground that the statute's prohibition against revocation of a license based solely on nonpayment of a debt cannot be negated by the presence of some further motive beyond the nonpayment, lest section 525 lose all force.

Avoiding Powers

A. Introduction

This is a subject on which you're likely going to spend a lot of class time. So, let's begin by setting out some basics:

- The avoiding powers are exercised to achieve certain key objectives in a bankruptcy case, most notably the goal of equitable treatment among creditors. In bankruptcy, it is frequently said that "equality equals equity" (or "equity equals equality," we can never remember which way it goes, but we don't think it matters).

- The power to bring an avoidance action—by which we mean undo or set aside some pre or post-filing transfer—belongs to the trustee. However, bear in mind two things: (1) in Chapter 11 the debtor in possession has the powers of a trustee, and (2) if the debtor in possession fails to act, the court can authorize a creditor or committee of creditors to bring the action.

- The avoiding powers are not automatic. The ability to avoid must be established by proof adduced in an adversary proceeding brought by the estate representative—either the trustee or the debtor in possession. As a result, if a dead-bang preference exists, but the trustee does not pursue it, the transaction will not be avoided.

- Even when a transaction is avoided, the avoidance of a transfer does not automatically result in an increase in the size of the estate. If a transfer avoided was the creation of a lien, the property subject to lien was already in the estate. If the transfer was an absolute transfer of the debtor's property (Ponoroff paid Markell $100 the day before filing bankruptcy), then the transfer must not just be set aside (avoided), but the property also *recovered,* which implicates section 550 of the Code. Under section 550, not only can the transfer (or its value) be recovered from the transferee (or any transferee of the initial transfer), but also from anyone for whose benefit the transfer was made.

- The time period (statute of limitations) for bringing an avoidance action is governed by section 546(a), which provides that the trustee has the lesser of two years after entry of an order for relief or the time the case is closed or dismissed within which to bring avoidance actions, subject to possible extension in cases where the trustee is not first appointed until more than one year (but before two years) after entry of the order for relief.

- With the exception of the power to avoid fraudulent transfers, all of the avoiding powers contained in

Chapter 5 of the Code are basically unique to bankruptcy.

- There is also one *debtor* avoiding power contained in section 522(f) that we will take up separately in Unit 6.

- Maybe your casebook is (like ours) anally retentive and has a section 502(d) problem. Under that provision, if a creditor received an avoidable transfer that has not yet been recovered under section 550, then any unsecured claim of that creditor is disallowed. So, assume Markell owes Ponoroff $10,000 and, prepetition, made a preferential payment on that debt of $50. If that $50 preference is not returned by Ponoroff, his entire claim for the balance—$9,950—is disallowed. Creates some incentive to pony up, huh?

The most important avoiding powers, and the ones on which we will spend most of our time on in this Unit, are the trustee's ability to avoid (1) unrecorded or untimely recorded transfers, (2) fraudulent transfers, and (3) preferential transfers. Once through those three topics, we will mention briefly some of the trustee's other avoiding powers and related matters.

B. Unrecorded Transfers (Herein of the Trustee's "Strong-Arm" Powers)

Bankruptcy itself does not call for the recording of a transfer of an interest in the debtor's property, but state law does. If you are taking, or have already taken, the Secured Transaction course, you know that public recording (i.e., filing a financing statement) is the principal mechanism that the U.C.C. Article 9 employs to deal with the problem of *ostensible ownership*. By this we mean the potentially misleading effect that can result when a debtor grants a security interest in its property to a creditor but retains possession of that property. If not aware of the secured creditor's interest, other creditors might be misled into believing that the debtor is more creditworthy than it really is by virtue of the debtor's apparent ownership of that property. Public recording of that interest, whether an Article 9 security interest or a real property mortgage or deed of trust, is how our law deals with the problem of ostensible ownership in the case of nonpossessory security interests. Thus, failure to provide notice of an interest through recording will typically result in avoidance of that interest.

How does this occur, you ask? Section 544(a)(1) of the Code confers on the trustee the status of a hypothetical lien creditor whose lien arises as of the moment of filing. While this status derives from federal law, what the trustee can do with that status depends on state or applicable nonfederal bankruptcy law. Think of it this way, the Bankruptcy Code says, "trustee, you have the rights and powers of a lien creditor. Now go and stomp on anyone who would lose to a lien creditor." So much for pick on someone your own size. . . .

Most vulnerable under the trustee's strong-arm power will be an unperfected security interest in personal property or a mortgage on real property. With respect to personal property, a security interest arises under Article 9 of the U.C.C. (enacted more or less uniformly in all 50 states, and so something that is fair game in a federal bankruptcy class) when it *attaches*; perfection occurs when the secured party takes the steps necessary to establish its priority vis-à-vis third parties. Most often, this will entail filing a financing statement in the state's U.C.C filing system. More importantly, however, for our purposes, under U.C.C. § 9-317(a)(2) an unperfected security interest is subordinate to a lien creditor. This means that the trustee, who has the rights and powers of a judicial lien creditor under section 544(a)(1), can avoid (set aside) the security interest, the effect of which is to leave the creditor with a wholly unsecured claim. The theory is that if the secured creditor failed to take the minimum steps necessary to establish its rights against third parties under state law, it should not be able to assert the existence of that security interest in bankruptcy to take priority in that collateral over other unsecured creditors. Note that this result follows even though unsecured creditors do *not* have priority over an unperfected security interest under Article 9.

This outcome is subject to an important exception. Suppose Markell sells Ponoroff a new Trek Performance racing bicycle in return for a small downpayment and Ponoroff's promissory note for the balance of the purchase price. Markell reserves a security interest in the bike as collateral for Ponoroff's obligation under the note. Ponoroff promptly uses the bike to ride to the bankruptcy court and file a Chapter 7 petition before Markell can perfect his security interest by filing a financing statement. Two days later Markell gets around to filing his financing statement and the questions are (1) can Markell's security interest be set aside under section 544(a)(1), and (2) did Markell violate the automatic stay by perfecting his security interest? The answers are "no" and "no."

The first "no" is due to the fact that section 546(b) makes the trustee's strong-arm powers subject to any applicable nonbankruptcy rules where the priority established by filing is deemed to relate back to an earlier time—and if that earlier time is prior to the bankruptcy filing, then the trustee will not be able to avoid the lien. The most common example of this is the provision in U.C.C. § 9-317(e) that says if a purchase money security interest is perfected by filing within 20 days after the debtor receives possession of the collateral, the perfection is deemed to occur not upon filing the financing statement but rather *relates back* to the earlier date of attachment. The second "no" is due to section 362(b)(3), which creates an exception to the stay in this situation in order to permit the filing of a financing statement after the bankruptcy petition is filed.

So, now, let suppose that on May 1, Markell advances Ponoroff $1,000 to buy a special edition Peyton Manning jersey and takes a security interest in the jersey as collateral. If Ponoroff buys the jersey the same day (and why wouldn't he) that is when the security interest "attaches" under U.C.C. § 9-203(b). Next, assume Ponoroff files for bankruptcy before Markell files his financing statement. Easy case for application of § 544(a), *unless* Markell files before May 21, in which case his perfection will be deemed to relate back to March 1, thus thwarting the trustee in Ponoroff's bankruptcy case.

While paragraph (1) of section 544(a) is the most commonly invoked provision, there are two additional paragraphs in the statute. Under section 544(a)(2), which hardly ever comes up, the trustee is given the status of a creditor with an execution against the debtor returned unsatisfied. Section 544(a)(3) confers on the trustee the status of a bona fide purchaser of real estate. Again, in both situations, what rights those statuses confer depends on applicable state law. Cases do come up under section 544(a)(3), and usually include the right to set aside unrecorded purchases of, and mortgages or deeds of trust on, real property. So if Ponoroff borrows money from Markell in return for a note secured by a mortgage on Ponoroff's property that Markell neglects to record in the real estate records, Markell's lien can be avoided should Ponoroff later file bankruptcy. Alternatively, if Markell bought the property but neglected to record the deed, section 544(a)(3) would also seem to apply, even though that transaction does not implicate the "secret lien" concern of the unrecorded mortgage.

In all three parts of section 544(a) the trustee's status is given "without regard to any knowledge of the trustee or of any creditor"—that's part of the hypothetical part of the hypothetical lien creditor. This may be important in a Chapter 11 case since the debtor in possession will almost certainly have knowledge of a transaction in which it engaged, but that actual knowledge will not preclude the debtor in possession from avoiding the lien. On the other hand, while the *specific* knowledge of the trustee is disregarded, if, in the case of real property, the lienor or buyer has done something to give general notice to the world, other than by recording, the trustee will not take free of this type of knowledge since it goes to her "bona fide" status. As a matter of state law, a bona fide person is generally one who takes in good faith, for value, and *without knowledge* of the prior interest. So, if Markell buys Ponoroff's property and immediately takes up residence, state law might regard open possession of the property as conferring the same kind of constructive notice as recording. If so, Ponoroff's trustee is out-of-luck. By contrast, in the case of personal property, knowledge is irrelevant to the priority that a lien creditor enjoys over an unperfected security interest under U.C.C. 9-317(a)(2)

C. Fraudulent Transfers

Fraudulent transfers, unlike the trustee's other avoiding powers, can be set aside outside of bankruptcy as well as in a bankruptcy case. Most states (although not New York) have adopted the Uniform Fraudulent Transfers Act ("UFTA"), which is likely in your statute book,[36] and is similar, but not identical, to the Code's fraudulent transfer statute: section 548. As we'll see, both state law and federal bankruptcy law talk not only about fraudulent *transfers*, but also fraudulent *obligations*. Neither is a good thing in the eyes of the law and, hence, can be undone by the trustee.

---

[36] On July 16, 2014, the Uniform Law Commission adopted the Uniform Voidable Transactions Act ("UVTA") to replace the UFTA. Largely the Act consists of a series of amendments to the UFTA designed, among other purposes, to achieve greater harmony with the bankruptcy law. As of this writing, the UVTA has been enacted in eight states and is pending in three others.

Fraudulent transfers (and obligations) come in two flavors—actual and constructive. Let's take a look at each.

1. *Actually Fraudulent Transfers*

These are transfers made (or obligations incurred) to "hinder, delay, or defraud" creditors. These are the kinds of transactions that normally come to mind when most people think about "fraudulent transfers." These are the most obvious kinds of fraudulent transfers. Suppose Ponoroff's creditors are bearing down on him and he's worried that one day one of them is going to have the sheriff grab his little BMW convertible, a thought he cannot bear. So he makes a "deal" with his buddy Markell to sell Markell the BMW for a one dollar, with the understanding that Ponoroff can continue to use it and that, when Ponoroff's troubles with his creditors are over, Markell will "sell" it back to him.

What was the purpose of this transaction? Duh, to thwart Ponoroff's creditors by placing his assets beyond their reach (they can't attach or levy upon something that isn't titled in or owned by their debtor, Ponoroff). If Ponoroff files bankruptcy any time in the next two years, the trustee in his case should be able to avoid this transaction under Code section 548(a)(1)(A), and recover the BMW or its value from Markell under section 550(a)(1). Note the key language in section 548(a)(1)(A)—that the transfer was made with *actual intent* to hinder, delay, or defraud. How does the trustee prove intent? Well, the trustee could place Ponoroff under oath and ask him, but we all know how far that will get the trustee. In fact, as in most instances where intent is an element of a cause, it is proved not directly, but inferentially from circumstantial evidence. In the case of fraudulent transfers, over the centuries, Anglo-American courts have developed certain factors, called "badges of fraud," which are treated by courts as strong indicators of intent.

Some of the most common badges of fraud are:

- That the transfer was made in secret

- That very little consideration was paid by the transferee

- That the transferor retained possession of the property

- That the transferee was someone close to the transferor, like a family member or friend

- That the transfer was made after a judgment was entered against the transferor.

Can you think of some other badges of fraud? The drafters of the UFTA came up with 11 of them in section 4(b) of that Act.

BAPCPA went after a particular kind of actually fraudulent transfer by adopting section 548(e)(1), which applies to transfers to a self-settled trust; that is, a trust for the benefit of the guy who sets up the trust (the "settlor"). Until 1997, debtors who wanted to hide their assets in a self-settled trust had to go offshore. These transfers were not recognized as proper trusts by the common law, but if the debtor went to an offshore trust haven that did not recognize U.S. judgments, it could be tough for the trustee to get the money back. In an effort to compete for some of these dollars, in 1997 Alaska adopted a law recognizing self-settled trusts set up with an Alaska bank as trustee. A few other states, including Delaware, followed suit. To address this new phenomenon, section 548(e)(1) makes the creation of such a trust set up with actual intent to defraud a recoverable fraudulent transfer. What's unique about this provision is that the reach back period is a full *ten years*! And it does not matter whether the debtor was trying to stiff his existing creditors or his future creditors; i.e., the new doctor who, fearing a big malpractice judgment one day, sets up one of these trusts upon opening her practice, may be vulnerable under section 548(e)(1) if a bankruptcy case is filed any time in the next ten years.

2. *Constructively Fraudulent Transfers*

a. In General

When we use the term "constructive" in the law, whatever follows is basically made up. In tax law, for example, we have the "constructive receipt" doctrine under which the taxpayer is deemed to have received income in the current year even though it won't *actually* be received until a later year. We're all familiar with the "constructive notice" doctrine in property law, where the recording of a deed or mortgage is deemed to put the whole world on notice of that interest, regardless of whether there's actual notice by any particular person. And so we have "constructive fraud" in the law of fraudulent transfers; transactions that may not involve actual fraud, but which will be deemed fraudulent because of their prejudicial effect on creditors.

Section 548(a)(1)(B) covers constructively fraudulent transfers. There are potentially four types of such transactions, but they all have *one thing* in common. In each case, the debtor must have received *less than* "reasonably equivalent value" in exchange for the transfer made or obligation incurred. Reasonably equivalent value is a factual matter, and thus we can't give you bright line rules. In essence, the court compares what the debtor received to what others might have paid or received for the same item, or the same obligation. Some things are clearly made without receiving reasonably equivalent value: gifts and corporate dividends are examples of transfers of property for less than reasonably equivalent value; co-signing a debt or guaranteeing a loan are examples of obligations incurred for less than reasonably equivalent value (assuming we are not dealing with a commercial surety who charges for bonds and other similar types of guaranties).

The most common of the four types of transactions that, when paired with a lack of reasonably equivalent value, is found in section 548(a)(1)(B)(ii)(I), which applies where the debtor was insolvent when the transfer was made or became insolvent as a result of the transfer. The provision reflects the adage that "a debtor must be just before she is generous." So, suppose Ponoroff's assets are less than his debts (not hard to imagine), but he does have some cash in his bank account. Recalling what a fine co-author Markell is (never late with his materials)[37] Ponoroff decides to buy and give Markell a $5,000 65-inch flat screen LED SmartTV on Markell's birthday. Six months later, with his creditors pressing in, Ponoroff files Chapter 7. It's easy to see how Ponoroff's innocent generosity has cost his creditors. Because the transfer occurred within two years of the filing, the trustee can seek to set it aside and, upon doing so, compel Markell under section 550(a)(1) to return the TV (or its value) to the estate.[38]

Note that under section 550(a)(2), even if Markell has since sold or given the TV to someone else, the trustee can still go after it (or after Markell for its value). However, if Markell sold the TV to his next-door neighbor, who paid fair market value, took in good faith, and without knowledge of the avoidability of the initial transfer, then Markell's innocent neighbor has a defense under section 550(b)(1) and the trustee is limited to pursuing Markell for the value of the TV.

Note also that determining the *time* the transfer occurs is important both in relation to the within two years of filing and the insolvency requirements. In the example above, it was pretty easy

---

[37] [Note from Markell: This is Ponoroff being passive-aggressive. Markell is reliably late with almost all his submissions.]

[38] Although Markell would have to give up the asset or its value, he would receive back a claim in the bankruptcy case. So if Markell pays the trustee $5,000, he gets a $5,000 claim against the estate. If the debtor was insolvent (and if it's Ponoroff, that's almost a lock), then Markell will not get anything like the $5,000 when the estate pays out its dividends.

to know when the transfer occurred—on Markell's birthday when Ponoroff showed up at his door with a large box. But now let's suppose Ponoroff transfers title to the house in which he and his spouse live, and which is titled solely in his name, to his wife on July 1, 2016. Because, however, it's a cozy deal, no one worries much about recording the deed and, in fact, Ponoroff's wife doesn't get around to doing so until September 1, 2016. Under section 548(d)(1), the transfer is treated as happening on September 1 because that's the date under state real property law that a bona fide purchaser of the property from Ponoroff could not obtain an interest in the property superior to Ponoroff's spouse. The point is that if Ponoroff wasn't insolvent on July 1, but became so by September 1, the transaction would be avoidable in a bankruptcy case filed by Ponoroff on or before August 31, 2018. Note that on these facts, including the relationship between the parties and the absence of consideration, the trustee would probably look closely at whether this kind of deal might also be challenged as *actually* fraudulent.

The other three kinds of transfers that the trustee may set aside under section 548(a)(1)(B)(ii) if insufficient value was not received in return, and there are where:

- The debtor was engaged or about to engage in a business for which the property remaining with the debtor was an unreasonably small capital (undercapitalized).

- The debtor intended to, or believed it would incur, debts beyond the debtor's ability to pay as they matured (equity-sense insolvency).

- The transfer was made to an insider under an employment contract and outside the ordinary course of business (a 2005 addition to the statute).

In all likelihood, this section of your casebook will (like ours) examine two types of corporate transactions potentially involving constructively fraudulent transfers: intracorporate guarantees and leveraged buyout transactions (LBOs). So let's take a brief look at the basics of each.

b.   Intracorporate Guaranties

Many businesses are operated through a family of affiliated companies that together represent a single, integrated economic enterprise. But our corporate law follows "entity theory"—each corporation forming part of this single enterprise is treated as a separate legal person. Thus, when one member of the corporate family guaranties the debt of another (incurs an obligation), fraudulent transfer issues are implicated should, for instance, the guaranty cause the company incurring the obligation to become insolvent.

Let's suppose Markell, Inc. has two wholly-owned subsidiaries: Larry Ltd. and Bruce Bros. Co. Three kinds of guaranties might occur between and among these affiliated companies. (1) Markell might guaranty a loan made by a bank to either Larry or Bruce (a "downstream guaranty"), (2) Larry or Bruce might guaranty a loan made by a bank to Markell (an "upstream guaranty"), or (3) Larry might guaranty a loan made by a bank to Bruce (or Bruce to Larry) (a "cross-stream guaranty"). Now if we assume in all cases that the party making the guaranty is (or is rendered) insolvent by taking on the obligation we have a problem, except in the first case, of reasonably equivalent value, since the loan proceeds—the value— are going to a different entity. The first case is not a problem because the parent who guaranties a subsidiary's debt is simply protecting its investment in that company; the extension of credit to the wholly-owned subsidiary represents sufficient return value. In the other two situations, however, there is obviously no benefit to the guarantor, at least no direct benefit.

Although the value given for the obligation goes to a third party and not the company incurring the obligation in these situations, the company making the guaranty may still be *benefited* in the sense that the larger economic enterprise, of which it is a part is better off as a result of the new credit. That is to say, it is benefitted indirectly. But is this *indirect benefit,* even if it counts as value, sufficient to constitute *reasonably equivalent* value? Making that determination can be a tricky exercise. Moreover, even if not, did the undertaking of the obligation render the debtor insolvent? In making that determination, you can't necessarily treat the guaranty obligation at face value, since it's a contingent obligation. Therefore, unless it is virtually certain that the debtor will be called upon on the guaranty, the amount of the debt has to be discounted in performing the solvency analysis. Suffice it to say, different courts take different views about how much certainty is required in proving both indirect benefit and the amount of the liability. What you need to do on your exam is recognize the issue of indirect value and talk about both the question of reasonably equivalent value and a triggering event, such as insolvency or insufficient capital to support business needs.

c.   LBOs

Ok, that was tough sledding, but the application of fraudulent transfer law to LBOs is even worse—maybe. Bear in mind that while LBOs come in a multitude of different forms, what they all have at their essence is that the assets of the company being sold and used to finance the purchase of the company.

A "simple" example: Markell is the sole shareholder of Markell, Inc. ("MI"). MI is a solvent company with lots of unsecured creditors. Ponoroff wishes to purchase MI from Markell and, to accomplish this he borrows the purchase price from Bank. As soon as Ponoroff acquires control of MI, he causes MI put up its assets as collateral for Ponoroff's loan. If MI later goes under and Ponoroff can't pay the debt, Bank will grab the assets and the unsecured creditors—who had been dealing with a solvent entity when they extended credit—now find themselves holding the bag. Assuming insolvency, did MI receive reasonably equivalent value for the lien it granted on its assets? Well, all it got in return was new management, which Ponoroff will probably claim was worth it, but since the company failed, the assertion is dubious. Instead, what really happened is that Markell's prior equity position was converted to secured debt at the expense of unsecured creditors. When this occurs, the lien may be avoided as a fraudulent transfer.

The effect of avoiding the transfer as a fraudulent transfer could be that the bank's lien is set aside. Alternatively, the value of the collateral might be recovered from Ponoroff, as the party benefitted by the transfer under section 550(a). Whether or not recovery can be had from Markell in the form of return of the purchase price paid for his stock will depend on whether Markell acted in bad faith, such as if he knew all of the terms of the deal and that the effect of the transfer would leave MI unable to pay its unsecured creditors. If, however, MI were a public company, the selling shareholders would be protected under section 546(e), something we daresay you probably won't cover in class!

3. *Use of State Fraudulent Transfer Law*

As we mentioned at the beginning of this section, fraudulent transfers are also avoidable under state law. So what does that have to do with bankruptcy? As it happens, quite a bit due to section 544(b) of the Code, which confers on the trustee the powers of an actual unsecured creditor to avoid transfers under nonbankruptcy law. This means that a transaction that could have been avoided by a creditor under *applicable law* (usually state law) can be avoided by the bankruptcy trustee. Because the trustee succeeds to the rights of an *actual* creditor under section 544(b), unlike under section 544(a) where the trustee succeeds to the rights of a *hypothetical* creditor, section 544(b)(1) requires that a creditor that had the power to avoid a transfer actually be in existence at the time of the filing. In addition, the creditor whose rights form the basis for the trustee's power under section 544(b) must be the holder of an allowed unsecured claim in the bankruptcy case.

So, what kinds of prefiling transfers are vulnerable under section 544(b)? The technical answer is *any transfer* that is avoidable by an existing unsecured creditor under state law. The practical answer, however, in the overwhelming majority of cases where section 544(b) is invoked, is a transfer that is avoidable under state fraudulent transfer law. But, since the Bankruptcy Code has its own fraudulent transfer statute, and that statute is pretty similar to the uniform state fraudulent transfer laws, of what utility is the added power? While there may, in a given case, be some esoteric differences in applicable state law, most importantly the power will be of utility where the transfer occurred more than two years prior to filing, which, you'll recall, is the period of vulnerability of transfers under section 548(a)(1). Section 9 of the Uniform Fraudulent Transfer Act, by contrast, has a four year statute of limitations.

Once the trustee establishes to entitlement succeed to the rights of an actual unsecured creditor, the challenged transfer is avoidable *in toto*, regardless of the amount of the claim of the creditor in whose shoes the trustee has stepped. Thus, it is often said that the trustee steps not just into the shoes of an actual creditor under section 544(b), but into the *overshoes* of that creditor. This is the principle established by the Supreme Court in *Moore v. Bay*.[39] For example, assume Ponoroff transfers to his wife, Monica, title to his palatial home with the intent to dodge his creditors, and three years later he files bankruptcy. At the time of

---

[39]   284 U.S. 4 (1931)

the transfer, Ponoroff was indebted to Markell for $50 Markell lent him so that Ponoroff could pay the balance on his DirecTV bill. Assuming the debt is still outstanding when Ponoroff files, the trustee could use Markell's $50 obligation under section 544(b) to recover the entire value of the house from Monica. Would it matter if Ponoroff had granted Markell a lien on his car to secure the $50 debt? You bet it would. Remember that the creditor to whose status the trustee succeeds under section 544(b) must not only still be in existence, but also must be the holder of an *unsecured* claim.

D. Preferential Transfers

You'll probably spend a lot of class time on preferences. Let's begin by noting that some preferences are aimed at rooting out secret liens, like the strong-arm power. We'll explain presently. In most cases, though, if the preferential transfer is not avoided, the recipient will gain a monetary advantage over all other creditors by virtue of the offending transfer to such creditor of cash or property in the shadow of bankruptcy. Thus, most preference challenges are aimed at ensuring that the bankruptcy goal of equality among similarly situated creditors is achieved.

Consider this: Ponoroff has five unsecured creditors, each owed $10,000, and he only has $10,000 of unencumbered assets. Ponoroff plans to file bankruptcy next week to deal with his debts. That weekend, Markell, who is one of the five creditors, stops by Ponoroff's house and says, "Hey, that $10,000 is gone as soon as you file, so why don't you pay me? Better I get it than those other guys." So Ponoroff pays him. That's a preference. Now, Ponoroff's other creditors, who would have received $2,000 each, get jack and Markell is $8,000 better off due to the payment. **Note:** if instead of giving Markell the $10,000 of assets, Ponoroff had granted Markell a lien on those assets, the effect would be *exactly the same*. Thus the preference statute, section 547(b), refers to the "transfer of an interest of the debtor in property."

1. Distinguished from Fraudulent Transfers

As we discussed earlier, it is important to recognize that a fraudulent transfer is most likely also illegal under state law. A preference generally is not. It involves, as in the example above, a transfer to pay a legitimate debt—something that state law actually encourages! In a fraudulent transfer situation, it is all of the debtor's creditors who are injured by a transfer of property to a noncreditor, whether purposefully to deceive, or simply for less than reasonable return value; i.e., a gift. Preferences, by contrast, involve intercreditor issues; one creditor has been advantaged at the expense of all of the other creditors. Return of the preferential transfer promotes creditor equality. In addition, the legislative history to the Code suggests that preferences have a second purpose; that is, to *deter* creditors from swooping in to grab assets from the financially-troubled debtor, thus precipitating the debtor's slide into bankruptcy. Finally, note that the application of both the fraudulent transfer and the preference provisions will have the effect of restoring assets to the estate for the benefit all of the debtor's unsecured creditors.

2. Elements of a Voidable Preference

Section 547(b) sets out the requirements for establishing a preference. When you look at it, it appears that there are five elements, but look more closely, because, in addition to the five numbered elements, there two additional requirements. So the seven elements of a preference are:

1.   A transfer (defined in section 101(54)),

2.   Of an interest of the debtor in property,

3. To or for the benefit of a creditor,

4. For or on account of an antecedent debt,

5. While the debtor was insolvent (defined in section 101(32)),

6. Made on or within 90 days of the filing of the petition (one year for "insiders"),

7. And that allows the creditor to receive more than the creditor would have received (a) had the transfer not been made, and (b) the debtor's estate liquidated in Chapter 7.

Element number (7) is referred to as the "greater amount test," or the "chapter 7 test" and, despite its wordiness, it doesn't amount to too much. Let's assume that Markell owes Ponoroff $1,000 and that, a few days before Markell files bankruptcy, Ponoroff threatens to "kick his rear" unless he pays at least half, and so Markell does. Now Ponoroff goes into Markell's bankruptcy case with a $500 claim. If unsecured creditors in Markell's bankruptcy case receive a 10 percent dividend, Ponoroff will end up being paid a total of $550 (the $500 payment and the $50 distribution) on his $1,000 debt. Had the payment not been made, Ponoroff would have had a $1,000 claim in Markell's case for which he would receive $100 (or slightly more than that because of the additional $500 in the estate). Clearly, Ponoroff is better off for the preference, so the greater amount test is met. In fact, in the case of an unsecured claim, the *only* time the greater amount test will not be met is when creditors are paid 100 cents on the dollar in the case (a bloody rare event).

In addition to solvent debtors, there are two other circumstances where the greater amount test will not be satisfied. Both involve secured creditors. The first is in the situation where the transfer is made to a fully secured creditor. In that case, the creditor was ultimately going to be paid in full anyway, and the payment results in a corresponding increase in value to the estate. To illustrate, assume Ponoroff is indebted to Markell for $10,000 and the obligation is secured by property worth $12,000. If Ponoroff makes a payment of $1,000 to Markell, the result is that there is now $3,000 in equity in the property available for the estate instead of $2,000. And, Markell, although he brings a smaller claim into the bankruptcy case, is no better off because had this payment not been made Markell still would have been paid in full from his collateral. The fact that he was paid sooner does not contravene the greater amount test; only when he is paid *more*.

Now contrast this situation from the case where Markell is undersecured. Same facts as above, except the collateral is worth $8,000, not $12,000. Is the $1,000 prefiling transfer a preference? You bet it is. Markell will now walk away from the case with a total $9,000—the payment plus the full value of the collateral (since there is no release of the collateral upon the payment)—*plus* whatever dividend is paid on his $1,000 unsecured claim (let's say 10 percent). Had the payment not been made, Markell would have come into the case with a $10,000 claim, $8,000 of which would be paid from the collateral. The $2,000 unsecured claim would be paid $200. So the payment has made Markell better off by $900 ($9,100 versus $8,200). What this means is any payment to an undersecured creditor will satisfy the greater amount test *until* the amount paid exceeds the amount of the unsecured deficiency ($2,000 in our example). The reason is at that point the additional payment is reducing the lien against the collateral and, in so doing, creating new value for the estate.

The second circumstance involving secured creditors where the greater amount test will not be satisfied is where what is transferred to an undersecured creditor is the collateral itself and not money. As far as unsecureds creditor are concerned, the transfer has not diminished the assets of the estate available for distribution to them. Using the hypothetical above, whether the $8,000 asset is transferred to Markell on his claim or not, Markell is going to end up with $8,200. Granted he'll get it sooner with the transfer, but, again, that doesn't factor in under the greater amount test or a preference analysis.

Now let's go back to elements (1) and (2). Because of the definition in section 101(54) includes *involuntary* transfers as well as voluntary transfers, when Markell acquires a judicial lien by having Ponoroff's property levied upon to satisfy Markell's judgment, a transfer has occurred just as surely as if Ponoroff delivered cash to Markell. This example also implicates element (2), which requires that the transfer need only be of *an interest of the debtor in property*. This means, once more, that the creation of a lien (an interest in the debtor's property) can give rise to a transfer just as plainly as an absolute transfer of cash.

However, if the transfer is of property *other than* of the debtor, no preference. So, if Markell's daughter pays off her father's debt to Ponoroff, there is no preference. Sure Ponoroff is better off than other creditors and happier than a tornado in a trailer park, but it's not at the expense of Markell's other creditors. Now suppose what happens is Markell's daughter gives the money to her dad and says, "now this is to be used to pay that nice man Ponoroff and not for any other purpose." Markell uses the money to pay Ponoroff. Preference? *Probably not.* This is an illustration of what's referred to as the "earmarking doctrine," which holds that even an insolvent debtor who pays a creditor does not make a preference if that payment is made with third-party funds clearly designated to pay that specific creditor—since, in that case, the transfer does not involve property of the debtor. Note that even if Markell's daughter gives him the money to pay Ponoroff as a loan, there's still no preference since all that's happened is one unsecured creditor has been substituted by another. The issue in the earmarking cases will be whether the debtor did or could have exercised control over how that third party money was used. On an exam, recognize facts possibly calling for application of the earmarking doctrine, mention control (if you're really daring say "dominion and control,") and you should be golden.

Element (3)—that the transfer be "to or for the benefit of a creditor"—means that a transfer *to* a third party can *benefit* a creditor and, thus, create a preference. We will discuss this in more depth in the subsection below concerning "Indirect Preferences," but, for now, just to illustrate, consider the following: Markell owns a piece of property worth $250,000. He has granted a first lien on the property to Ponoroff to secure a debt of $200,000. Markell has also granted a second lien on the property to Sixteenth National Bank to secure a debt of $100,000. Ponoroff is fully secured so a prefiling payment to him (let's say of $50,000), even if all the other elements of section 547(b) are satisfied, won't be preferential. But it will be a preference, indirectly, as to Sixteenth National because that $50,000 payment to the senior lienor increased Sixteenth National's secured claim in the property from $50,000 to $100,000, thus converting an unsecured claim into a secured claim—no different in effect than if Ponoroff had granted the bank a lien on other unencumbered assets during the preference period. By the way, the "creditor" requirement explains why a gift cannot be a preference, although it may be a fraudulent transfer as we saw above.

The antecedent debt requirement (element (4)) means that the transfer is given to pay or secure an already existing obligation. So, if Ponoroff owes Markell $400 because he bought Markell's 2006 Prius two months ago, and Ponoroff pays that debt while insolvent and a month before he files bankruptcy, a preference has occurred. However, if, in return for the $400 payment, Markell tenders the title to the Prius, then the transfer is not on account of an antecedent debt and cannot be a preference. Instead, the transfer is in exchange for "new value" within the meaning of section 547(a)(2).

Generally, the Code adopts the balance sheet sense of insolvency—liabilities in excess of assets; maybe you can relate to that situation. Proving another party's financial condition can be difficult, but the Code eases the trustee's burden considerably by incorporating a presumption of insolvency in section 547(f). Take heed, this presumption is rebuttable and only applies in the 90 days prior to filing; i.e., not during the extended insider preference period.

Lastly, we have the "within 90 days" element. This time period is, frankly, pretty arbitrary—under the former Bankruptcy Act it was 120 days. This 90-day period is extended to a year for "insiders." The rationale for the longer insider preference period is that, by virtue of being closer to the debtor, an insider is likely to become aware more quickly than third-party creditors of the debtor's financial troubles and use that advantage to favor their own debts. Also, there is a belief that an insider may be in a position to keep the debtor out of bankruptcy for more than 90 days in order to protect a transfer made to the insider, but probably not for a full year. The term "insider" is defined in section 101(31) to *include* lots of different categories of creditors—officers, directors, partners and others in control of the debtor (as well as affiliates—those with 20% common ownership), and if the debtor is an individual, relatives within the third degree of consanguinity (essentially, first cousins), but bear in mind that it is a nonexclusive list in that when the Code uses the term *includes* or *including*, section 102(3) says it is to be construed as "not limiting."

3.   *Time of Transfer*

As was the true in the case of fraudulent transfers, in order to assess whether of several of the elements of an avoidable preference are satisfied, we need to *when* the transfer occurs. That may seem simple, and it is in the case of an outright transfer of property. If Ponoroff pays Markell, an unsecured creditor of his, $50, the transfer occurs when that U.S. Grant passes from Ponoroff's hand and into Markell's eager mitts. But suppose, instead of making that payment, Ponoroff grants Markell a security interest in Ponoroff's used BMW. Now state law tells us clear enough that the transfer occurs when that security interest "attaches" under U.C.C. § 9-203(a) & (b), requiring that Ponoroff had received value from Markell, had rights in the property, and had authenticated a security agreement. But that's not necessarily when the transfer of the interest in Ponoroff's property will be deemed to occur for preference purposes. Rather, section 547(e)(2) says, in effect, that if the secured party has not taken the necessary steps to make the transfer effective against third parties within 30 days, the transfer will be deemed to occur when those steps are taken, or, if never taken, immediately before the filing of the bankruptcy petition The steps necessary to make the transfer effective against third parties (i.e., "perfection") will ordinarily entail the filing of a financing statement under Article 9 with respect to personal property liens, and the recording of the mortgage or deed of trust in the case of real property liens.

A simple example should help here. Let's say, on March 1, Ponoroff buys Markell's car paying partly in cash and partly by a promissory note. As security for the note, on the same date, Markell reserves an interest in the car. If Markell perfects his security interest on or before March 30, the transfer will be deemed to occur when it became effective between the parties; i.e., on March 1. Thus, if Ponoroff files for bankruptcy on June 6, the transfer of the security interest in the car will not be a preference because (1) it's outside the 90-day period, and (2) it isn't on account of an antecedent debt. *But*, if Markell doesn't get around to filing his financing statement until April 10, the transfer will be deemed to occur on that date, meaning it's now inside the preference period and on account of an antecedent debt. So, Markell's got a problem. This scenario reflects the role of preference law in regulating secret liens.

Now let's assume the same facts as above, but Ponoroff files bankruptcy on March 6. It remains true that if Markell perfects his security interest on or before March 30 the transfer will be deemed to occur on March 1 and, thus, would not be on account of an antecedent debt. But can Markell take the actions necessary to perfect without violating 362(a)(4)? The answer is "yes" under the exception in section 362(b)(3) for perfection occurring within the grace period allowed by section 547(e)(2). But Markell is probably not out of the woods insofar as losing his lien is concerned. Do you see it? Yup, that's right, the security interest was *unperfected* at filing, which usually means it can be avoided under section 544(a). However, this is a purchase money security interest for which there is a 20-day relation back period under state law (U.C.C. 9-317(e)) and as to which the trustee's strong-arm powers are, as we've seen, made subject under Code section 546(b)(1)(A). Therefore, if Markell were to perfect on March 25 (or any time after March 21 and before March 31), while there would be no avoidable preference, Markell would still be vulnerable to avoidance of his interests under the strong-arm clause of section 544(a). If you didn't see that go back and review Section B.1 of this Unit above dealing with "Unrecorded Transfers."

4. Preference Exceptions (or Defenses)

Section 547(c) contains nine exceptions or defenses to the trustee's ability to avoid a preferential transfer. *Note*: we never get to section 547(c) *unless* the transfer meets the definition of a preference in section 547(b). *Note also*: while the trustee has the burden of proof under section 547(b) (except with respect to insolvency in the 90 days prior to filing), it is the creditor against whom recovery is sought who bears the burden of proof to establish the nonavoidability of the transfer under one of the exceptions of section 547(c).

Some of these exceptions are intended to cover transactions that (1) meet the technical definition of a preference under section 547(b), but do not have preferential effect; i.e.,do not result in a diminution of the estate. Othersreflect a legislative judgment that a competing policy objective outweighs bankruptcy equality policy. Still other exceptions represent an attempt to prevent the trustee from bringing a preference claim as a nuisance suit primarily for its settlement value. Examples of the first category are the exceptions in sections 547(c)(1), (3), (4), & (5). The exceptions in section 547(c)(7) and the safe harbor in section 547(h) are examples of the second category.[40] The two low dollar safe harbors in sections (c)(8) and (9) are examples of defenses in the third group. Finally, and all by itself, is the all-important "ordinary course of business" defense in section 547(c)(2). Let's take a look at the most important of these exceptions; i.e., the ones you're most likely to encounter on your final exam!

---

[40] There are also safe harbors from avoidance actions under section 546(e) for certain transactions in the public commodities futures and securities markets. The purpose behind section 546(e) is to protect the nation's financial markets from the instability that might result from the reversal of settled securities transactions.

a. Substantially   Contemporaneous   Exchanges   for New Value

This exception is to protect transfers in cases where there is a slight gap between the incurring of the debt and the payment thereon. Thus, the payment technically constitutes a transfer on account of an antecedent debt, but is for all intents and purposes for new value. *But*, proximity in time is just *one* element of this defense; i.e., that the transfer and the return value are in fact substantially contemporaneous. The second element is that the parties must have *intended* the transfer to be made in exchange for contemporaneous new value.

Consider the case where Ponoroff calls the bank he regularly does business with at 9:00 a.m. and says, "I'm in Markell's office and he's agreed to sell me his vintage Prius. If you'd wire the money to his account, I'll stop by the bank later today or tomorrow and sign a security agreement granting you a lien on the car, and give you the title." The transfer of the security interest to bank is technically on account of an antecedent debt, so that if Ponoroff files bankruptcy a month later and the other elements of section 547(b) are satisfied, a preferential transfer has occurred. It is in this circumstances that section 547(c)(1) might well offer the bank a defense if the trustee seeks to set aside its lien. Now contrast this with the situation where, with no understanding about a lien, the bank wires the money to Markell's account at Ponoroff's request. An hour later, the bank officer who sent the money learns that Ponoroff has been missing payments to multiple creditors. So, he calls Ponoroff and demands that Ponoroff come down to the bank immediately and give the bank a lien on the Prius to secure the obligation. The temporal delay between the making of the loan and the grant of the lien may be identical, but in this case the bank would have no defense under section 547(c)(1) upon Ponoroff's later bankruptcy because they parties did not intend for the loan and the grant of the lien to be contemporaneous. Initially, even though only for an hour or two, the bank intended to make an unsecured loan.

b. Ordinary Course Transfers

Section 547(c)(2), the ordinary course of business defense, is the most litigated, the most important, and the most controversial of the preference exceptions. According to the legislative history, its purpose is to "leave normal financial relations undisturbed." Thus, if an obligation is incurred by the debtor in a transaction that was in the usual course of business (meaning, normal or routine from the debtor's perspective) *and* a payment on that obligation is made *either* in the normal course of business between the debtor and the creditor (typical of the way in which they have done business with one another in the past) *or* according to "ordinary business terms" (typical in the industry), it will be shielded from preference recovery. Until 2005, the payment had to be ordinary *both* as measured by the parties' past practice and industry standards, but now if the payment is ordinary measured either subjectively or objectively, it will be immune from recovery.

So, assume Markell Widgets ("MW") has been a supplier to Ponoroff, Inc. ("PI") for the past six years and during that time PI always paid invoices from MW within 20 to 30 days of receipt. PI has just filed for bankruptcy and, in the 90 days preceding the filing, it paid two invoices received from MW for the earlier sale of widgets: one for $5,000 and one for $7,500. If the $5,000 payment was made 22 days after receipt of the invoice for that amount, it will likely qualify for protection under section 547(c)(2), assuming (as we are) that the obligation was incurred in the ordinary course.

If the $7,500 payment, however, was made 60 days after receipt of the invoice, it would probably be deemed outside of the ordinary course of dealings between the parties and, thus, have been recoverable prior to 2005. Now, however, MW might still be able to employ the defense if it is able to show that payments 60-days following invoice are not extraordinary in the widget industry And so, too, would the converse be true where industry standards were stricter than the pattern characterizing the practices established between PI and MW. Don't forget, though, the debt on which the payment was made must have come about in a transaction that wasa typical for both parties. Thus, you can think of the elements of section 547(c)(2) as follows: (1) plus (2) or (3), with (1) being incurred in the usual course, (2) being paid in the normal course of business for the parties, and (3) being paid in a manner that is typical in the industry.

While the length of time from invoice to payment measured against historic averages is the most significant factor bearing on whether a payment falls within the protection of section 547(c)(2)(A), other considerations, including unusual creditor collection pressure, may be taken into account by the court. With respect to section 547(c)(2)(B), compatibility with "ordinary business terms" is generally considered to be met if the circumstances surrounding the transfer in question are similar in some general way to the range of terns that encompass the practices in which firms similar to the debtor and creditor engage.[41] A few courts have suggested that this lenient standard for defining ordinary business terms should only apply to protect a preferential transfer when there is no established course of dealings between the parties, but that view seems to belie the language of the statute.

c. Enabling Loans

This is an exception that will potentially apply in connection with secured transactions that, under state law, we would call "purchase money"; which is to say the collateral secures its

---

[41] The seminal case expounding of "ordinary business terms" is *In re* Tolona Pizza Prods., 3 F.3d 1029 (7th Cir. 1993).

purchase price. Recall that under Article 9 there is a grace period during which the perfection of a purchase money security interest will relate back to the time the security interest was created, and thus take priority over intervening liens. Specifically, as you'll recall from our discussion of the trustee's strong-arm powers in Section B above, under U.C.C. § 9-317(e), so long as the creditor is perfected within 20 days of the time the debtor receives delivery of the collateral, its priority will relate back to the time the security interest attached. Section 547(c)(3) of the Bankruptcy Code is similar, but *not identical* to the U.C.C. provision. It provides that if a security interest secures new value (1) given at or after the signing of a security interest describing the collateral, (2) given by the secured party, (3) that enables the debtor to acquire the collateral, and (4) the security interest is perfected on or before 30 days after the debtor receives the collateral, then the transfer of the security interest may not be avoided as a preference

Now, you may recall that under section 547(e)(2) a transfer of a lien on the debtor's property will be deemed to occur when it becomes effective between the parties provided that the lien is perfected at or within 30 days of that time. So, what additional protection does section 547(c)(3) add to that? The answer lies in section 547(e)(3), which says that in no case can a transfer occur before the debtor has rights in the collateral. That is to say, the transfer of a security interest in after acquired-property does not relate back, as it does under state law, to the original perfection. Thus, assume on Day 1, Ponoroff advances Markell funds to enable Markell to buy a new beanie with a helicopter propeller on top of it and Markell in return grants Ponoroff a security interest in the beanie under a written security agreement. Ponoroff immediately files a financing statement, but Markell doesn't get around to actually buying the beanie (acquiring rights in it) until Day 40. At that point, the security interest attaches and is automatically perfected because of the earlier filing, but, under section 547(e)(2), the transfer is deemed to occur on Day 40 and, thus, is on account of an antecedent debt. This is where the exception (c)(3) applies since all of its conditions have been met.

The other circumstance where section 547(c)(3) may come into play is a function of the fact that the language concerning when the 30-day grace period in sections 547(c)(3) and (e)(2) begin to run is not the same. As noted, under subsection (c)(3), the 30 days runs from the time the debtor receives possession of the collateral. Under subsection (e)(2), however, it's 30 days from the time the transfer becomes effective between the parties, which under Article 9 can occur as soon as the debtor *acquires rights* in the collateral; i.e., before actual possession of the collateral. So, let's say Markell loans Ponoroff $500 to purchase a new motor scooter to get back and forth to school on, and Markell reserves a security interest in the scooter. That same day, Ponoroff orders the scooter from Scooter's Unlimited, thereby acquiring rights in scooter under state law. The scooter arrives 10 days later. If Markell perfects his security interest in the ensuing 20 days, the transfer will not be a preference because it will not be deemed on account of an antecedent debt. But, if Markell perfects between 20 to 30 days after Ponoroff receives the scooter, it will be a preference, *but* Markell should be able to invoke the defense in section 547(c)(3). Thus, the difference in language between the two subsections has, in this scenario, effectively operated to extend Markell's time to perfect from the usual 30 days to 40 days.

d. Subsequent Advances

Ok, let's assume that on the 85th day before his bankruptcy filing, Ponoroff, while insolvent, makes a $10,000 payment to Markell, one of his suppliers, on an existing unsecured open account debt. No question we have a preference. However, on the 25th day before bankruptcy, Markell sells Ponoroff $5,000 worth of new goods on unsecured credit; that is, he sends the goods without immediate payment on the understanding that Ponoroff will send the purchase price within a certain time, usually 30 days. Under section 547(c)(4), Markell will have a defense to the earlier preference in the amount of the new value provided; i.e., $5,000. Makes sense—during the entirety of the preference period Markell is only $5,000 better off— and pretty simple. But stick around.

Now let's change the dates so the credit sale of the new goods occurs on the 85th day and the payment on the 25th day before filing. What is the amount of the preference that can be recovered? The answer is the full $10,000, even though viewed from the perspective of the entire preference period, Markell was only advantaged to the extent of $5,000. Here's the point: section 547(c)(4) is *not* a net result rule; it's a *subsequent* advance rule.

Now go back to the original scenario but assume Markell demands and receives a security interest in the goods sold on the 25th day before filing. What's the amount of preference that can be recovered? It depends on whether that security interest is perfected in a timely manner. If so, then the recovery is $10,000 because, under section 547(c)(4)(A), the new value must not be secured by an otherwise unavoidable security interest. If Markell properly perfects the security interest, this requirement is not met because (if you excuse the double or triple negative) the new value is not not secured by an otherwise unavoidable security interest. If Markell fails to perfect, however, then the security interest is avoidable under section 544(a) and, in that case, section 547(c)(4)(A) is satisfied so that the value of the new goods would be an offset against the earlier preference. Once more, this makes sense in that $5,000 of value was restored to the estate after the preferential transfer occurred.

Finally, under section 547(c)(4)(B), the new value must remain unpaid in order for the exception to apply. What this basically means is that if, in our original example, Ponoroff had paid cash for the $5,000 of goods sold to him by Markell on the 25th day prior to bankruptcy, none of that value would qualify under section 547(c)(4) and the entire $10,000 preference could be recovered.

e. Net Improvement in Position

Here you need to bear in mind two things: (1) when the collateral for a security interest is the debtor's inventory and receivables, that collateral is constantly changing as receivables are paid, new inventory is purchased and sold, and new receivables generated—this is the so-called "floating lien," because the security interest is said to float over an ever-shifting mass of collateral; and (2) section 547(e)(3) says that in no event can the transfer be deemed to occur until the debtor has rights in the collateral. This means, for example, in the case of a borrower with a high inventory turnover rate, all of the inventory and receivables collateral on an earlier-created security interest may have been acquired in the 90 days before filing, and are thus deemed as having been transferred on account of an antecedent debt, even though the value of the collateral on the date of filing is no greater than the value 90 days earlier—it's just *different* stuff.

Because the creditor hasn't really improved its position at the expense of other creditors in this situation, section 547(c)(5) comes to the secured creditor's rescue and says there is no preference *except to the extent* the creditor has *improved its position* between day 90 and the date of filing. Improvement in position, in turn, is measured by the reduction, if any, in the creditor's unsecured deficiency between the beginning of the preference period (or the date on which new value was first given under the security interest) and the date of filing. To illustrate, let's look at a couple of simple examples.

	90 Days Before Filing	Date of Filing
Amount of Debt	$500,000	$500,000
Value of Collateral	$400,000	$475,000
Unsecured Deficiency	$100,000	$25,000

As you can see, the creditor's unsecured deficiency was reduced by $75,000 during the two measuring periods. Thus, this is the amount of the avoidable preference—even if *all* of the inventory and receivables representing that $475,000 was acquired inside of the 90-day period.

Next consider:

	90 Days Before Filing	Date of Filing
Amount of Debt	$500,000	$450,000
Value of Collateral	$400,000	$300,000
Unsecured Deficiency	$100,000	$150,000

Ok, now what is the amount of the avoidable preference? Why nothing, of course, even though the debt was reduced by $50,000. But, because the value of the collateral went down by twice that amount, the creditor's unsecured deficiency actually increased between the two measuring points. That is to say, the creditor is no better off. And, again, we say that just looking at these two points in time; it doesn't matter if, let's say 30 days before filing, the unsecured deficiency was only $50,000.

Now there's a couple of other things to say here and then we can move on. First, if the creditor is fully secured 90 days before filing, there will be no preference no matter what happens. If your unsecured deficiency is zero, it can't get decrease any further. Second, section 547(c)(5) requires not just a reduction in the unsecured deficiency, but a reduction that operates to the prejudice of unsecured creditors. Thus, if the secured creditor's position improves (its deficiency is reduced) because of appreciation in the value of existing inventory, and not due to the acquisition of new inventory, there is no prejudice to other creditors and no preference. By the way, under these circumstances there is probably also no preference because there is no "transfer."

5. *Indirect Preferences*

So far, the preference situations we've examined have involved two parties: the debtor and the transferee-creditor. But the language of section 547(b) refers to a transfer "to or for the benefit of a creditor." This means that sometimes the analysis of a preference will involve three parties: the debtor, the transferee-creditor, and a third party *benefited* by the transfer. Bear in mind that section 550(a)(1) also says that an avoided preference may be recovered from *either* the transferee *or* the party benefited by the transfer.

How do these provisions operate? Let's assume Markell has borrowed money from Ponoroff, and the debt is guaranteed by Markell's spouse, Emily (in an inexplicable moment of temporary insanity on her part). In any case, you will recall from our discussion of claims that both Ponoroff and Emily have claims against Markell if he files bankruptcy (Markell a direct claim on the debt; Emily a contingent claim for reimbursement from Markell if she has to pay the bum's debt). But suppose, a few day before filing, Markell, while insolvent, pays Ponoroff (thinking about matrimonial harmony). Obviously Ponoroff has received a preference, but so has Emily, a person clearly benefitted by the payment since the payment to Ponoroff has discharged her contingent liability. This means that, under section 550(a)(1), the trustee can recover the payment from *either* Ponoroff or Emily.

Now, change the facts just slightly so that the payment occurs 120 days before Markell's filing. Viewed solely from the perspective of Ponoroff, the transfer was not a preference since it was not made within 90 days of filing. However, it was also a transfer for the benefit, indirectly, of Emily, as we've seen, as to whom it is a preference since she's an insider. Can the trustee recover from Ponoroff, even though Ponoroff is not an insider and the transfer was not a preference from his perspective? In the infamous case of *In re V.N. Deprizio Constr. Co.*, 874 F.2d 1186 (7th Cir. 1989), the court held in the affirmative. In essence, *Deprizio* viewed sections 547 and 550 as independent provisions to be applied independently. That is, the party responsible under section 550(a) does not have to be the same party as to whom the transfer was preferential. Put yet a third way, the question of was the transfer avoidable is separate from the analysis of from whom the transfer, once determined to be preferential, may be recovered.

The lending community went berserk at the prospect that they could be exposed to preference recovery for up to a year simply because they had obtained a guaranty that happened to be made by an insider. The irony was that the whole purpose for taking the guaranty to begin with was to *reduce* risk. So the lending community did what they do best and lobbied Congress to change the law, which Congress did in 1994 by adopting section 550(c), which prohibits recovery of the preference from a noninsider creditor in these circumstances.

But, oops, Congress forgot that section 550(c) would be of no help where the transfer was of an interest in property rather than an outright payment. In other words, Markell grants Ponoroff a security interest in collateral 120 days prior to his filing. Because that transfer is a preference (as to Emily) it could be set aside and there is no *recovery* necessary. So, section 550(c) never comes into play. Therefore, Congress finally finished the job in 2005 by adopting section 547(i), which statutorily makes a transfer nonavoidable as to a noninsider creditor if it occurs more than 90 days prior to filing. So, in our example, Ponoroff keeps his lien, but the value thereof could still be recovered from Emily.

There are two other circumstances where indirect preferences still occur. The first, which we described earlier, involves multiple liens on the same property. Let's take another look. Suppose Markell and Ponoroff are both owed $150,000 by their co-author Epstein, and each has a lien on Epstein's house, which has a value of $200,000—Ponoroff lien was filed first. Now if Epstein pays Ponoroff $25,000, alone that is not preferential because Ponoroff is fully secured. *But* the reduction of Ponoroff's lien against the property by $25,000 increases the secured portion of Markell's junior claim from $50,000 to $75,000. So the payment was preferential from the perspective of Markell—the party benefitted from the transfer. Under the reasoning of *Deprizio,* if Ponoroff files bankruptcy say 30 days later, the trustee should be able to recover the $25,000 from *either* Markell or Ponoroff.

The second circumstances is a little trickier. Now let's assume Ponoroff owes Markell $100,000. If, while insolvent and within 90 days of filing bankruptcy, Ponoroff either pays Markell or grants him a lien on Ponoroff's property, the transaction will of course be an avoidable preference. But, suppose, what Ponoroff does is convinces Last Nat'l Bank ("LNB") to issue a letter of credit ("LOC") on June 1 for the benefit of Markell, under the terms of which LNB commits to pay Markell $100,000, if on or after July 1, Markell delivers a document to LNB confirming that Ponoroff has not paid his outstanding debt to Markell. Why would LNB do that? Well, it won't unless it receives a fee and a "back-up" promissory note from Ponoroff that becomes activated if LNB pays under the LOC.

Now, if we assume Markell delivers notice of nonpayment on July 1, LNB pays, and 30 days thereafter Ponoroff files for bankruptcy, has a preference occurred? No, all that's happened is one unsecured creditor has been substituted for another; there's been no net diminution of the value of the estate. But next let's assume LNB won't issue the LOC unless Ponoroff also provides collateral for the back-up note with a value equal to the face amount of the LOC. Now when the note gets activated, a secured creditor has been substituted for an unsecured creditor. That's definitely preferential and, under the theory of *Deprizio*, should be recoverable from either Markell or LNB, even though LNB gave new value for the secured loan. Perhaps your casebook contains the opinion in of *Kellogg v. Blue Quail Energy, Inc. (In re Compton Corp.)*,[42] where the court only permitted recovery against the party paid under the letter of credit; analyzing the effect of the preferential transfer (of the security interest) separately from the perspective of both the direct and indirect transferee. But *Kellogg* was decided before *Deprizio* and might well come out differently today.

E. Setoff

1. *What Is a Setoff and the "Right of Setoff"?*

A setoff is simply a netting or canceling out of mutual obligations. So, if Ponoroff one weekend makes two bets with Markell, taking the Bears and the Lions, and the Lions win but the Bears don't, then Ponoroff and Markell might simply cancel the debt each owes to the other from the losing bet and end up square. From a commercial law perspective, the most notable right of setoff is the common law right of banks to set off against a deposit account (which is really the bank's obligation to pay the depositor) any amounts owed to the bank by the owner of the account.

Assume Markell maintains a checking account at Ponoroff Federal Savings & Loan ("PFSL"). Markell then borrows money from PFSL for a new four-wheel drive SUV (hybrid of course). Several

---

[42] 831 F.2d 586, (5th Cir. 1987)

months later, Markell defaults on his car loan, with a balance of $18,000 still outstanding. At the same time, the balance in his checking account with PFSL is $7,000. Exercising its common law right of setoff, PFSL may debit the account for the entire balance and apply it to Markell's loan, thereby reducing the amount due to $11,000.

2. Setoff in Bankruptcy

The bankruptcy law does not create a right of setoff. Rather, section 553(a) preserves a creditor's right outside of bankruptcy to set off mutual *prepetition* debts. A couple of other provisions of the Code also bear on the right of setoff.

First, under section 506(a), the right of setoff is treated as a secured claim. It's as if, in the example above, PFSL's loan is secured by Markell's checking account. This means that PFSL will get precisely the same recovery in bankruptcy as, hypothetically, creditor X, who is also owed $18,000 and has a first lien on other property owned by Markell worth $7,000.

Second, because of section 362(a)(7), a creditor that did not exercise its setoff right prior to the debtor's filing for bankruptcy cannot exercise the right of setoff after the bankruptcy filing without first obtaining relief from the stay from the bankruptcy court. That requires cause under section 362(d)(1), remember?

Although section 553(a) generally recognizes a nonbankruptcy right of setoff, it also imposes certain limitations on that right. Specifically, subsections (a)(1), (2), and (3) each provide different circumstances under which setoff will be denied to a creditor, either in whole or in part; and subsection (b) provides a basis for avoiding certain prefiling setoffs. Like the preference law, these provisions are intended to assure that one creditor does not obtain an unfair advantage over other creditors, we will consider each of these limitations.

a.   The Section 553(a) Limitations

Let's say Ponoroff is a regular supplier of blank DVDs to Markell's Awesome Video Shop, Inc. ("MADV"). Because MADV is still using DVDs rather than streaming, its business has suffered and it has now had to file under Chapter 11. Ponoroff had recently purchased $500 worth of Markell's finished products for his personal viewing, for which he has yet to pay. At the time of the filing, MADV owed Ponoroff $500 on open account, but MADV can show that half of the DVDs were defective, giving rise to a claim for breach of warranty. If Ponoroff seeks to withhold payment for the videos based on MADV's outstanding debt to him in the same amount, section 553(a)(1) will come into play. It prohibits setoff of a claim that is disallowed. Because half of Ponoroff's claim is not allowed under section 502(b)(1), Ponoroff will only be entitled to set off the remaining $250 balance due from MADV against what he owes to the estate. The other half of the obligation must be turned over to the debtor in possession.

Section 523(a)(2) and (a)(3) both prevent a creditor from building up a right to setoff in the 90 days prior to filing. The former deals with a situation where a creditor that owes money to the debtor purchases the claim of another unsecured creditor of the debtor at a discount in order to create a right of setoff. Thus, assume Markell owes Ponoroff $500, and Ponoroff owes Smith $500. Ponoroff is insolvent and it appears likely that Ponoroff's creditors will get ten cents on the dollar at best. So Markell approaches Smith and offers to buy his claim against Ponoroff for $100 (20 cents on the dollar). Smith should be and is thrilled. But now Markell seeks to use the full value of the purchased debt to claim a setoff against what he owes to Ponoroff. This is like taking $450 out of the estate (what Markell would have had to pay the estate, less the $50 the estate would otherwise have had to pay Smith). For all intents and purposes, it's the same as a $450 preferential transfer to Smith that also benefits Markell, so, section 553(a)(2) says Markell cannot use the debt he acquired from Smith in the 90 days prior to filing as a setoff against his debt to Ponoroff.

Section 553(a)(3) deals with just the opposite scenario. Instead of acquiring a claim to use as a setoff to a debt owed to the debtor, the section 553(a)(3) scenario applies when a creditor of the debtor, within of 90 days of filing and while the debtor was insolvent, incurs a debt to the debtor so as to create a right of setoff. Let's assume Markell Nat'l Bank ("MNB") has an unsecured loan to Ponoroff with a balance of $10,000. MNB learns Ponoroff is in a financial mess and likely will file bankruptcy soon. MNB knows that if it just pressures Ponoroff to pay the loan or come up with collateral such a transfer would be avoidable as a preference. So, MNB hits on a plan and instead of demanding payment from Ponoroff, it insists Ponoroff open up a deposit account at LMB, which Ponoroff does with a $5,000 deposit made 30 days before his bankruptcy filing. It is obvious that MNB has converted half of its claim from unsecured to secured, and that won't do. So, section 553(a)(3) precludes the setoff to prevent a $5,000 reduction in the size of the estate during the 90 days prior to filing..

There is one notable difference between subsections (a)(2) and (a)(3); namely, (a)(3) has an intent requirement. That is, subsection (a)(3)(C) requires that the debt to the debtor be acquired *for the purpose of obtaining a right of setoff*. Subsection (a)(2) contains no similar requirement. Thus, if Ponoroff, of his own accord, decided to open an account at MNB, or add a deposit to an existing account, the increment in MNB's right of setoff might not be barred.

b.   Section 553(b) and Reduction in the "Insufficiency"

Let's go back to our situation where MNB induced Ponoroff to open an account at MNB and deposit $5,000. The only difference is that now let's assume MNB immediately exercises its right of setoff;

that is, before Ponoroff's bankruptcy case was filed. By its terms, section 553(a)(3) will not apply since it only relates to an attempt assert a right of setoff *after* bankruptcy is filed. However, this is where section 553(b) comes to the trustee's rescue; and if you notice an eerie similarity to section 547(c)(5), well, we like the way you're thinking.

Section 553(b) applies to *prepetition* setoffs that occur in the 90-days before filing and while the debtor is insolvent. The amount setoff can be recovered *to the extent* that the action results in an improvement in the creditor's position, described as a reduction in the creditor's insufficiency. In this context, "insufficiency" is used to mean the excess of the amount owed by the debtor over the amount owed by the creditor to the debtor. So, going back to our example, on the 90th day before filing, MNB's insufficiency was $10,000—the full amount owed. The next measuring date is the date of setoff, when the insufficiency is only $5,000. Thus, the whole $5,000 can be recovered by the trustee.

The first measuring date is the date (up to 90 days prior to the bankruptcy filing) on which there is first an insufficiency. So if Ponoroff had an existing account at MNB with a balance in excess of $10,000 on the 90th day before filing, and it did not fall below that level until it was reduced to $8,000 on the 75th date before filing, and we again assume a $5,000 deposit the 30th day before filing and a setoff of $10,000 on the 5th day before bankruptcy, how much can the trustee recover under section 553(b)? Right! $2,000—which is the reduction in the insufficiency between the 75th day (the date of the first insufficiency) and the date of setoff. Just like under section 547(c)(5) we only look at those two dates and ignore whatever else might happen in between.

The last point to be aware of is that 553(c) creates a presumption of insolvency during the 90 days preceding the bankruptcy filing. This presumption works the same way as the presumption of insolvency under section 547(f) in preference case, shifting the burden of proof on the issue from the trustee to the creditor who exercised or is seeking to exercise a right of setoff. The presumption in section 547(c) applies in cases under section 553(a)(2), 553(a)(3), and 553(b).

F. Postpetition Transfers

As we know, as soon as a case is filed, all property in which the debtor has an interest becomes property of the estate. Thus, it stands to reason that any transfers by the debtor made *after* the case is commenced should be avoidable by the trustee. Section 549(a) so states, subject to the provisos that the transfer was (a) not authorized by the Code or the court, or (b) only authorized under section 303(f) or 542(c). The meaning of the first of these limitations is pretty clear; namely, the trustee can only avoid *unauthorized* transfers. Thus, a sale of assets, for example, approved under section 363, could not be avoided. The second proviso is more obscure in that it permits avoidance of two types of transfers that are *authorized* under the Code. What's that all about?

The first such authorized transfer is one made in an involuntary case after the filing of the petition but prior to entry of the order for relief. Section 303(f) authorizes the debtor to continue to acquire and dispose of property free of the constraints imposed by section 363 until entry of the order for relief. This is intended to prevent avoid the filing of involuntary petition from becoming a self-fulfilling prophesy. But, even though authorized, gap period transfers are subject to avoidance under section 549(2)(1)(A). That seems counterintuitive until one considers the exception in section 549(b) that bars avoidance to the extent of any value given by the transferee.

To illustrate, if, while an involuntary petition is pending against Ponoroff, he sells a large piece of business machinery to

Markell for $150,000 cash, roughly its fair market value, section 549(b) will prevent avoidance of that transfer under subsection (a). On the other hand, if the transfer is made in satisfaction of a debt of $150,000 owed by Ponoroff to Markell, the exclusion in subsection (b) regarding "satisfaction of a prepetition debt" will apply and the trustee could proceed under subsection (a) to avoid the transfer and recover the machinery (or its value) from Markell pursuant to section 550(a)—when and if the order for relief eventually is entered. This makes sense from a policy point of view since the first transaction is like any old prefiling transfer for new value, whereas the latter is like a preferential transfer. Finally, for purposes of the exception in section 549(b), it does not matter whether the transferee was or was not aware of the pendency of the involuntary petition.

The second authorized postpetition transfer that may be set aside involves a good faith transfer of estate property (or payment of a debt owing to the debtor) to someone *other than* the trustee by a person who was unaware of the bankruptcy case. Section 542(c) creates an exception for the transferor in that situation from the turnover requirements of section 542(a). However, even though the transfer was authorized, recovery of the property may still be had from the *transferee* because of section 549(a)(2)(A).

Lastly, section 549(c) creates a safe harbor from recovery under section 549(a) for a transfer of real estate in which the transferee purchased in good faith, without knowledge of the bankruptcy case, and for "present fair equivalent value," provided that the conveyance was recorded in the appropriate real estate records prior to recordation of notice of the bankruptcy filing. Note, however, that the exception in section 549(c) is limited to real estate. Thus, if shortly after filing bankruptcy, Markell sells his Prius to Ponoroff for the absurdly high price of $20,000, the car can be recovered by Markell's trustee under section 549(a) and Ponoroff has no recourse against the estate (such as a lien on the car) for the money he paid Markell. Instead, he simply has a postpetition breach of contract claim against Markell. Good luck with that!

G. Statutory Liens and Reclamation

1. *Disguised State Priorities*

Section 545 of the Code deals with the trustee's power to avoid statutory liens—as defined in section 101(53). While it's a little broader than just this, what you need to know about this section it is that it permits the trustee to set aside the fixing of a statutory lien that arises *only* upon the debtor's bankruptcy filing or some other indicator of financial distress.

Now bear in mind that a state can favor a certain category of creditors by providing them lien rights if they are not paid—such as a garageman's lien on the vehicle that the car repair shop worked on or repaired. If the owner files bankruptcy, the repair shop's claim is secured. What a state cannot do, however, is favor its creditors *just in* bankruptcy by enacting a lien statute that says the lien shall arise "when and if the customer files bankruptcy" That's really a disguised priority dressed up to look like a lien, and won't be tolerated. States are aware of this rule, so the issue does not come up very often.

You might also note that liens for rent are avoidable under sections 545(3) and (4) even if not tied to the tenant's financial condition. The rational is the same as the explanation for the cap rent claims under section 502(b)(6); that is, concerns that the case not be overwhelmed by ginormous rent claims arising out of long-term leases.

2. Seller of Goods' Right of Reclamation

Ordinarily, an unpaid seller of goods has no rights against those goods once delivered to the buyer unless the seller has reserved a security interest in the goods. A limited exception to this rule has long existed in the form of a right of reclamation, currently codified in U.C.C. § 2-702(2), when it happens that the buyer was insolvent when the goods were received and prompt demand (within 10 days) is made for their return. As originally enacted in 1978, section 546(c) of the Code simply recognized the nonbankruptcy right of reclamation by making clear that the trustee's avoiding powers were subordinate to the right; that is, could not avoided as a preference, a statutory lien, etc.

Section 546(c) was re-written by BAPCPA to make the elements of the right of reclamation quite a bit different than under the U.C.C. Perhaps, most notable, the period for making demand (which under the Code must be in writing) is now 45 days (or within 20 days of the bankruptcy filing if the 45-day period has not expired as of the filing). In addition, the goods must have been sold in the ordinary course of the seller's business. So if Ponoroff sells his lawnmower to his next-door neighbor Markell, who is insolvent, and the next day Markell files bankruptcy, Ponoroff cannot recover the lawnmower under section 546(c).

The revised version of section 546(c) now makes explicit what had previously been the practice in the case law, which is that the seller's right of reclamation is subject to the claim of a secured creditor of the buyer with a security interest in the goods sold. Thus, suppose Ponoroff sells inventory goods on credit to an insolvent Markell, who has previously granted a security interest in all of his existing and after-acquired inventory to Last National Bank ("LNB). LNB's security interest will attach under U.C.C. Article 9 as soon as Markell has rights in those inventory goods. Therefore, it has priority over Ponoroff's reclamation claim, such that, if the value of all of

Markell's inventory is less than what is owed to LNB, Ponoroff's reclamation claim will be worthless.

In addition, even when the secured creditor's prepetition claim is paid off as part of the same lender's advance of postpetition financing for the debtor in possession, and the same collateral is used to secure the new loan (a so-called "roll-up"), the majority view seems to be that the "prior lien"defense in section 546(c)(1) still applies.[43] Finally, the ability that the bankruptcy courts used to possess to deny a reclamation claim when the goods were necessary for an effective reorganization and, in lieu thereof, award a lien or administrative priority, was eliminated in 2005. Some have people have questioned the wisdom of this decision based on its potential to impair the prospects for a successful reorganization in some cases.

As a practical matter, the right of reclamation is probably less important today than it was earlier, because, you'll recall, BAPCPA also adopted an administrative expense priority for the value of goods received by the debtor in the 20 days prior to the filing of the case where the goods were sold to the debtor in the ordinary course of its business. This is likely to be a simpler remedy for sellers, thus limiting, in most instances, reclamation to claims for goods received between 21 and 45 days prior to the commencement of the case.

---

[43] *See, e.g., In re Dana Corp.*, 567 B.R. 409 (Bankr. S.D.N.Y. 2007).

Executory Contracts

A. What's the Point?

Executory contracts are the subject of section 365 of the Bankruptcy Code. They are a part of every bankruptcy case.[44] Before we look at section 365, let's figure out why the section is important.

First, what is an executory contract? We'll deal this this shortly, but the big picture is that an executory contract is a mixed asset and liability of the estate (note, we said "mixed," not "mixed up"). Let's break that down. We know assets. Things like land, goods, copyrights, etc. We know liabilities. Things like notes, guaranties, unpaid bills, etc. When are they ever mixed? Easy—when they are in the same contract and that contract isn't over yet.

The classic example of an executory contract is a lease of real property, like an apartment, or a business' storefront. The lease is an asset—it represents the debtor's right to occupy the premises and, in the case of the business, conduct its business there. The lease is also a liability—the debtor has to pay its monthly rent in

---

[44] You know this. Why? The section number—365—indicates that it is in chapter 3, and we know that chapter 3 applies in all cases under the Code.

order to stay in the premises. We call the lease a mixed asset because while it represent a property right, that right comes with a cost (the monthly rent).

Why do we focus on these mixed assets? Because they may be valuable . . . or not. One of the functions of section 365 is to give the estate the option to keep valuable executory contracts, and shed costly ones.

How do you know which is which? Well, you as a student do not. You have to be given information about the contract before you can know whether it is valuable or not. For example, the rental rate for business premises varies, but over time tends to go up. If a debtor has a 20-year lease on its premises, and is in its 15th year of the lease, chances are that the contract rate is less than the market rate. And that's what makes the lease—the executory contract— valuable. The debtor is paying less for the premises than it would if it entered into new negotiations for the same space. Conversely, if the debtor entered into the lease just before a real estate bubble burst, chances are that the contract rate is higher than the market rate. So the lease is a dud.

Section 365 gives the estate[45] the ability to keep and perform those deals that are beneficial to the estate (keep the below-market rate lease) and ditch the deals that aren't. And it does this in a way that is very beneficial to the estate.

Recall that when we studied claims, we said that postpetition claims were treated better than prepetition claims. Indeed, if the postpetition claims qualify as administrative claims, they get paid in full before any prepetition claim gets paid a penny. As we will see, the executory contract process allows the estate time to

---

[45] In this Unit we talk about the "estate" rather than the debtor because executory contracts affect *all* who are involved in the case, not just the debtor. As a consequence, the decisions should be made by the estate representative. Who's that? Generally, it will be the Chapter 7 trustee in a Chapter 7 case, the debtor in a Chapter 13 case, and the debtor in possession in a Chapter 11 case. See 11 U.S.C. § 323.

evaluate its contracts (and receive their benefits) during the case. And, if the estate decides the executory contract is too costly, to get rid of it and classify all damages as *pre-petition* claims, even if the decision to get rid of the contract was made *post-petition*. Conversely, if the estate decides that the executory contract is a good one, it can force the non-debtor party to accept the estate's performance, *even if* the debtor was in default pre-petition, and *even if* the executory contract had a clause in it that allowed the non-debtor party to terminate the contract if the debtor filed bankruptcy.

How does section 365 do all this? Read on . . .

B. Just What Is an Executory Contract, Anyway?

Before we look in detail at how executory contracts work, we need to reach some sort of working understanding of what an executory contract is. And the key to that is to understand what makes a contract "executory." What does that mean? Well, you may recall from Contracts that "executory" implies that there are duties left to be executed; that is, that neither side has completed what it committed to do when it signed the contract. A lease that has not expired is executory. A supply contract that has not yet been terminated is executory. A license to use property is executory if both sides have unperformed duties—the licensee has obligations to pay, and the licensor has the duty to protect title to the property licensed. A contract to build a house is executory if the house isn't yet built and the owner hasn't yet paid.

1. What Isn't an Executory Contract

So what isn't executory? Contracts under which one side has fully performed, but the other side hasn't. For example, if the only obligation left unperformed is the debtor's duty is to pay money, the contract is not executory. A contract to purchase goods, as is, for $2,500 is not executory if the seller has delivered the goods and all that remains to be done is for the buyer to pay. A promissory note under which a bank lent money and is merely expecting to be repaid by the debtor is not executory. The bank has no further duties. In each of these cases, the nondebtor party has a claim, and nothing more, in the bankruptcy. It will simply file a proof of claim, and wait for its bankruptcy dividend, if any.

2. *Countryman Definition*

So what is executory? Most courts now adopt what has come to be called the "Countryman Test," named after Vern Countryman, the Harvard law professor who suggested it. His formulation was as follows: "a contract under which the obligations of both the bankrupt[46] and the other party to the contract are so far unperformed that the failure of either to complete performance would constitute a material breach excusing the performance of the other."[47]

Ok. Don't be scared. Yes, this definition does require you to go back to the dim and dark recesses of your mind to call up what you learned (or were exposed to—hopefully) in your first year Contracts class: the concept of "material breach." Material breach requires that both parties—the debtor and the non-debtor—have unperformed obligations under the contract as of the filing of the bankruptcy case. It also requires that those unperformed duties— the executory obligations—be something more than trivial. That is, failure to perform these unperformed obligations when due would give rise to a "material" breach of contract.

---

[46] "Bankrupt" was the somewhat unflattering term used in bankruptcy legislation prior to the current Code to refer to the party that we know call the debtor. This is our footnote, by the way; it's not part of the Countryman article.

[47] Vern Countryman, *Executory Contracts in Bankruptcy (Part I)*, 57 MINN. L. REV. 439, 460 (1973).

What's a material breach? We'll leave an exhaustive examination of that to the Contracts *Short and Happy Guide* (which we also partially co-author), but for now let's define a material breach is one that deprives the other party of the basic benefits of the contract. It takes away the reason for the contract in the first place. When rent isn't paid, that deprives the landlord of its benefit of the lease. When a delivery of goods isn't made, the buyer doesn't get what it bargained for.

So what about Ponoroff's contract to build a house for Markell, with Markell to pay the price over time? If, after the house is done, Markell files bankruptcy, is the contract executory? It might look like it's *not* executory—although Markell has duties (to pay money), what are the Ponoroff's? He's finished the house. But this just shows that you have to look at the deal. Ponoroff probably made warranties in the contract as to durability and quality of the house's features. If the stove breaks, or if the roof leaks, Ponoroff has a obligation to fix these problems. Even though these warranties might be contingent claims, if Ponoroff didn't perform required warranty service, he would be a material breach of his building contract. And thus the contract would be executory.

The issue of "executoriness" has come up in licenses of intellectual property. Once the licensor signs the license, what are the licensor's continuing duties that might make the contract executory? Some early courts found that the licensor's contingent obligation to protect its rights in the property licensed to be sufficiently unperformed and material. Such an obligation is usually part of every license; you wouldn't want Microsoft or Apple to be able to just say "too bad" if they lost the rights you licensed from them. See *Lubrizol Enterprises, Inc. v. Richmond Metal Finishers, Inc.*, 756 F.2d 1043 (4th Cir. 1985). The current trend, however, is to focus on whether the unperformed obligation would give rise to a *material* breach, as opposed to just a regular old breach.[48]

An example of this is *In re Exide Techs.*[49] In that case, Exide had granted a trademark license in connection with the prepetition sale of substantially all of its industrial battery business. Under the terms of the license, the licensee, EnerSys, had a "perpetual, exclusive, royalty-free license to use the Exide trademark."

The Second Circuit found that the trademark agreement was integrated with the related sale agreements and that EnerSys had substantially performed its obligations under the agreement, primarily relying on the not insubstantial fact that EnerSys had already paid the full $135 million purchase price, had assumed liabilities in connection with the business, and had operated under the Exide Agreement for ten years. The Third Circuit determined that, under New York law (which governed the Exide Agreement), a "material breach" must be "a breach which is so substantial as to defeat the purpose of the entire transaction" and that no material breach can occur if the breaching party has already "substantially performed" under the contract. Since EnerSys had substantially performed, the court concluded that there could be no material breach.[50]

---

[48]   The difference is that while a nonbreaching party can always obtain damages for a breach, the nonbreaching party can only suspend or cancel its remaining (i.e., executory) obligations if the breach was material.

[49]   607 F.3d 957 (2d Cir. 2010).

[50]   That's part of contract law. If there is substantial performance by one party, that party cannot be in "material" breach. Regular breach, sure. But not material breach.

C. What Are the Three Things You Can Do with Executory Contracts, and What Are the Differences Among Them?

Things now get technical. There are three things the estate can do with an executory contract. They are:

- Reject it

- Assume it and retain it

- Assume it and assign it to a third party

Every executory contract issue will deal with one of these three actions.

1. Reject

The estate's first option is that it can "reject" an executory contract. Although "rejection" sounds like someone has a broken heart, it is simpler than that: it means that estate can breach the contract. Ho hum. Anyone can breach a contract. But the kicker here is that if the estate decides to breach the contract, any damages will be pre-petition, unsecured damages. They can be paid in small, less-than-100%-on-the-dollar, bankruptcy dollars. See section 365(g)(1). The benefit here is that the estate gets time *after* it files bankruptcy to determine whether the damages will be calculated as if they occurred *before* the filing.

How does the estate make this decision? The standard is fairly low. All the estate has to show is that it is exercising its good faith business judgment that the executory contract is a burden to the estate; that is, that it will cost more to perform under it that it is worth.[51] Against this standard, most nondebtors don't have a chance. Challenging the exercise of business judgment is, well,

---

[51] This standard is not set forth in the Code. It has evolved in the case law under Section 365.

challenging. As the Ninth Circuit has said, "rejection should be approved unless the decision is so manifestly unreasonable that it could not be based on sound business judgment, but only on bad faith, whim, or caprice." *In re Pomona Valley Medical Group.*[52] Tough standard for nondebtors to meet.

Rejection is a public affair; the estate must seek court permission to reject most contracts, and usually seeks this permission by motion. The only exception for this is in Chapter 7 cases and certain types of executory contracts in Chapter 11, which we will get to later in subsection (1) and (2) of Section E below.

Why would a nondebtor ever bother to challenge the rejection of an executory contract? Well, executory contracts are a zero-sum game. What is a loss to the estate is a gain to the nondebtor party. So the non-debtor party wants the estate to continue to perform. That occurs, however, only if the estate assumes the contract, which we take up next.

2. *Assume and Retain*

The estate's second option is to assume the contract, and retain its benefits. Assumption sounds ponderous, and just like rejection is a fancy word for what is going on (*breach*), assumption is an overstuffed word for what the estate wishes to do: *perform*. That is, when an estate elects to assume a contract, it elects to perform the contract, and hold the nondebtor to its performance. Like rejection, assumption is accomplished by court order after notice and a hearing.

What are the consequence of assumption? They are serious. Assumption of a contract binds the estate to perform the contract's terms, with the consequence that any breach thereafter will result

---

[52] 476 F.3d 665, 670 (9th Cir. 2007). There is a different standard for labor contracts in chapter 11 provided by section 1113. That is way beyond what most introductory courses cover, however.

in administrative expense liability. *See* section 365(g)(2). That's full, 100% dollars; accept no substitutes. So if the estate miscalculates the benefit of an executory contract, and assumes it, the estate's creditors will suffer if the estate later breaches.

For such serious consequences, there are two different standards for assumption: one if the debtor was in default at the time of the filing, and the other if the debtor was not in default. Let's take the easy case first.

a. If Contract Is Not in Default

If the debtor was not in default under the executory contract when the debtor filed its bankruptcy case, the test of the propriety of the estate's decision is whether the estate representative exercised good faith business judgment when making the decision to assume. This is the same test as for rejection, and like rejection, it is a judicially-imposed requirement. Nothing in section 365(a) sets forth this standard. So if the estate wants to assume the lease of its business premises, and the lease was not in default (no missed rent payments, for example), then all the estate has to do is (1) request that the court approve the assumption, (2) notify the nondebtor party, and (3) support the decision by evidence of the exercise of its good faith business judgments (usually done by the declaration of the estate representative or one of its agents). That's it.

So if Ponoroff's survival knife business, Ponoroff's Points, Inc. (PPI) files bankruptcy, and wants to retain its below market lease of its headquarters, can it do so over landlord Markell's objection? (Markell does not like pointy things like Ponoroff's . . . wares.) Yes, so long as PPI was not in default when PPI filed bankruptcy. All PPI has to do is request assumption from the court (usually by a motion), and support that request with a declaration from Ponoroff that he believes assumption of the lease is in PPI's best interests because the rental rate is below market. Markell has no defense. Ouch. To paraphrase Bryan Adams, it cuts like a knife.

b.   If Contract Is in Default

But this is bankruptcy. If a PPI was honoring all of its contracts, it likely would not have to file bankruptcy. Could PPI, as estate representative, assume the lease if it were two months behind in its rent (that is, in default under the lease)? The answer is not obvious initially. Recall that the test for whether a contract is executory is whether the nonperformance of unperformed terms would constitute a material breach under non-bankruptcy law. Under nonbankruptcy law, one consequence of material breach is that the non-breaching party can terminate the contract. So if the prepetition breach was material, can the non-debtor now terminate the contract? Despite the right to terminate under nonbankruptcy law, the answer is clearly that PPI *can* assume: Section 365(b) allows an estate to assume a contract in default. Markell is again out of luck.

How does section 365(b) work? It allows an estate to assume and retain an executory contract that is in default, but only if the estate meets certain conditions. Those conditions are listed in section 365(b)(1). They require the estate to:

- Cure, or promptly cure, the default

- Compensate the nondebtor party for damages related to the default; *and*

- Provide adequate assurance of future performance of the contract

Cure means that the estate must remedy the breach. If, as indicated above, PPI is two months in arrears of its rent, it has to pay those two month's rent as part of the assumption process.

Compensate means that the estate must pay additional funds to put the nondebtor party in the position it would have been in had the default or breach not occurred. Normally, in uncomplicated matters, this can be done by paying interest on the cure amount (the remedy for the non-payment of money is usually interest for the time during which the money was not paid).

Adequate assurance of future performance is trickier. In short, the Code has adopted a version of UCC § 2-609, which requires a party to provide "adequate assurance" of future performance if the other party is reasonably doubtful about continued adherence to contract terms. What forms do adequate assurance take under section 365(b)(1)? Courts are all over the map on this, and the following is only a partial list: (1) whether the financial terms of the agreement are at or below the prevailing rate (the more favorable the terms are to the estate, the greater the chances the estate will perform to retain their benefits); (2) the general outlook in the debtor's industry; (3) a plan that would earmark money exclusively for the nondebtor party to the agreement; (4) evidence of profitability; (5) the presence of a security deposit; (6) the presence of a guaranty; and (7) the debtor's payment history. *See In re M. Fine Lumber Co.*[53]

Most courts look to give the nondebtor assurances equivalent to those that were in place at the time of contracting; the nondebtor party should not do better than it did initially. So if the contract was risky to begin with, the estate only need demonstrate that it is providing the same assurances as were in place when the contract was made.

So let's continue with PPI. Assume that it is two months in arrears. To assume this contract, PPI will have to show that assumption is in its good faith business judgment, provide the two

---

[53] 383 B.R. 565, 573 (Bankr. E.D.N.Y. 2008).

month's back rent (cure), provide interest on the back rent (compensate), and provide adequate assurance that it will perform in the future. How will it prove this last element? Perhaps by declaration from Ponoroff as to the business prospects, and how they are now equivalent to what they were when the lease was signed. Or, it might require showing a feasible plan of reorganization. Another method might require a guaranty of payment from Ponoroff himself (although that undoubtedly would be of minuscule worth).[54] Finally, it might require PPI to show a reasonable budget that includes the rental payment prominently.

If PPI does all this, Markell again has no defense. He will have to allow PPI to stay in place, and can't toss the bum out. That's the point here. Section 365(b) allows estates to stay in place, or to retain the benefits of contracts, by looking only at whether it makes sense for the *estate* to do so. The nondebtor party's wishes are irrelevant.

There are, of course, many nuances and exceptions to these rules. We'll get to them in the rest of this Unit, but first let's look at the third option: assumption and assignment.

3. *Assume and Assign*

The third option an estate has involves assuming the contract, and then assigning it to a third party. First, you should ask yourself why an estate would want to do this. The answer is pretty easy: to make money. Say, for example, that a debtor has overextended itself and needs to downsize its operations. It has some locations that it no longer wants, but which are subject to a below market lease. There's value there—and the question is who gets it, the estate, or the landlord. The landlord would get the value if the lease were rejected, as it would re-let the premises at the higher, market

---

[54] *Comment from Ponoroff*: Although Markell wrote this to be cheeky, sadly it's true and will remain so unless you get lots more of your friends to buy this book!

rate, to a third party. The estate, however, would get it if it could assign, or sell, the lease to that same third party—who would presumably be willing to pay something for the ability to take over a below-market lease.

a. Requirements

So what does an estate have to do to assign this lease? That is section 365(f)'s domain. First, the estate must assume the lease, using analysis described above. With assumption, the lease will be current. Next, it must be shown that the assignee—the buyer of the lease—will provide adequate assurance of its performance under the lease. That's all. Again, a fairly simple process, or at least a process not very different than if the estate were going to assume a defaulted contract.[55]

But what if the lease itself says that it cannot be assigned? Many leases have such anti-assignment clauses. Section 365(f) essentially neutralizes these types of provisions. It says that the estate can assign a lease or executory contract "notwithstanding a provision in an executory contract or unexpired lease of the debtor, or in applicable law, that prohibits, restricts, or conditions the assignment of such contract or lease." *See* section 365(f)(1). Further, section 365(f)(3) confirms this right by providing that the nondebtor party can't terminate the lease or executory contract after assumption or assignment based on an anti-assignment clause.

How does this work in practice? Again, assume that Ponoroff's Points, Inc. (PPI) is in bankruptcy, and wants to downsize. It needs to reduce its locations from ten to five. Each location, for purposes of this hypothetical, is leased from Markell at rates that were at market when the leases were entered into, but are now way below market. Each lease has unperformed obligations (the landlord has

---

[55] Note that adequate assurance must be provided even if the lease or executory contract is not in default. This is a difference from the straight assumption decision.

to allow access; PPI has to pay rent), so section 365 will govern each lease.

First, PPI will assume the leases that it wishes to keep. If it is not in default of these leases, that is, if it is current on its rent and all other provisions, it is the simple process described above. Markell loses. If PPI is behind in rent, and thus in default, same result, except now PPI will have to cut through Markell's cries of despair and bring the rent current, pay interest on the back rent, and show that the downsized PPI is just as good a tenant as PPI was when the leases were originally signed (that would be the provision of adequate assurance).

What about the five leases it doesn't want? Even if PPI spurns them, others will want them given their below-market lease rates. Using section 365(f), PPI can "sell" those leases—assign them—over Markell's objection. The leases will have to be assumed (any back rent brought current, etc.) and the new leases—the purchasers from PPI—will have to show that they can provide adequate assurance. If those points can be shown, Markell will lose (again). This will be the case even if each lease says "This lease may not be assigned." Section 365(f) overrides those provisions.

b. Sales of Assets

Section 365(f) is also important in asset sales under section 363 of the Code. If a debtor wishes to sell a unit of its business, or all of its business, it will not just sell hard assets. It will also attempt to transfer the benefit of the contracts the debtor has with others. The only way to do that is to assign the contracts, and the only way to do that assignment in bankruptcy is through section 365(f). So not only can section 365(f) be used to realize value on unnecessary assets, but it can be used to facilitate sales of businesses.

c.   Release of Liability

One might hesitate a bit about the benefits of assignment. At common law, when a party assigned its rights and delegated its' duties under a contract, the assignor remained liable on the contract. Section 365(k) anticipates this, and modifies the common law to release the estate from *all* liability under the assigned contract. So, in the hypothetical above, PPI will not be liable on the assigned leases from and after the assignment.

D. What Are the Limitations and Exceptions?

Are there any limitations and exceptions to rejection and assumption other than the good faith business judgment rule? Of course. When drafting the Code, Congress inserted provisions that benefit the estate by closing loopholes that might have allowed parties to evade the workings of section 365. Congress also limited section 365 by excluding certain contracts from its reach. Since the devil is in the details, let's look at those benefits and restrictions.

1. Restrictions Which Benefit the Estate

Contracts are private obligations. May parties anticipate bankruptcy and contract out of section 365? No. There are several provisions that restrict parties from opting out in their agreements.

a.   Ipso Facto Clauses Do Not Bar Assumption

The first restriction is Congress' invalidation of so-called "ipso facto" clauses. These clauses seek to terminate a contract simply because the debtor filed bankruptcy.[56] The prohibited clauses also include clauses that seek to enable one party to terminate the contract for the other party's financial condition (such as when one

---

[56] The term "ipso facto" is from the Latin phrase meaning "by the fact itself," and so an ipso facto clause would terminate the contract by the fact itself of the filing of the bankruptcy case.

party can terminate if the other's net worth drops below a certain level) or the debtor's use of (or subjection to) some other collective debt relief remedy such as a receivership. So long as the debtor is current and not otherwise in default under the contract, the Bankruptcy Code deems ipso facto clauses invalid in bankruptcy.[57]

It does this in two ways. First, section 365(b)(2) states that the presence of such clauses cannot be used to block assumption. Thus, even if a contract says that filing bankruptcy terminates the contract, the estate can still assume the contract because section 365(b)(2) will invalidate it. Second, section 365(e) takes away the ability of the nondebtor party to use such clauses to terminate or modify the contract during bankruptcy.

Sections 365(b)(2) and 365(e) work as follows. Assume our friend Ponoroff Points, Inc. (PPI) files bankruptcy. It has a steel supply contract with Markell under which Markell has agreed, for the next two years, to supply PPI with so much steel per month at a set price. That price is now below market (steel has risen in price) and PPI wants to keep the contract. Markell, however, points to two provisions in the contract: one that allows him to terminate the contract if PPI files bankruptcy, and another that requires PPI to maintain a net worth of $1 million dollars. When PPI seeks to assume this contract, Markell opposes, citing these two clauses.

Markell will lose. First, the ipso facto clause is specifically overridden by section 365(b)(2)(B), which allows assumption despite a clause that terminates the contract upon "the commencement of a case under this title." Second, section 365(e)(1)(A) overrides clauses which terminate the contract on "the insolvency *or financial condition* of the debtor at any time before the closing of the case." So PPI can assume.

---

[57] There are exceptions for various types of financial contracts such as derivatives and repurchase agreements, but we won't go into those here. If you knew what we know about those types of deals, you'd thank us.

But now Markell is steamed. Section 365(b)(2) just talks about assumption. It doesn't speak to ongoing operations. So it now raises both clauses as excuses for Markell's continued performance, and declines to deliver more steel. Does Markell fare any better?

Nope. Section 365(e) now controls. Using the same language as section 365(b)(2), it provides an executory contract cannot be "terminated or modified, [or] any right or obligation under such contract of lease . . . terminated or modified . . . solely because" of an ipso facto and financial condition clause. So Markell will have to continue to perform.

b. Non-Monetary Defaults and the Impossibility of Cure

What if the contract between Markell and PPI has other defaults that can no longer be cured? Many leases, for example, contain what are called "going dark" clauses. These clauses allow the landlord to terminate the lease if the tenant closes up shop for a certain period of time; that is, "goes dark."[58] If the tenant later resumes business and files bankruptcy, can that lease be assumed?

The argument against is that there is a default—the tenant went dark—and that this default cannot be cured. You can't go back in time and change facts. Once the bell has been rung, you can't un-ring it. Once the eggs are scrambled. . . . Ok, you get the point.

That's where section 365(b)(1)(A) comes in. It excuses the obligation to cure a non-monetary default "if it is impossible for the trustee to cure such default by performing nonmonetary acts at and after the time of assumption. . . ." So no cure is necessary, although to the extent possible the estate will need to compensate the nondebtor party for the fallout from the breach of the non-monetary terms.

---

[58] These are usually found in leases in which the rent includes an amount based on the tenant's revenue (so-called percentage rent), so if the tenant "goes dark," it deprives the landlord of a portion of the bargained rent.

2. Restrictions Which Limit Assumption

So far, we've seen bankruptcy law make it easier for the estate to assume or assign an executory contract and reap its benefits. Are there any limitations on that ability; or, put another way, do nondebtors have any rights?

They do. This section explores those rights.

a. Personal Service and Other Non-Assignable Contracts Cannot Be Assumed or Assigned

Section 365(c)(1)(A) prohibits estates from assuming or assigning executory contracts in which "applicable law excuses a party, other than the debtor, to such contract or lease from accepting performance from or rendering performance to an entity other than the debtor or the debtor in possession." This is sometimes mistakenly referred to as the "personal services" contract exception, because under the common law, obligations under contracts for personal services—such as a contract with an artist to paint your portrait, or a contract with a famous architect to design your new house—cannot be delegated. That makes sense; if you hire Markell to paint your visage; you sure as heck don't want him to delegate the task to Ponoroff—who has hasn't been praised for his artistry since kindergarten.

The limitation, however, brings in nonbankruptcy law— "applicable law" in the words of the statute—as a test of what can be assumed (or assigned) and what can't. That means on an exam your instructor will either assume that you know the nonbankruptcy law or will tell you what it is. If he or she doesn't tell you, the test, according to section 317(2)(a) of the *Restatement of Contracts (Second)*, is that a contract cannot be assigned if the assignment would "materially increase the burden or risk imposed on [the obligor] by his contract, or materially impair his chance of obtaining return performance."

The distinction is sometimes relevant under government contracts. Such contracts typically have non-assignability clauses, and, as they are with the government, the government typically ensures that "applicable law" makes such contracts non-assignable.

Courts have developed two competing tests to decide whether an estate may assume a government contract: the actual test and the hypothetical test. Under the actual test, the estate (or, more usually, the debtor in possession) is treated as an actual assignee, and courts apply section 365(c)(1)(A) to prohibit assignment to the estate. Under the hypothetical test, by contrast, assignment is prohibited only if the debtor in possession lacks authority to assign the contract to someone else, which would be a hypothetical person (hence the name) since the only relevant entities are the debtor, and its successor the debtor in possession. *In re Catapult Entertainment, Inc.*[59] The so-called "hypothetical test" is preferred by a majority of the other Courts of Appeals that have addressed this question.[60]

b. Contracts of Financial Accommodation Cannot Be Assumed or Assigned

Also excluded from the types of executory contracts that can be assumed or assigned are contracts of "financial accommodation." These are things like loan agreements or contracts under which the nondebtor has agreed to extend some sort of financial benefit to the debtor. They just can't be assumed; no one thinks you should force a bank to lend more money to someone in bankruptcy without complying with section 364, the Code's section which directly addresses postpetition lending.

---

[59] 165 F.3d 747 (9th Cir. 1999).

[60] At least two Justices of the Supreme Court think this issue is sufficiently important that the whole Court should grant certiorari on it. *N.C.P. Marketing Group, Inc. v. BG Star Productions, Inc.* 556 U.S. 1145 (2009) (Kennedy, J, with Breyer, J, joining, on denial of certiorari).

c. Adequate Assurance and Shopping Center Leases

Shopping centers are singled out for special treatment in section 365.[61] We'll see later how they have priority with respect to timing; in this section, however, we focus on Congress' special requirements for assumption of a lease in a shopping center when the debtor is in default.

We saw above that if the debtor was in default prepetition, it had to among other things give adequate assurance of future performance. In most contexts, that is an open-textured, contextual inquiry. With leases of spaces in shopping centers, it is not.

Section 365(b)(3) requires that when a defaulting debtor assumes a shopping center lease (either for purposes of retention or for assignment): (1) any percentage rent due under the lease will not decline substantially; (2) assumption or assignment of the lease will not alter the non-monetary terms of the lease, including terms on location, use, or exclusivity; and (3) that assumption or assignment of such lease will not disrupt any tenant mix or balance in the shopping center.

So if Ponoroff Points, Inc. (PPI), our favorite knife vendor, wants to assume and assign its below market lease at a local mall to the local chapter of Pacifists, Inc. (PI) (an organization opposed to pointy objects), and if PI would not fit in the mix of tenants already at the mall, PPI cannot provide adequate assurance of future performance. It thus cannot assume or assign the lease. Done.

---

[61] Congress did not define the term "shopping center." In determining whether a lease is a shopping center lease, courts have looked to such factors as (1) multiple leases held by a single landlord; (2) spaces being leased to commercial retailers, (3) a common parking area, (4) requirements for common operating hours, (5) common areas for patrons, and (6) common advertising.

E. What Are the Time Limits for Accomplishing the Three Actions?

Section 365 has lots to say about when the estate can assume or reject, and some deadlines that vary by chapter. We examine those here.

1. Chapter 7 Cases

In Chapter 7 cases, if the trustee is going to assume a contract, it must do so within the first 60 days of the case. *See* section 365(d)(1). If the trustee does nothing, the executory contract or lease is automatically rejected. The trustee can seek an extension of this 60-day deadline, but the court must grant the extension before the expiration of the 60-day period or it's too late.

2. All Other Cases

In all other cases (that is, cases filed under Chapters 9, 11, 12, or 13), the estate representative has until the confirmation of the plan to assume or reject executory contracts or leases. *See* section 365(d)(2). Nondebtor parties to the contract or lease may request that the estate make an earlier determination, but such requests require the court to balance the nondebtor's need for a decision against the debtor's right to reorganize, and things rarely go well for the nondebtor party in those circumstances.

There is a special exception for "nonresidential real property leases." This ungainly term refers to lease of business properties, such as spaces in a mall or other shopping center, but also more broadly to any lease of real property that is not being used for humans to live in.

This exception puts outside limits on the amount of time an estate has to decide whether to assume or reject such leases. The time period is 120 days from the order for relief, with one possible extension of an additional 90 days if the estate or the landlord shows cause, and if the court enters the extension order within the 120-day period. *See* section 365(d)(4). If the estate misses these deadlines, the consequences are severe: the statute requires that the estate "shall immediately surrender that nonresidential real property to the lessor."

So assume that Ponoroff Points, Inc. (PPI) has 150 stores it leases in various parts of the country. It needs to reorganize; its finances are not that sharp.[62] If it files, it has to assess the viability of each of the 150 stores within this 120-day time frame (or maybe 210 days if it can get an extension). If it does not timely make this assessment, or otherwise misses the deadline, it has to surrender the stores not designated. Congress imposed this limit in 2005, and most agree that it has adversely affect large reorganizations of retail operations such as PPI, or, in the real world, Circuit City or Radio Shack.

3. *What Happens in the Meantime?*

The deadlines are relatively clear, and so are the consequences. But what happens in the meantime? Put another way, what is the status of a non-assumed, non-rejected executory contract after filing and before the court orders assumption or rejection?

a. Business as Usual

The general rule is that an executory contract remains in effect pending assumption or rejection by a debtor. Indeed, the Supreme Court has indicated that, before the estate assumes or rejects, the contract is enforceable by, but not against, the debtor. *NLRB v. Bildisco & Bildisco.*[63]

---

[62] "I want to make clear that Markell wrote that." /s/ Ponoroff.

[63] 465 U.S. 513, 531–32 (1984).

As a consequence, the nondebtor party must generally continue to perform its obligations under the contract prior to assumption or rejection, but the debtor is not bound by the provisions of the contract unless the contract is subsequently assumed.

Courts have thus held that executory contracts are property of the estate entitled to the protection of the automatic stay that cannot be terminated by the nondebtor party, at least not without first obtaining stay relief. So if Markell tries to terminate its supply contract with Ponoroff Points, Inc. for failure to pay invoices without first seeking relief from the automatic stay, he will face possible damages for such a violation.

b.   Nondebtor Rights and Remedies

Non-debtor parties are not without some additional remedies. They can request early decision by the estate under section 365(d)(2). In addition, to the extent that they provide goods or services, they also obtain an administrative expense claim to the extent they confer benefit upon the estate, albeit perhaps not at the contract rate. As the Supreme Court has stated, "[I]f the debtor-in-possession elects to continue to receive benefits from the other party to an executory contract pending a decision to reject or assume the contract, the debtor-in-possession is obligated to pay for the reasonable value of those services, . . . which, depending on the circumstances of a particular contract, may be what is specified in the contract. . . . Should the debtor-in-possession elect to assume the executory contract, however, it assumes the contract *cum onere*,[64] . . . and the expenses and liabilities incurred may be

---

[64] Fancy Latin for "with all burdens." This reinforces what we said when we started this Unit, long ago: an executory contract is a mixed asset. It comes with benefits and burdens.

treated as administrative expenses, which are afforded the highest priority on the debtor's estate, 11 U.S.C. § 503(b)(1)(A)."[65]

Lessors of personal property in Chapter 11 also have different and better rights. Section 365(d)(5) requires timely performance of all obligations under such leases beginning on the 61st day *after* the entry of the order for relief. Courts have read this provision to mean that they should grant administrative priority status—without requiring the usual showing of actual benefit to the estate under Section 503(b)(1)—to all unperformed obligations under a personal property lease to the extent that such obligations arise from and after the 61st day *after* entry of the order for relief. So say our favorite knife vendor, PPI, leases a knife sharpening machine from Markell at $1,000 a month. It can continue using that machine for 60 days after it files a chapter 11 case, and all it has to pay is the fair market value of its use. After that time, however, PPI has to perform the obligation in full, that is, it has to pay the full $1,000, even if the machine is broken and not useful and even if PPI ultimately rejects the lease.

Finally, some courts have held that section 365(d)(3) requires payment in full of all lease obligations on nonresidential real property leases even if the lease rates exceed the benefit to estate; in short, these courts read that section 365(d)(3) overrides the requirements of section 503(b) for administrative claims.

F. Exotic Situations

Section 365 has been the subject of much lobbying. As a result, there are special provisions that affect special situations—or exotic situations as we call them.

---

[65] Bildisco, 465 U.S. at 531-32.

1. Debtor as Lessor of Real Property; Rights of Lessee

What happens if the debtor is a landlord, and not a tenant? Does the landlord obtain the ability upon filing bankruptcy to reject the lease and toss the tenant out?

No. Section 365(h) provides protection for tenants. It provides that the tenant of a rejected lease has an option. It can treat the lease as terminated if a breach by the landlord would permit it to terminate under applicable nonbankruptcy law. Or, it can elect to remain, and can offset its damages arising from the landlord's rejection/breach against future rental obligations. The point to be made is rejection does not mean termination; it just means, well, rejection.

2. Debtor as Licensee of Intellectual Property; Rights of Licensee

Licensees of intellectual property[66] have similar rights. Under section 365(n), if the licensor rejects, the licensee may treat the license as terminated, or may continue to use the property subject to the terms of the license (and for the contractual life of the license), and may deduct from any license fees any damages suffered as a result of the rejection. Rejection does not mean termination. If this provision looks similar to the treatment of tenants under section 365(h), then give yourself a prize; it was patterned after that section.

---

[66] For reasons too detailed to reprint here and still remain short (and happy), trademark licenses are not within the scope of this section. Patent and copyright licenses, in contrast, are.

G. Basic Checklist for Executory Contracts

As a bonus, here is a basic Checklist of the decision process for typical executory contracts or leases. It does not contain detailed descriptions of, or account for, some of the limitations discussed above. But it should serve as a good basic review of the chapter.

- Is the contract executory?
  - o If not, § 365 does not apply
- Does the estate want to reject?
  - o If yes, apply business judgment test and contract reject. § 365(a)
  - o Consequences of rejection:
    - ▪ Rejection treated as breach.
    - ▪ All damages treated as pre-petition unsecured damages. § 365(g)(1)
- Does the estate wish to assume?
  - o Can contract be assigned under § 365(c)?
    - ▪ If no, then no assumption
  - o If contract can assigned, was the debtor current and not in default on the filing date?
    - ▪ If yes, then apply business judgment rule and contract assumed. § 365(a)
  - o If contract can be assigned, was the debtor in default on the filing date?
    - ▪ If yes, debtor may still assume (§ 365(b)), but only if:
      - ▪ Debtor cures default
      - ▪ Debtor compensates for default

- Debtor provides adequate assurance of future performance
    - Consequences of assumption
        - Contract in full force
        - Any breach is treated as administrative expense. § 365(g)(2)
- Does the estate wish to assign the contract?
    - If yes, then must assume and provide adequate assurance that assignee will perform in future. § 365(f)
    - Estate relieved of any liability for future breaches. § 365(k)

Special Issues in Chapter 7

A. Overview

The overwhelming number—about 70 percent—of bankruptcy filings are Chapter 7 cases. Of these, the overwhelming number are filed by individuals—about 99 percent—and the overwhelming number of these—better than 90 percent—are so-called "no asset" cases, meaning that there are insufficient assets to cover even the costs of administration, so there will not be any distribution to general unsecured creditors.

As we noted back in Unit 1, at its core, a Chapter 7 case involves the surrender of the debtor's assets to the trustee for liquidation and distribution to creditors, in return for which the debtor receives a discharge of all debts arising prior to the filing of the bankruptcy petition; or, stated in other terms, a fresh start. This means that the principal issues surrounding Chapter 7 cases involve: (1) what steps can or is the debtor entitled to take in order to keep some of her property; (2) when will the debtor be denied a discharge; (3) under what circumstances will the debtor's discharge be denied; and, if the discharge is not denied, (4) what debts are excepted from the discharge.

Recall also from Unit 2, that an individual debtor is no longer automatically eligible for relief under Chapter 7. An individual debtor must pass the means test in section 707(b)(2) before relief will be granted under Chapter 7. If the debtor fails the means test, the debtor's bankruptcy recourse will usually be Chapter 13. Most debtors easily pass the means test, but all debtors must take it nonetheless. This has added some expense and complication to Chapter 7. It's time now to address the operation of the means test, so steel your minds and gird your loins.

B. Why You Gotta Be So Mean?

Before 2005, section 707(b) provided that the bankruptcy court could dismiss a Chapter 7 filing if it found that the granting of relief would constitute a "substantial abuse." An important factor in this analysis was the debtor's ability to repay his debts under Chapter 13. But Congress believed that the bankruptcy courts weren't doing enough to steer debtors who could pay some reasonable portion of their debts away from Chapter 7 and into Chapter 13. So Congress decided to take matters into its own hands (and out of the hands of the bankruptcy judges) by coming up with the "means test," now codified in section 707(b)(2), as one way in which the granting of relief would constitute an "abuse" of Chapter 7 for purposes of section 707(b)(1), and, as such, grounds for dismissal or conversion.

The means test is pretty complicated and we're trying to keep things simple here (if not happy), so let's see if we can boil it down to its primary features. Only bankruptcy filers with primarily consumer debts, not business debts, need to take the means test, and for these purposes household mortgage debt is considered consumer debt.

The first step in the means test is to calculate "current monthly income," a term defined in section 101(10A) as the debtor's average income over the six calendar months before filing for bankruptcy. If the debtor's current monthly income is less than the median income for a household of her size in her state (a number conveniently compiled by the Office of the United States Trustee),[67] she passes the means test. Period. She's done. The debtor does not need to complete the rest of the means test and the case may proceed under Chapter 7

If the debtor earns more than the applicable median, things get more complex, as it must next be determined if she has enough *disposable income* to repay some portion of her unsecured debts. To determine disposable income requires that certain "allowed monthly expenses" be deducted from current monthly income. Some of these expenses are *actual* expenses, but most are determined by reference to Standards promulgated by the Internal Revenue Service for purposes of ascertaining a taxpayer's ability to repay delinquent taxes. These data are also available on the OUST website: http://www.justice.gov/ust/means-testing.

Once the debtor's disposable monthly income is determined it is multiplied by 60 (the life of a typical Chapter 13 plan for high-income individuals is 60 months). This represents what the debtor is able to apply toward unsecured debts under a Chapter 13 plan. If that amount is $12,475 or more, the debtor has failed the means

---

[67] The Office of the United States Trustee ("OUST") and the U.S Trustees who are appointed by the Attorney General to serve in 21 local regions (each comprised of one or more federal judicial districts) should not be confused with the "trustee" appointed to represent the bankruptcy estate. The OUST is a branch of the Department of Justice charged with responsibility to carry out sundry administrative duties in bankruptcy cases, such as to appoint a panel of private trustees to serve in bankruptcy cases, monitor the debtor's filings of required reports, monitor plans in rehabilitation proceedings, etc. The activities of the U.S. Trustees around the country are overseen by an Executive Director. Alabama and North Carolina are not part of the OUST system. Instead, the duties of the U.S. Trustee in the six federal judicial districts of those states are carried out by Bankruptcy Administrators appointed under the Bankruptcy Administrator Program, which is a judicial rather than an executive agency.

test and there is a presumption of abuse—which may be rebutted based on special circumstances, such as unusual medical expenses. If the number is under $7,475, there is no presumption of abuse. Note that these numbers adjust every four years under section 104(a), and will adjust again on April 1, 2016. If the debtor's disposable income is in-between these floor and ceiling amounts, there is a presumption of abuse if the debtor's disposable income is sufficient to pay 25 percent or more of her nonpriority unsecured debt.

Note further that because median income levels vary by state and household size, and each county and metropolitan region has different allowed amounts for categories of allowed expenses, such as housing and transportation, what it takes to pass (or fail) the means test can vary widely from debtor-to-debtor. Also, even if you pass the means test, the case can *still* be dismissed under section 707(b)(3) if the court finds either that (1) the filing was in bad faith, or (2) the totality of the circumstances surrounding the debtor's financial situation demonstrates abuse. An example of a case in the second category might include the situation where the debtor engaged in unlawful pre-bankruptcy planning as discussed more fully below in Section C.12.d.

C. Keeping Property in Chapter 7

1. Exemptions

a. Understanding Exempt Property

Generally speaking, we say that in Chapter 7 the debtor surrenders her property for a discharge, and in Chapters 11, 12 & 13, the debtor retains her property in return for paying off her debts under some type of rehabilitation plan. However, the more accurate statement is that in Chapter 7 the debtor surrenders her unencumbered, nonexempt assets for liquidation and distribution by the trustee. "Unencumbered" because, as we have seen, for the most part perfected liens pass through the bankruptcy case unaffected. "Nonexempt" because, by law, certain assets (although initially property of the estate) remain with the debtor to assist with her fresh start.

Exemptions apply only to individual debtors (corporations, for example, don't get them). They can also be important in individual Chapter 11 and 13 cases, even though those debtors don't need exemptions in order to keep their property. This is because Chapter 13 and Chapter 11 both use a liquidation baseline for evaluating whether a rehabilitation plan can be confirmed by the court, and in setting that baseline exemptions factor into the calculation. Thus, as we'll see when we get to the Units dealing with those kinds of cases, it will be important to know how much would have been distributed to general creditors had the Chapter 11 or 13 debtor's estate been liquidated in a Chapter 7 case. Again, more on that later.

Exemptions are not limited to bankruptcy. Every state has its own list of property that is placed beyond the reach of execution by judgment creditors. Similarly, there are some nonbankruptcy federal exemptions. The idea behind exemption statutes generally is to leave the judgment debtor with at least enough to support herself and her dependents.

Exemptions can be defined by (1) type of property interest; e.g., the family bible, or (2) a dollar amount; e.g., personal property not to exceed X dollars in value; or (3) a combination of the two—an automobile not to exceed $10,000 in value. In the last example, if the debtor's car is worth $15,000 it will be sold and the first $10,000 of proceeds turned over to the debtor, who will presumably have to buy a cheaper car—like Markell's Prius.

Exemptions can extend to personal property, real property (the "homestead" exemption), and income streams, such as retirement or disability payments. Also, it's very important to remember that exemptions cannot be asserted against creditors with a lien on the exempt property, except to the extent section 522(f), which we examine in Section C.1.e below, applies. So, if Markell takes a mortgage on Ponoroff's house to secure a debt of $100,000, and Ponoroff has a homestead exemption of $40,000 and the house is worth $100,000, Ponoroff is not going to see any of his exemption. The exemption, it is said, is subordinate to the lien. However, a general waiver of (or agreement to subordinate) exemptions to an *unsecured* extension of credit is unenforceable as a matter of public policy *See* section 522(e). So, in the above example, if Markell did not take a lien to secure his debt and instead reduced the claim to judgment and arranged for a foreclosure sale of Ponoroff's house, the first $40,000 of proceeds from the sale would go to Ponoroff. And this would be true even if the promissory note Ponoroff signed said that he agreed Markell's debt would be superior to Ponoroff's right to any exemption claim in his property.

Exemptions vary pretty wildly from state to state both in scope and amount. While some states offer relatively miserly exemptions to their judgment debtors, the state exemptions that draw the most attention are exemptions that are unlimited in amount and, in particular, unlimited homestead exemptions, such as in Texas, Florida, and Kansas. When an unlimited homestead exemption applies in a bankruptcy case, it is important to appreciate that this is more significant than assertion of the same exemption under state law. That's because under state law, the value is only exempt so long as it's held in exempt form. But, in bankruptcy, once the discharge is granted, the value is forever free from creditors, even once the homestead is sold and the proceeds used to acquire other assets. *See* section 522(c). But, why would a state's homestead exemption apply in bankruptcy? Read on, brothers and sisters.

b.   **Law Determining Exempt Property**

Section 522(d) of the Code contains a list of federal bankruptcy exemptions. Surprisingly, however, they apply in relatively few actual bankruptcy cases. This is because of section 522(b) contains two elections. Under section 522(b)(1), a debtor may elect to have her exemptions determined either under section 522(d) (and thus get the federal exemptions) or under applicable state and nonbankruptcy federal law (whatever the debtor's state provides), together with certain retirement funds defined in section 522(b)(3)(C)). In the case of a joint filing by spouses, the debtors must both elect to have their exemptions determined under state or federal law, and, if they can't agree, the federal bankruptcy exemptions will apply.

So why is it unusual for section 522(d) to control the determination of exemptions? Because section 522(b)(2) allows the states to elect to restrict their debtors to the state law exemptions (i.e., to take away their resident debtors' election under section 522(b)(1)). About two-thirds of the states have exercised this right to "opt-out" of the federal bankruptcy exemptions. To further confuse matters, about ten states now, including both opt-out and nonopt-out jurisdictions, have enacted special exemptions that apply or are available only to their residents who file bankruptcy. For the most part, these bankruptcy-specific exemptions are more generous than the states' general exemptions from judgment execution.

Because state law will control exemptions in most bankruptcy cases, it becomes rather important to determine which state law is the "applicable law." This is also not so easy. Until 2005, the rule was to use the exemptions of the state where the debtor was domiciled for the 180-day period prior to the filing of the petition (or the state where debtor was domiciled for the greater portion of that sixth-month period). Concerned about the possibility that some debtors were changing their residence from State A to State B in advance of filing to take advantage of State B's more generous exemptions, in 2005 Congress amended section 522(b)(3)(A) to change the rule governing which state's law applies. Now it will be the law of the state where the debtor's domicile was located for the 730 days (roughly two years) prior to filing, or, if the debtor was domiciled in more than one state during this period, then the state where the debtor was domiciled for the 180-day period preceding the 730-day period. If the debtor was domiciled in more than one jurisdiction during this 180-day period as well, then her exemptions will be determined under the law of the state where she was domiciled longer during that time than in any other place. That's simple enough, huh? Maybe a hypo or two will be helpful

Markell was a life-long resident of California until about eighteen months ago when he decided he was sick of quiche and sprouts and moved to Texas to open a cattle ranch. Unfortunately, Markell knew nothing about the cattle ranching business and he now has to file bankruptcy. Markell, who has purchased an expensive home, would like to claim his exemptions under Texas law to take advantage of the state's generous homestead exemption. Can he do so? Of course not, section 522(b)(3) precludes Markell from using the Texas exemptions. What about the federal exemptions in section 522(d)? No, unless California is a nonopt-out jurisdiction, but it's not. Suppose California law says that its exemptions are limited to "residents of the state," of which Markell is no longer one. Now what does Markell do since he's barred by section 522(b)(3)(A) from using Texas exemptions and barred by California law from using *either* the state or federal exemptions? There is an answer in the last paragraph of section 522(b)(3), which says the debtor in these circumstances may elect to use the exemptions under subsection (d). In addition, some (but by no means all) courts to address the question have held that a state's attempt to restrict its exemptions to current residents of that state is preempted by section 522(b)(3)(A).

c. Application of Exemptions

Because there's so much variation from state to state, let's use the section 522(d) exemptions for purposes of example; your professor will likely give you or tell you if you are to use any specific state's exemptions on an exam. Two things should be noted about this exemption list, which is otherwise pretty typical in its definition of most exemptions by both "type" and "value." First, section 522(d)(5) contains a "wildcard" permitting the debtor to apply $1,225 in value (plus up to $11,500 of any unused homestead exemption) to any property interest that the debtor chooses. Second, all of the dollar limitations in subsection (d) adjust every three years under section 104(a).

Now let's suppose Ponoroff, a down-on-his-luck lawyer who doesn't own a home, has just filed under Chapter 7 and he owns the following personal property: (1) a 2001 BMW Z3 3.0i Roadster worth $12,000, (2) a gold watch worth $1,200, (3) 20 suits worth a total of $2,500, (4) 20 pairs of suspenders worth $12 each, (5) a flat screen TV worth $1,500, (6) household furnishing worth $12,000, and (7) law books with an aggregate value of $5,000. Which items of property can Ponoroff keep?

Bearing in mind we're using the exemption amounts that went into effect on April 1, 2013, here's how the analysis might look. First, Ponoroff is way over the value limit for the motor vehicle exemption in section 522(d)(2), so he's going to have to use $8,325 of his combined $12,725 subsection (d)(5) wildcard and unused homestead exemption if he wants to keep the Bimmer. Second, the gold watch is under the subsection (d)(4) jewelry limit, so he's ok there. The $2,500 of suits would fall under the $12,250 exemption in subsection (d)(3), which includes wearing apparel, as would the suspenders. But Ponoroff has a problem with the TV, as it's over the $575 per item limit in subsection (d)(3) for household goods and apparel, and the rest of his household goods (even if no other single item is worth over $575) put him way over the (d)(3) maximum. He can use another $925 from subsection (d)(5) to cover the TV, but now he's down to $3,475 left, of which he's going to need $2,015 to cover the rest of his household goods that exceed the (d)(3) limit. The law books would probably constitute tools of the trade under subsection (d)(6), but that exemption is capped at $2,300 and Ponoroff doesn't have enough (d)(5) value left to cover the $2,700 needed. Something is going to have to be sold, maybe the car, with the first $3,675 in proceeds going to Ponoroff so he can buy a used Prius or something. Certainly can't let that TV go. Law books? Hmm; maybe he can connect to Westlaw. And so it goes.

d.   Conversion of Nonexempt Property to Exempt Form

As mentioned earlier, section 522(c) provides that exempt property is immune from collection not only during the case but *after* it as well. This protection for exempt property extends even to most nondischargeable debts. Therefore, it is very much in the debtor's interest to hold as much of her property as possible in exempt form, and this is something that can be controlled to an extent prior to filing. Suppose, for example, Markell has $10,000 in a nonexempt savings account. If, the day before filing, he withdraws those funds and either buys exempt property or pays down a lien against exempt property, can Ponoroff, a creditor of Markell, successfully challenge that action in Markell's bankruptcy case on the ground that now there is going to be $10,000 less available for distribution to all creditors?

The answer is not so clear-cut.[68] It is clear that the conversion of nonexempt property to exempt form on the eve of bankruptcy is

---

[68] This is likely not a preference as to any seller of property given the—remember?—fact that the seller is not a creditor or that the exchange was intended

not alone enough to cause the exemption to be denied, or worse. However, if there is other evidence tending to show that the conversion was done with the intent to defraud, then not only might the exemption be denied, but the debtor may be denied a discharge altogether under section 727(a)(2) (discussed later in this Unit), which makes a fraudulent transfer within a year of bankruptcy grounds for denial of discharge. But what's the difference between a mere conversion of assets and a conversion accompanied by fraud? Many cases have tackled that question and, although no clear picture has emerged, a couple of things can be said. First, deliberately lying to or misleading creditors about one's assets or one's intentions with respect to those assets will ordinarily satisfy the requirement of extrinsic evidence of fraud. Secondly, even though it has nothing technically to do with fraud, there seems little doubt that the amount of property converted will be a factor.

So in our example above, Markell is probably ok, absent any other evidence of bad intent. If, however, in the six months before filing, Markell, a Florida resident, undertakes a plan to liquidate virtually all of his nonexempt property and then use the proceeds to buy a multimillion dollar expensive residence outside Miami, which, under state law, is exempt without limitation, he may lose the exemption and/or his discharge. This approach of "just too much," is sometimes summed up in the old adage that "pigs get fat, but hogs get slaughtered."

In 2005, at the same time that Congress attempted to control debtors from moving from a less to a more generous state in anticipation of bankruptcy, Congress also placed some controls on the debtor's ability to take advantage of an unlimited or large homestead exemption even when it does apply. First, section 522(o)

---

to and was substantially contemporaneous. As to the lien paydown, whether or not it's a preference will depend on whether the creditor was oversecured. If it was, it is not preferential; if it wasn't (or if it was undersecured), it would be preferential. But we are focusing on the effect on the debtor here.

was added to the Code. It provides that the value of the debtor's state law homestead exemption shall be reduced by the value of any nonexempt property that the debtor disposed of in the ten years preceding filing with intent to defraud her creditors. This codifies the case law holding that "fraudulent" asset conversions can be effectively undone. The ten-year look-back period is considerable; could a debtor really plan that far in advance of her bankruptcy filing? Probably not, but all the statute requires is *intent* to hinder, delay, or defraud creditors, not that the conversion be done specifically in anticipation of bankruptcy. Finally, note that this limitation only applies when assets are converted to an exempt homestead (or burial plot) and not any other form of exempt asset.

Second, BAPCPA added subsection (p)(1) to Code section 522. It provides that, regardless of state law, the homestead exemption is capped at, currently, $155,675 with respect to property acquired during the 1215-day period prior to filing bankruptcy. There is, however, an exception to the limitation in subsection (p)(2) for (A) the principal residence of a family farmer, and (B) any amount representing the proceeds from the sale of the debtor's previous principal residence (provided that it was acquired outside the 1215-day period) if both the previous and the current residences are located in the same state.

To illustrate the logic (and perhaps illogic) of section 522(p), assume Ponoroff is employed by Less for More Law School ("LMLS") in Midland, Texas. LMLS decides to open a new campus in Niceville, Florida and asks Ponoroff to transfer to the new school. Ponoroff agrees and sells his lovely, long-time Midland home for $1,000,000 and buys a house of comparable value in Niceville. Sadly, the new law school turns out to be a bust after three years and Ponoroff is shown the door. If he files Chapter 7, can Ponoroff claim his residence as wholly exempt under Florida's unlimited homestead exemption? The answer is "no," if 1215 days have not passed since

Ponoroff purchased the house. In other words, Ponoroff gets caught in the section 522(p)(1) net capping his homestead exemption at $155,675,, even though, in this example, he had no abusive motive. Moreover, the exception in section 522(p)(2) is of no help since Ponoroff's previous residence was in Texas, not Florida.

e.   Avoiding Exemption-Impairing Liens

Section 522(f) is a special provision that augments the debtor's exemptions by providing debtors with another vehicle for improving their post-bankruptcy economic position and, thereby, promoting the fresh start. It operates as an exception to the basic rule that perfected liens survive bankruptcy and take priority over exemption claims. Specifically, to the extent it impairs an exemption, 522(f)(1) permits a debtor to avoid:

A.   a judicial lien, and/or

B.   a non-purchase money, non-possessory consensual lien in: (i) certain consumer goods, (ii) tools of the trade, and (iii) prescribed health aids

The effect of this unique debtor avoiding power is to render the creditor's claim in bankruptcy unsecured and preserve the property for the debtor free of the encumbrance. The policy justification for denying the creditor of its property interest is that (1) in the case a judicial liens, the creditor is a non-consensual, non-reliance creditor (check the definition of "judicial lien": it picks up most liens acquired prepetition by levy and execution under state law); and (2) in the case of non-purchase money, non-possessory liens in household goods, the lien is merely a "leverage lien," in the sense that the creditor might use it to try to extract a reaffirmation, but is not likely to actually foreclose since the value of the collateral typically would be insufficient to even cover the costs involved in doing so. In fact, such liens are no longer even permitted by virtue of Federal Trade Commission rule and Federal Reserve Board Regulation.[69]

The 2005 amendments added sections 522(f)(4)(A) & (B) to the Code, which list items that are included and excluded from the category of "household goods" for purposes of section 522(f)(1)(B). Note: this is not a list of what can be exempted; but rather a list of what constitutes household goods solely for purposes of section 522(f)(1)(B) avoidance, and it is more restrictive than the general category of "household goods"—the idea being to preclude debtor's from using the lien avoidance power in section 522(f) on the really good stuff like works of art and expensive electronic equipment.

Now that we've identified the *type* of lien that can be avoided, the next question is *when* and to *what extent* can it be avoided? Prior to 1994, there was a great deal of disagreement and confusion over whether a lien "impaired" an exemption, particularly in cases where the property was also subject to other nonavoidable liens. Some, albeit not all, of the confusion was relieved by adoption of a statutory formula in section 522(f)(2) for determining the existence and amount of impairment.

Under subsection (f)(2), you need to do a bit math to determine whether a lien is deemed to impair an exemption. Fortunately, that math is fairly simple—even by law student standards. An exemption is impaired to the extent the sum of (1) the lien, (2) all other liens on the property, and (3) the amount of the exemption the debtor would enjoy if there were no liens on the property, exceeds the value that the debtor's interest in the property would have in the absence of any liens. Here's how that definition operates:

Let's presume Markell owns a home worth $100,000 on which Ponoroff holds a judicial lien securing a judgment debt of $100,000.

---

[69] *See* 16 C.F.R. § 444.2(4) (FTC); 12 C.F.R. § 227.13(d) (FRB).

Markell's state allows a $25,000 homestead exemption. Under section 522(f)(2), Markell can reduce Ponoroff's lien to $75,000, because $25,000 of the lien impairs Markell's homestead exemption. That is, we add the amount of the lien—$100,000—plus all other liens—$0—and the amount of the exemption—$25,000 = $125,000. From this we subtract the value of the property—$100,000—and our formula tells us that the lien impairs to the extent of $25,000. Note that this permits Markell to enjoy the full $25,000 homestead exemption, which has been carved out of Ponoroff's lien.

Now assume the same facts, except that Markell's house is also subject to a first mortgage securing a debt of $50,000. Under section 522(f)(2) we add together the two liens—$150,000—and the exemption amount—$25,000 = $175,000. From this we subtract the value of the property—$100,000 = $75,000. Thus, Ponoroff's lien will be set aside to that extent. The result is the first mortgage retains its priority, Markell has his $25,000 exemption, and the balance of the value of the property goes to Ponoroff. In a sense, we again carved the exemption out of Ponoroff's lien.

You may do some other hypos in class involving multiple judicial liens and/or non-avoidable liens that are more complex and the answers less clear. But once you know the basics you should be good to go.

2. Redemption

Another way in which a Chapter 7 debtor may be able to retain certain property is through "redemption" under Code section 722. This entails the purchase of exempt property from a lienor, the amount of whose lien exceeds the value of the collateral. In that case, section 722 permits an individual debtor to extinguish the lien by paying the lienholder the full amount of its allowed secured claim as determined under section 506. Note this right applies only to "tangible personal property intended for personal, family, or household use" that secures a consumer debt. So, neither real estate nor commercial collateral may be redeemed under this provision.

Here's sort of how it works. Let's assume that Ponoroff Finance Corp ("PFC") holds a purchase money security interest in Markell's Prius securing a debt of $10,000. The most liberal estimate of the Prius's retail value is $6,000. Because the security interest is consensual and purchase money it cannot be avoided under section 522(f)(2). Because there is no value in the car above the amount of PFC's lien, the trustee will likely abandon the vehicle under Code section 554, which would then permit PFC to go ahead and foreclose. However, by virtue of section 722, Markell can retain the Prius free of Ponoroff's lien by paying Ponoroff $6,000—the amount of its allowed secured claim. And, why not, as this is at least as much—and probably more—than PFC would have realized on foreclosure. Where Markell would get the $6,000 is another story, but sometimes even the most miserable wretch has soft-hearted relatives.

Note that even if the value of the property is *less* than the amount of the lien, the trustee might still abandon it if the sum of the lien and any exemption to which Markell is entitled exceed the value of the Prius. For example, if the Prius is worth $12,000, and Markell is entitled to claim an exemption of up to $6,000 in one motor vehicle, there is still nothing in it for the estate. Thus, Markell can redeem, but to do so (assuming he has the cash) he will have to pay PFC in full. If, however, the property is not exempt and there is value above the lien, then redemption will not be available since that equity will be claimed by the estate. Read section 722 and see if you can identify the language that makes this so.

Let's be clear that redemption requires payment in cash in a lump-sum. Moreover, because of section 506(a)(2), the amount to be paid to redeem will be determined using a "replacement value" standard. Where will Markell get the money to do so? Maybe a soft-hearted relative or friend, as suggested above, or a hard-hearted new lender (they often charge 20% to 30% for redemption loans), but in most cases he will not be able to gin up the cash. This makes redemption a somewhat limited solution for debtors that want to keep their property, thus bringing us to the next alterative that a debtor, who can neither avoid the lien nor redeem, might consider.

3. *Reaffirmation*

Section 524(c) allows a debtor and secured creditor to enter into a *reaffirmation agreement*, under the terms of which the debtor agrees to continue his personal liability on the debt (i.e., the discharge will not apply to the reaffirmed debt) and, in return, is permitted to retain possession of the collateral so long as he makes all required payments due to the creditor under the agreement.

With regard to reaffirmations:

First, it is important to note the ways in which reaffirmation *differs* from redemption.

Second, we need to identify why it is that a debtor might want to reaffirm a debt.

Third, we have to look at the process for reaffirming a debt, and there is quite a bit of process.

a. **Compared to Redemption**

As we discussed, redemption is limited to individual debtors and applies only to liens on consumer property that secures a dischargeable consumer debt. In addition, the property subject to the lien must be either exempt or abandoned by the trustee. Reaffirmation is not limited to individuals, nor to secured debts, nor to consumer debts. It is also not limited to Chapter 7 cases, although, by far, most reaffirmations take place in liquidation cases. Reaffirmation, does, however, require an *agreement* between the debtor and the creditor. That means the debtor cannot reaffirm if the creditor prefers to just call it a day and be done with the debtor despite the debtor's amenability to reaffirming the debt.

If a secured creditor is open to a reaffirmation agreement it might insist on full payment of the debt, regardless of the value of the underlying collateral. Sometimes, the creditor will condition its agreement to reaffirm the debt that the debtor *wants* to reaffirm on the debtor also agreeing to reaffirm other obligations to that creditor that the debtor does *not want* to reaffirm. Although negotiations concerning reaffirmations generally do not run alone run afoul of the automatic stay, creditors insisting on such terms run perilously close to crossing the line into a willful violation of section 362(a).

One big benefit of reaffirmation over redemption for the debtor is that payment does not have to be in cash. Typically, the reaffirmation agreement will just call for continuation of the debtor's periodic payments under the terms of the original obligation. Also, sometimes a creditor that is eager to have its debt reaffirmed will offer the debtor a "sweetener," such as a slight reduction in the obligation owed, more favorable payment terms than the original obligation, or a modest amount of postpetition credit.

b.   Why Reaffirm?

It has been suggested that since reaffirming a debt undermines the goal of providing the debtor with a fresh start, and can sometimes be a source of creditor abuse, no reaffirmations should be tolerated under the Code—realizing that nothing stops a debtor who can and wants voluntarily to repay a debt from doing so. However, that would probably be a bit too paternalistic, as there may be good reason to reaffirm in some situations. For example, not uncommonly, a debtor who wants to retain property subject to a lien, but who can't raise the cash to redeem, assuming that's even an option, will fall back on reaffirmation as the only alternative.

But why would a debtor ever reaffirm an otherwise dischargeable *unsecured* debt? And debtors do just that in surprisingly high numbers. One not uncommon reason is to protect a co-debtor on the obligation who is a close friend or relative. Markell knows that, unless he reaffirms his debt to Last National Bank ("LNB"), the bank will pursue Ponoroff, who had generously agreed to guaranty the obligation. Correctly believing that Ponoroff had already done enough for him, Markell might approach LNB with an offer to reaffirm. Sometimes a debtor will reaffirm in order to preserve an important relationship. For example, if Ponoroff owes his cannabis supplier[70] $5,000 at the time he files his bankruptcy case, Ponoroff may be willing to reaffirm the debt just to ensure that that the supplier doesn't cut him off in the future.

Sometimes, while there is no selfish motive driving the decision to reaffirm, a debtor will do so simply out of a sense of particular moral obligation to this creditor—repeat the cannibas supplier hypo here?[71] Finally, reaffirmation agreements are often used as de facto settlement agreements in dischargeability litigation (*see infra* Section C.3). For instance, suppose Ponoroff has brought a suit alleging that Markell's debt to him is nondischargeable. Given the risk of an adverse determination, plus the cost of the defense, Markell might offer to settle by agreeing to reaffirm a portion of the debt. And, for the same reasons, Ponoroff might accept.

---

[70] Assuming Ponoroff lives in a state in which this is legal, such as Colorado. If it's not legal, then Ponoroff would have a basis to object to the claim (under section 502(b)(1) it would be an illegal debt), and a court might not permit the reaffirmation.

[71] [Note from Markell: One wonders what Ponoroff, who wrote this sentence, was smoking when he conceived of a debt to a dealer as a moral obligation!]

c.   Procedure for Reaffirming

Because of the potential for reaffirmation agreements to be abused by creditors taking advantage of naïve or desperate debtors, section 524(c) sets forth a number of requirements that must be met for a reaffirmation agreement to be enforceable. These requirements were augmented in BAPCPA by adoption of the provisions in sections 524(k) through (m). The following is an overview of the detailed requirements governing enforceable reaffirmations:

First, per section 524(c)(1), the agreement must be entered into *before* the debtor's discharge is granted. Second, the debtor must have received all of the extensive disclosures and warnings required by section 524(k). Third, the reaffirmation agreement must be filed with the court to allow the court to ensure all of the requirements of an enforceable reaffirmation have been met. Fourth, if the debtor is represented by an attorney in connection with the negotiation of the reaffirmation agreement, section 524(c)(3) requires that the attorney supply a declaration or affidavit that: (a) the agreement represents the informed, voluntary agreement of the debtor, (b) that the agreement will not impose an undue hardship on the debtor or a dependent of the debtor, and (c) that the attorney fully counseled the debtor about the potential consequences of entering into the agreement. Furthermore, in a case in which a presumption of hardship arises under subsection (m) because the debtor's disposable monthly income is less than the monthly payment under the reaffirmation agreement, the attorney must also certify that the debtor will be able to meet the monthly payment—but how? By scrimping on other expenses? Oddly, however, this presumption only lasts for 60 days after the agreement is filed with the court.

The obligation of the debtor's attorney to be the watchdog for deciding that it is in the debtor's best interest—i.e., does not impose an undue hardship—to enter into the reaffirmation agreement can place the lawyer in an awkward position vis-à-vis his or her client. In other words, suppose Ponoroff wants to reaffirm his debt to Best Buy for a three-year old computer on which a balance remains of $1,500, even though Ponoroff could get a brand new computer for less than that amount. Ponoroff's lawyer, Markell, points this out to him but Ponoroff is insistent saying, "but I know how this computer *works*, I'm not sure I'll know how to use a new one." What does Markell do? Is he going to come over to Ponoroff's house once a week to do computer training lessons?[72]

What if the debtor is not represented by an attorney, or the debtor's bankruptcy attorney declines to represent the debtor in negotiating the reaffirmation agreement—which is perhaps what Markell might decide to do in the above example. In that situation, the Code places the onus on the court. Under section 524(c)(6) and (d)(2), if the debt is not a consumer debt secured by real property, the court must make the finding that the reaffirmation will not pose an undue hardship *and* that it is in the debtor's "best interest." Also, in the case of a *pro se* debtor (i.e., one not represented by a debtor, which is about 10 to 40 percent of all filers, depending on where you are), section 524(d)(1) requires the court to hold hearing, which the debtor must attend, and at which the court will explain again to the debtor the legal consequences of his or her decision to reaffirm. In addition to all of the above, whether or not the debtor is represented by an attorney, he has the right to rescind the reaffirmation agreement up to the later of the time discharge is granted or 60 days after the agreement is filed with the court. *See* section 524(c)(4).

---

[72] Don't count on your bankruptcy course—or indeed any law school course—to teach you how to make the types of determinations this statute requires, especially whether reaffirming an obligation will impose an "undue hardship" on your client.

4.   Ride-Through (Nevermore)

Before BAPCPA, some courts (but by no means all) held that there was yet a third option—beyond redemption and reaffirmation—available for a Chapter 7 debtor to retain her property, provided the debtor was not in default on the obligation secured by that property. These courts based their holdings on the language of prior section 521(2), which required that a debtor state his intention with respect to collateral securing a consumer debt to surrender, reaffirm, or redeem, and then perform in accord with that stated intention. However, prior to 2005, the Code neither provided any consequence for the failure to comply with section 521(2) nor made explicit that surrender, redemption, and reaffirmation were the only options. Some courts thus said that if the debtor was current on his payments, he could simply "ride-through" bankruptcy and keep the collateral so long as he remained current on the debt. The effect was like reaffirmation *but* without personal liability.

Although this option was not necessarily a bad alternative for the secured lender, since it was getting paid and could grab its collateral should those payments cease, lenders still didn't like it. Thus, as part of BAPCPA, in addition to some tinkering with the language of section 521(a)(2)(B), a couple of new provisions were added to the Code to put an end to ride-through. First, as we have already seen, section 362(h)(1) now provides a remedy—in the form of automatic relief from stay—if the individual debtor fails to state his intention with respect to collateral that secures a debt (no longer just a consumer debt) as required by section 521(a)(2)(A) or fails to perform in accordance with his stated intention within the time set forth in section 521(a)(2)(B). Second, in the case where the collateral is personal property that secures its purchase price, section 521(a)(6) provides that the debtor who has not timely (no later than 45 days after the first meeting of creditors) either reaffirmed or redeemed may not retain possession of the property. A bit obscure, but again, if the debtor may "not retain the property" then presumably the purchase money lender is entitled to relief from stay

A creative argument that a couple of courts have accepted is that when the debtor offers to reaffirm but the court refused to approve the reaffirmation agreement, the debtor has met his duty under section 521(a)(2). Therefore, the obligation may still ride-through bankruptcy and the creditor may not repossess the collateral so long as the debtor remains current. Clearly, that's not what Congress had in mind and, while we applaud the try, we think it's headed for the trash heap. Another possibility exists if the security agreement does not make the fact of insolvency and/or a bankruptcy filing an event of default. This is unlikely to be the case when dealing with documents prepared by professional lenders, and thus is uncommon.

Nonetheless, suppose Ponoroff has a security interest in Markell's Prius. Markell is current on the note secured by the car, but, for other reasons, enters bankruptcy. During the case, Markell continues the payments but does not state an intention to surrender, redeem, or reaffirm. This means that the stay is lifted under section 362(h)(1), but if Ponoroff did not make the bankruptcy filing an event of default, he has no grounds under state law to repossess the car and foreclose. On the other hand, if Ponoroff did make the act of bankruptcy an event of default—a so-called *ipso facto* clause—section 521(d) makes that clause enforceable, even though elsewhere throughout the Code *ipso facto* clauses are frowned upon.

D. The Chapter 7 Discharge

1. In General

Certainly discharge, which we first introduced back in Unit 3, is the end game for the individual debtor in Chapter 7, but discharge is important for all types of debtors and under all chapters of the Code. There are some ways, however, in which the discharge operates differently for different kinds of debtors and under the different chapters of the Code. So let's get some basics out of the way right up front:

First, who gets a discharge and when will depend on who is the debtor and what chapter the case is proceeding under. For instance, only individuals are entitled to discharge in Chapter 7. Corporations (and other forms of business association such as partnerships and limited liability companies) cannot, we repeat cannot,-obtain a discharge in Chapter 7. *See* section 727(a)(1). Their only hope for a discharge is Chapter 11.

Second, per section 727(b), a Chapter 7 discharge applies to all debts arising *prior* to entry of the order for relief. As discussed in more depth in the separate Units below concerning Chapters 11 and 13, discharges in those chapters occur for individuals after completion of their plans in most cases.

Third, the discharge only applies to the debtor's *personal liability* on the debt. The debt itself is not wiped out. Therefore, if there is a co-debtor, or a guarantor, or the debt is secured, the creditor can seek collection from the nondebtor and/or also assert whatever *in rem* rights against any collateral. Let us *repeat* that it is important to distinguish a creditor's *in personam* rights against the debtor, from the creditor's rights against both nondebtors and rights against the debtor's property.

Fourth, some categories of debt do or may survive discharge. Thus, it is important to distinguish between discharge—which is a status to which the debtor may or may not be entitled—from dischargeability—which relates to whether the debtor's discharge will extend to a particular debt. We discuss dischargeability in Section C.3 below, but note that the issue of dischargeability never arises *unless and until* it is determined that the debtor is entitled to a discharge.

Fifth, recall from our discussion in Unit 3, that the entry of discharge operates as an injunction under section 524(a) against any effort to collect the debt from the debtor. Therefore, violations of the discharge will constitute a contempt of court—serious business.

2. *Denial of Discharge*

Sections 727(a) deals with denial of discharge. These provisions apply only in Chapter 7 cases, with the limited exception in section 1141(a)(3), which incorporates section 727(a) provisions in individual Chapter 11 cases under certain circumstances. More on that in Unit 8.

Turning to the 12 grounds in section 727(a) on which the trustee, a creditor, or the U.S. Trustee may object to the granting of discharge in Chapter 7, some have to do with what the debtor did *before* the bankruptcy case while others are based on something the debtor did or did not do *during* the bankruptcy case. We will look at the most important of these grounds for objection to discharge in the material that follows.

However, before we do so, note that the consequences of having discharge denied are pretty extreme. If the court finds that the debtor should be denied discharge, this does not means the case is over. Rather, the estate is administered, the assets liquidated, and the proceeds distributed to creditors. But of course, the debtor remains personally liable for whatever portion of his creditors' claims remain unpaid at the end of the case. Thus, the debtor's lawyer *should* carefully consider the risk of denial of discharge before proceeding with the filing.

a.   Stuff the Debtor Did Before Filing

Section 727(a)(2)—Fraudulent Transfers: Of the all the things a debtor can do to mess up his right to discharge before filing, probably the most important, and surely most litigated, is the transfer of property occurring within one year of filing made with intent to hinder, delay, or defraud creditors. Recall that these are the same words used in section 548 to describe an actually fraudulent transfer—and so such a transfer could give rise not only to recovery of the assets so transferred, but also to loss of discharge. A double whammy. Hence, bringing together some material from past Units, let's suppose Ponoroff, in advance of filing Chapter 7, and while promising his creditors that he'll pay them something if they just give him a bit more time, secretly liquidates all of his nonexempt assets and uses the proceeds to buy annuity policies, which in his state are exempt without limitation. Markell, one of Ponoroff's creditors points out that Ponoroff lied and committed fraud, and thus given Ponoroff's deceit and skullduggery, he moves to have Ponoroff's discharge denied under section 727(a)(2)(A). If successful, Ponoroff may not only lose the exemption for the annuities, but obviously will not get a discharge either.

Now, let's take a different hypothetical. Assume Markell has got himself in a financial jam—yet again. He knows he's going to have to file bankruptcy, so in what he believes is a clever move, he transfers his one-half interest in his house to his spouse for one dollar. Several days later, Markell goes to see Ponoroff, a bankruptcy attorney, about filing a Chapter 7 case. Ponoroff agrees to represent him, but says, "Chapter 7 can help you get rid of a lot of debt, *but* you made a fraudulent transfer of your interest in your home and that could cause your discharge to be denied. I want you to undo that transfer before we file your petition." Markell agrees and has the one-half interest in the property transferred back to him. In his bankruptcy schedules, Markell lists his interest in the house as an asset and, as he is required to do, discloses the transfers to and from his spouse. The trustee then files a complaint to have Markell's discharge denied based on section 727(a)(2). What result would you say? If you said "it depends" you'd be right! There are two circuit court decisions addressing this issue. In one, the Ninth Circuit said that section 727(a)(2) requires that the property be transferred *and remain transferred*, in order for an objection under section 727(a)(2) to be granted.[73] The Eleventh Circuit, however, took a contrary view based on the statutory language, holding that once the prohibited transfer occurs, the discharge is lost even though the debtor tries to atone before filing.[74] Should the penalty for making a fraudulent transfer under section 727(a) actually be greater than the remedy for a fraudulent transfer, which, ordinarily, is simply return of the property? It's up to you on the final exam to make the argument for or against denial of discharge.

Section 772(a)(3)—Bad Books: Discharge might be denied if the debtor has failed to keep or preserve adequate records regarding her financial condition and prior business dealings. The statutory language offers little guidance as to what type of records must be maintained. The courts, however, generally apply a "sliding scale," according to which more will be expected of financially sophisticated debtors than of consumer and other nonbusiness debtors. Finally, even if the objecting party establishes that grounds for denial of discharge exist based on section 727(a)(3), the court may still not grant relief if it finds that the debtor's action or failure to act "was justified under all of the circumstances of the case."

---

[73] *In re* Adeed, 787 F.2d 1339 (9th Cir. 1986).
[74] *In re* Davis, 911 F.2d 560 (11th Cir. 1990).

Section 727(a)(5)—The Dog Ate My Assets: Recall that Chapter 7 involves a bargain of sorts under which the debtor receives a discharge in return for turning over all of his nonexempt assets to his creditors. Thus, if the debtor is unable to explain to the court's satisfaction what happened to property the debtor had before filing but now no longer does, the debtor might be deprived of his end of the deal under section 727(a)(5). Note that what the debtor must come up with is a credible explanation, not necessarily a good one. So, if Ponoroff can produce the losing ticket on the 100 to 1 shot in the Kentucky Derby on which he bet his entire tax refund two days before filing bankruptcy, he probably keeps his discharge.

Sections 727(a)(8) & (9)—Earlier Discharge: The Bankruptcy Code has a number of provisions that attempt to control what is perceived to be the abuse of serial filings—although not all serial filings are necessarily abusive. In any case, if the debtor received a discharge in a Chapter 7 or Chapter 11 case filed within eight years of the filing of the current case, discharge can be denied under section 547(a)(8). Note that the measuring date is the date of the prior filing and *not* the date the discharge was actually granted. Thus, if Markell received a discharge on June 1, 2008 in an earlier Chapter 7 case filed on April 1, 2006, and he files another Chapter 7 case on May 1, 2016, he is still eligible for a discharge in the current case, asmore than eight years elapsed between the two filings.

Section 727(a)(9) imposes a similar limitation on discharge in the situation where the debtor received a discharge in a prior Chapter 12 or 13 case filed within six years of the commencement of the current case. There is, however, an escape hatch for the debtor if the payments under the earlier plan totaled 100 percent of unsecured claims, or 70 percent of such claims *and* the plan had been proposed in good faith and represented the debtor's best effort.

b. Stuff the Debtor Did or Didn't Do on or After Filing

Section 727(a)(4)—Dishonesty: If a debtor "knowingly and fraudulently" engages in one or more of the four actions specified in section 727(a)(4) "in or in connection with a case" she may have her discharge denied. The acts include: (1) making a false oath or account, (2) making a false claims, (2) attempting to gain personal advantage by acting or forbearing to act, and (4) withholding necessary books or records from the estate. The key aspect here is in paragraph (1)—making a false oath. When a debtor files a bankruptcy case, he or she files a schedule of all his or her assets and this schedule is filed under oath. If that list is cooked, so is the debtor's discharge. By the way, commission of any of these actions might also expose the debtor to prosecution by the U.S. Attorney under the bankruptcy crimes statute—18 U.S.C. § 152, making for a really bad day.

Section 727(a)(6)—Refusal to Obey or Testify: Grounds for objection to discharge also include that the debtor scorned a lawful order issued by the court, including a failure to respond to a material question posed by the court or to testify (other than a refusal based on valid exercise of the privilege against self-incrimination). Thus, if, at Ponoroff's first meeting of creditors, he refuses to explain what he paid for at Larry Flynt's Hustler's Club, this would likely not cause him to lose his discharge since Ponoroff is just exercising his Fifth Amendment right not to incriminate himself.[75] On the other hand, if Ponoroff continues to refuse even after the prosecutor's office has offered immunity for any actions that may have occurred at the club, he may well lose his discharge.

Section 727(a)(10)—Waiver: Discharge will also be denied if the debtor voluntarily waives her right to receive a discharge. Why would a debtor do this? Well, it's not common, but somethings a

---

[75] [Note from Markell: Just what do they sell at that club? I have no idea.]

dirty debtor has a change of heart, realizes he or she won't get a discharge, but alsos realizes that using a bankruptcy will likely increase the average returns to all creditors so that the amount of debt left over is less. To be enforceable, however, such a waiver must be in writing *and* approved by the court. Note: the waiver must also have been executed *after* the filing of the case. A prefiling waiver is *not* enforceable.

Section 727(a)(11)—Financial Management Instruction: BAPCPA was big on financial education for debtors—which is an ok thing when done right. You will recall, for instance, that section 109(h) requires individual debtors, as a condition to eligibility to file, to have received *before* filing a briefing outlining opportunities available for credit counseling and budget assistance. Section 727(a)(11) expands on this concept by requiring, at the risk of loss of the discharge, that the debtor *after* filing have completed an instructional course in personal financial management from a provider approved in accordance with section 111. A list of these approved providers can be found on the U.S. Trustee's website. This course can be completed over the Internet, and generally does not take more than two hours.

3. *Revocation of Discharge*

Chances are you won't talk about revocation of discharge in your bankruptcy class. But it is a possibility. Revocation of discharge is covered by section 727(d), which sets forth the grounds on which the debtor's discharge, once granted, may be revoked, and section 727(e), which sets the outside dates by which the trustee, the U.S. Trustee, or a creditor may request revocation.

Generally speaking, revocation may be ordered on a showing that the debtor did something that would have been grounds for denial of discharge under section 727(a), but it was not discovered until after the discharge had already been granted. Thus, assume

Markell failed to disclose in his Chapter 7 case a prepetition transfer of valuable assets to Ponoroff for no consideration, and that Markell continued to possess and use. The trustee did not learn of Markell's perfidy until six months after discharge was granted. By virtue of sections 727(d)(1) and 727(e)(1), the trustee should be able to cause Markell's discharge to be revoked.

4. *Dischargeability of Particular Debts*

Unlike the grounds for objection to discharge in section 727(a), the categories of debt that may be carved out of the discharge apply (pretty much) in all individual bankruptcy cases. Recall that if there is a successful *objection* to discharge, then the discharge exceptions become irrelevant. On the other hand, from the perspective of any particular creditor you would much rather have *your* debt determined to be nondischargeable than see the debtor's discharge denied *in toto*—meaning everyone's debt is not discharged.

The types of debt that are subject to exception to discharge are listed in section 523(a). There are now 18 separate categories of such debts—more than can be individually examined in a *Short & Happy Guide*! But there are a few general points worth making and then we can look at the most important (that is, most likely to come up on your exam) exceptions. So, on to the general points:

First, some of the discharge exceptions, like some of the grounds for denial of discharge, are based on debtor misbehavior, such as fraud or breach of fiduciary duty. Remember the adage (that appears nowhere in the Code) that the bankruptcy discharge is for the *honest but unfortunate* debtor. Other exceptions, such as domestic support obligations, taxes, and the provisions regarding student loans, are based on the nature of the debt and a legislative judgment that a competing social policy interest outweighs the bankruptcy fresh start policy.

Second, three of the types of debt that are nondischargeable— those in sections 523(a)(2), 523(a)(4), and 523(a)(6)—will be discharged *unless* the creditor timely files, and is successful, in an adversary proceeding in the bankruptcy court (not state court) to have the debt declared nondischargeable. *See* section 523(c)(1). The time for bringing an action under section 523(c) is governed by Bankr. Rule 4007, which currently sets a deadline of 60 days after the date first set for the initial meeting of creditors under section 341(a). Since the first meeting of creditors is set within 20 to 40 days of the date the debtor's petition was filed, this means that these actions must usually be filed within the first three months of a case (when the clerk sends out the notice of bankruptcy, the notice includes the exact deadline).

With respect to the other categories of nondischargeable debt, the creditor need not take any action in bankruptcy court, although sometimes creditors will file a dischargeability complaint in bankruptcy court in order to have an adjudication that the debt is nondischargeable before the case closes. The point, however, is that the matter can always be resolved later and also be resolved in state court; as the state courts have concurrent jurisdiction with respect to all of the categories of nondischargeable debt, except for those listed in section 523(c)(1).

Third, dischargeability litigation must be by adversary proceeding (something approximating a real lawsuit), and will often entail application of "principles of preclusion"; i.e., *res judicata* (claim preclusion) and collateral estoppel (issue preclusion). Maybe you thought you left those concepts behind in Civil Procedure, but here they are again. Let us assume that Ponoroff fraudulently induces Markell to purchase Ponoroff's car by turning back the odometer. Later, Markell learns of Ponoroff's dastardly act and sues Ponoroff for damages, based on the difference between the contract price and the market value of the car with the true mileage, on the alternative theories of breach of contract and fraud.

Ponoroff sees the handwriting on the wall and offers to settle the case in an amount that is agreeable to Markell. So, the parties enter into a settlement agreement providing for entry of a consent judgment by the court in the agreed sum. Because all he cares about is getting his judgment, Markell does not insist that the agreement and judgment refer to fraud as opposed to breach of contract. However, before Markell can collect the settlement amount, Ponoroff files a Chapter 7 case. If Markell brings an action to have the debt declared nondischargeable based on fraud (section 523(a)(2)), can Ponoroff defend on the ground of *res judicata*? In *Brown v. Felson*,[76] the Supreme Court said "no," holding that claim preclusion did not prevent the bankruptcy court from looking beyond the documents terminating the state court proceeding in order to ascertain if the debt at issue was obtained by fraud.

Next, let's assume that Markell was a little more on the ball and required that the settlement agreement contain a provision in which Ponoroff acknowledged his fraudulent conduct. Once more, Ponoroff files Chapter 7 and Markell seeks to have the debt determined to be nondischargeable under section 523(a)(2). When Ponoroff attempts to deny that his conduct was fraudulent, Markell, argues that Ponoroff is collaterally estopped from "relitigating" the issue of fraud? Who's right? Sadly, Markell.[77] Once more, the answer comes from a Supreme Court decision holding that principles of collateral estoppel do apply in bankruptcy dischargeability litigation.[78] Generally, this means that so long as the issue was actually litigated in the earlier action, it will be treated as final in a subsequent dischargeability proceeding. Of course, Markell must

---

[76]   442 U.S. 127 (1979).

[77]   [Note from Markell: Ponoroff obviously was the main author of this section.]

[78]   Grogan v. Garner, 498 U.S. 279 (1991)

still establish the rest of the elements of his claim for relief, but having the issue of fraud resolved in advance is a big leg up.

With these general principles behind us, let's look at some of the more common nondischargeable claims.

a.   Taxes

The taxes that are excepted from discharge by section 523(a)(1) are (a) the taxes entitled to priority under sections 507(a)(3) and (a)(8); (b) taxes for which a return was either never filed or filed late and within two years before the bankruptcy filing or thereafter; and (c) tax claims based on fraud or tax evasion. The fact that some nondischargeable tax debt also receives priority under section 507(a) is a good thing for the debtor since it is in the debtor's interest to see as much of these claims as possible paid from the bankruptcy estate (after all, those dollars were already gone). The same thing is true with respect to domestic support obligations excepted from discharge under sections 523(a)(5), as discussed below, and entitled to priority under section 507(a)(1), as discussed back in Section A.3.a.ii of Unit 3.

So, assume Ponoroff files bankruptcy on April 10, 2016. He filed his tax returns for 2011 and 2012 in timely fashion, but did not pay the taxes due for either year. Are either of these tax debts nondischargeable? As for the 2011 taxes, for which the return was due April 15, 2012, the answer is "no," since it does not fall within the after three years before the date of the filing of the petition in bankruptcy that would entitle it to priority under section 507(a)(8)(A)(i). Since, however, the "after three year before date" is April 10, 2013, the 2012 taxes (due on 4/15/2013) are nondischargeable. Note: had Ponoroff waited an additional six days before filing his bankruptcy case, these taxes would have been discharged, too. What was his lawyer thinking? Perhaps he was representing himself; that would explain it!

Now, let's suppose Ponoroff didn't file his 2011 return until June 1, 2014, even though he had not requested or been granted an extension from the IRS. The tax debt is not entitled to priority under section 507(a)(8)(A)(i), *but,* because the late return was filed within two years before the bankruptcy petition, the debt is nondischargeable under section 523(a)(1)(B). The same would be true if Ponoroff never filed a return for the 2011 taxes. Finally, if Ponoroff timely filed the return for the 2011 taxes, but deliberately omitted the huge royalty income he received that year from sales of *A Short & Happy Guide to Bankruptcy*, discharge of the claim, which also would not qualify for priority, would be denied under section 523(a)(1)(C).

b. Debts Incurred by Fraud

While the nondischaergeability of tax claims reflects a legislative judgment to put protection of the public *fisc* ahead of bankruptcy fresh start policy, the exception in section 523(a)(2) for fraudulently incurred obligations is quite obviously based on disapproved conduct by the debtor. Section 523(a)(2) is divided into three paragraphs: (A) debts based upon "false pretenses, a false representation, or actual fraud, *other than a statement respecting the debtor's or an insider's financial condition*"; (B) debts obtained based on a false written statement "respecting the debtor's or an insider's financial condition"; and (C) debts for luxury goods and services and debts for cash advances that are "presumed to be nondischargeable."

The first category of fraud in section 523(a)(2)(A) does not specify what is required to prove fraud or false pretenses. However, in *Fields v. Mans,*[79] the Supreme Court held that the elements of the common law tort of fraud pertain, which would include proof of

---

[79] 516 U.S. 59 (1995)

intent to deceive and *justifiable* reliance.[80] By contrast, subsection (2)(B) lays out all of the elements of nondischargeability thereunder, which includes *reasonable* reliance on the false written statement. So, what's the difference between *justifiable* reliance and *reasonable* reliance? To be perfectly honest, we're not really sure, but formulation of the latter presumably includes some investigation into the truth of the false statement rather than just subjective reliance.So, justifiable reliance is a lesser standard, although it seems clear that mere *actual* reliance alone is not enough. In other words, even under a justifiable reliance standard the creditor can't put its head in the sand.

Finally, subsection (2)(C) creates a presumption (no proof of reliance needed) of nondischargeability in section 523(a)(2)(A) cases for (1) consumer debts for luxury goods and services totaling more than, currently, $650 incurred by an individual debtor within 90 days of filing; and (2) cash advances totaling more than, currently, $925 for cash advances under an open-ended credit pan (like your VISA or MasterCard) and obtained within 70 days before the bankruptcy filing. In both instances, the focus of the subsection is to thwart debtors who deliberately "load up" in anticipation of filing bankruptcy. Now the big questions under subsection (2)(C) are what constitutes a luxury good or service, and how is the presumption rebutted. Does Markell keep his Prius but Ponoroff has to give up the BMW (even though it's used and cost much less than a new Prius)? Can a Prius ever be a luxury good? How about a loaded Honda Civic? If Ponoroff can show when he borrowed the money for the BMW he fully intended to repay and was not even thinking about filing bankruptcy, is that enough to rebut the presumption of

---

[80] As of this writing, the Supreme Court has granted *certiorari* to review the Fifth Circuit's decision in *Husky Int'l Elecs., Inc. v. Ritz (In re Ritz)*, 787 F.3d 312 (2015), holding that the "actual fraud") bar to discharge under section 523(a)(2)(A) does not apply unless the debtor makes a false representation to the creditor.

nondischargeability? Probably, but how will he prove that? Would you believe him?

Returning to the relationship between subsections (2)(A) and (2)(B), consider this scenario: Ponoroff approaches Markell Finance ("MF") about a loan. MF decides that, based on his balance sheet and income, Ponoroff does not look like a good credit risk. Ponoroff then offers to provide a guaranty from his Aunt Thelma, who Ponoroff claims is a "wealthy widow." MF asks to meet with Aunt Thelma and, at this meeting, inquires about her assets and liabilities. Thelma assures MF that she is quite well off. Satisfied, MF makes the loan to Ponoroff who—yes, you guessed it—files bankruptcy shortly thereafter. When MF proceeds to go after Aunt Thelma on her guaranty, they lo and behold discover that Thelma is just as insolvent as her nephew. Not to be thwarted, MF files a complaint in Ponoroff's bankruptcy case to have its debt determined nondischargeable under sections 523(a)(2)(A) and (B). What result? Now, try to work it out yourself by carefully reading the statutory language before we spill the beans.

Ok, MF will lose under section 523(a)(2)(A) because, even if all the elements of common law fraud can be proved, the false statement at issue—"Aunt Thelma is a wealthy widow"—related to the financial condition of an *insider*.[81] As for subsection (a)(2)(B), we agree that there is an issue about reasonable reliance—actually a big issue—but we never get there. Why not? Because the false statement concerning Thelma's financial situation was not in *writing* as required by subsection (a)(2)(B). Thus, MF is just out-of-luck, and has hopefully learned a valuable lesson about doing some due diligence before taking people at their word. To quote Ronald

---

[81] "Insider" as defined in section 101(31) includes "relative." A "relative" under section 101(45) is anyone within the third degree of consanguinity. That includes great grandparents, grandparents, parents, sons, daughters, grandchildren, great-grandchildren (direct lines of consanguinity), as well as great aunts and uncles, aunts and uncles, and first cousins (indirect lines of consanguinity). And the spouses of each. Since an aunt is in this group, an aunt is a relative and thus an insider. Whew.

Reagan, speaking in connection with a nuclear disarmament treaty with the then Soviet Union, "trust, but verify."

A lot of the cases arising under section 523(a)(2) involve credit card debt. If the debtor obtained the card by submitting a fraudulent application or financial statement, that probably falls under section 523(a)(2)(B), and will likely turn on the reasonableness of the issuer's reliance. But most of the credit cards cases involve claims by the issuer that the debtor maxed out the card in anticipation of filing bankruptcy and knowing all along that she could never pay the charges being rung up. This type of case has to be analyzed under section 523(a)(2)(A). In any event, credit card use does not neatly fit into the section 523(a)(2) scheme insofar as the requirements of "a representation," "intent to deceive," and "reliance' are concerned. Most courts deal with the first issue by finding an implied representation of intent to pay with each use of the card. Intent to deceive must then be proved by inference from circumstantial evidence, such as unusual activity just prior to filing, etc. A minority of courts take the view that only continued use of the card by the debtor after being given notice of its revocation by the card issuer will give rise to nondischargeability.

Perhaps most problematic in dealing with credit card cases is establishing justifiable reliance on the implied representation to repay. In fact, there is no real reliance by the issuer when the card is used. Thus, once more, reliance will be implied by many courts, provided that the account was not already in default when the card was used or a routine credit investigation would have made the creditor aware of the risk associated with issuance of the card to the debtor. Given the way that most credit card lending is done—on an actuarial basis and often without any in-depth credit analysis— that last factor can represent a significant hurdler for the card issuer to overcome. Of course, to the extent the card is used to obtain cash advances within 70 days of filing, section 523(a)(2)(C) makes it much easier for the issuer to establish nondischargeability as to those transactions.

c.   Unscheduled Debts

When the debtor initiates her bankruptcy case, or shortly thereafter, she is required to file lots of lists and schedules regarding her financial situation, including, of course, a list of all of her creditors. It is the scheduled creditors who then receive notice of the case under Bankr. R. 2002, which alerts them to the existence of the case and of the necessity of filing a proof of claim. It makes sense, therefore, that if a creditor is not properly listed by the debtor, and therefore never receives notification of the case, its debt should be carved out of the discharge. This is accomplished by section 523(a)(3).

An important exception, however, to this ground for nondischargeability exists in both subsections (3)(A) and (3)(B) by virtue of the language "unless such creditor had notice or actual knowledge of the case" in time to file a proof of claim and, if the debt is of the kind falling under sections 523(a)(2), (a)(4), or (a)(6), in time to file a request to have dischargeability denied. In these situations, the Code places the onus on the unscheduled creditor to find out what the applicable deadlines are in the case and to follow them at the risk of having its claim discharged despite the lack of formal notice.

d.   Debts Based on Fiduciary Misconduct, Embezzlement, or Larceny

Section 523(a)(4) covers three kinds of debt obligations. Debts for embezzlement or larceny involve the debtor's appropriation of property of another—with the only difference being that, in an embezzlement scenario, the debtor's initial possession will have been lawful. The third kind of debt covered by this exception arises out of fraud or defalcation committed while the debtor was acting in a fiduciary capacity. It is well understood that "fraud" entails intentional conduct. For quite a while it was less clear what state of mind must accompany an act in question for it to constitute a "defalcation." In 2013, the Supreme Court finally resolved the matter by holding that, for purposes of section 523(a)(4), the term requires a showing of knowledge or gross recklessness with regard to the fiduciary behavior at issue.[82] This means, as the Court noted, it will be more difficult to find debts based on the conduct of nonprofessional trustees nondischargeable, inasmuch as they do not possess the same level of understanding as to the responsibilities of a fiduciary as, for example, a lawyer or a bank trust company.

e.   Domestic Support Obligations and Related Debts

Missed some alimony payments? Behind on child support? Think bankruptcy is going to help you? Think again. The combination of section 523(a)(5) and (15) assure that almost any kind of debt incurred as part of a divorce decree or settlement agreement is going to survive the discharge—so the louse is still on the hook. Section 523(a)(5) simply carves all "domestic support obligations" out of the discharge. You will recall that domestic support obligations, which also receive a first priority under section 507(a)(1), are defined in section 101(14A) to include obligations owing to a spouse, former spouse, or child of the debtor that is in the nature of alimony, maintenance, or support. These debts are not only nondischargeable, but they may even be enforced against the debtor's exempt property. *See* section 522(c)(1).

Although the definition of domestic support obligation is far-reaching, it does not encompass debts arising from a property division or settlement agreement entered in connection with a domestic relations proceeding. That's where section 523(a)(15) enters the picture and carves those obligations out of the discharge

---

[82]   Bullock v. BankChampaign, N.A, 133 S.Ct. 1754 (2013).

as well. You might wonder why all of these types of debt are not just included in a single subsection of section 523(a). Well, for one thing, they were enacted at different times, and, for another, until 2005, debts falling under section 523(a)(15) were one of the types of nondischargeable debts that, under section 523(c)(1), had to be established exclusively in the bankruptcy court. Now that this is no longer true they could all be in the same subsection—except they're not.

f. Debts Arising from Willful and Malicious Injury

The exception in section 523(a)(6) generally covers debts arising out of various intentional torts, although not all intentional tort claims will be shielded by this exception as it has come to be interpreted. Like debts arising under sections 523(a)(2) and (a)(4), an exception for debts based on "willful and malicious" conduct under section 523(a)(6) must be adjudicated as such by the bankruptcy court or it will be discharged.

The basic issue under section 523(a)(6) has been whether it is sufficient that the debtor intended to commit the act that resulted in the injury, or whether it is necessary to prove that the debtor also specifically intended to injure. In other words, if Markell deliberately and recklessly throws a bat in the direction of Ponoroff, which in fact strikes Ponoroff causing severe brain damage, is the resulting tort obligation dischargeable once Ponoroff shows that Markell threw the bat intentionally, or must he also prove that Markell intentionally threw the bat toward him with the intent of injuring Ponoroff. In *Kawaauhu v. Geiger*,[83] the Supreme Court adopted the latter view, holding that the term "willful" in the statute modifies the word "injury," such that a willful act alone is not sufficient to satisfy the exception. This means that some intentional tort victims will see their debts discharged despite

---

[83] 523 U.S. 57 (1998).

section 523(a)(6). It also means that "malicious" doesn't add much to "willful," and vice versa.

For a time, there was some disagreement in the case law as to whether section 523(a)(6) could be used to hold debts arising out of injuries caused by intoxicated drivers nondischargeable. Under the *Geiger* standard, the answer would seem to be "no," but it no longer matters since, in 1984, Congress added a special discharge exception in section 523(a)(9) for death or personal injuries caused by the operation of motor vehicle (or vessel or aircraft) while intoxicated.

g. Educational Debt

For some reason that has never been clear to us, students seem particularly interested in this discharge exception! The exception for educational loans has gone through a number of permutations. Originally, such debts were dischargeable after five years and applied only to loans made or subsidized by a governmental unit. Gradually, however, Congress (the same body that authorizes most of these loans) has made the standard tougher and tougher, until now discharge is denied for virtually all forms of educational loans and the only relief from nondischargeability is if the debtor can prove that continuation of the debt would impose "a substantial hardship on the debtor and the debtor's dependents." The key question under section 523(a)(8), then, is what constitutes a substantial hardship.

Two tests have been developed by the circuit courts. The most widely adopted standard is what's called the *Brunner* test, which derives from a Second Circuit case by that name.[84] Under *Brunner*, the debtor must make three showings: (a) inability to maintain a minimal standard of living at his or her current level of income; (b)

---

[84] Brunner v. N.Y. State Higher Education Servs. Corp., 831 F.3d 395 (2d cir. 1987).

likelihood that this inability will persist for a significant portion of the repayment period; and (c) he or she has made good faith efforts to repay. The second test, followed in the Eighth and First Circuits, is a "totality of the circumstances" test, which looks to the debtor's reasonably reliable future financial resources, reasonably necessary living expenses, and any other relevant facts. Even though the two test are pretty similar in their formulation, lender's generally favor the *Brunner* test since it reduces the amount of discretion that can be exercised by the court.

Under the language of section 523(a)(8), it is not necessary for the debtor actually to be the student for the exception from discharge to apply. A few courts, however, noting that the legislative history seemed focused on recent (mostly professional school) graduates who, on the verge of accepting lucrative employment, would file bankruptcy, have not extended its application to the situation where a parent (or other third party) incurs the debt to finance another's education.

Special Problems in Chapter 13

Chapter 13 is a special chapter for individuals only. No corporations, partnerships or limited liability companies need apply. For qualified individuals, it presents a stark contrast to Chapter 7 practice and Chapter 7 relief. Why? Let's start with a quick review of that question.

A. Policy Issues: The Reasons for Chapter 13

Chapter 7 has some problems, for both creditors and debtors. For creditors, a lot of Chapter 7 cases for individuals do not return *anything* to creditors. And by a lot, we mean over 90% of all Chapter 7 cases return no dividends to creditors. Zero returns; zilch; nada. On the other side, Chapter 7 does not give debtors a lot of flexibility for secured debts like car and mortgage loans. Recall that the only options for debtors under Chapter 7 is to reaffirm, redeem or surrender their collateral. So unless they give up their discharge for any deficiency claims, pay the debt in full, or just give back the collateral, Chapter 7 offers little help for the types of things that are basic to American life: a car and a house. On top of that, nonbankruptcy law in many states does not permit reinstatement of secured debt—that is, the ability to make up past due payments and return to the original payment plan. The debtor is left to state law; if such law does not permit reinstatement for mortgage debt, the debtor loses the house unless he or she can redeem. And no state permits reinstatement under Uniform Commercial Code Article 9 for debt secured by personal property such as cars.

So Chapter 13 exists. As might be expected, it has a distinctly different approach than Chapter 7. Whereas Chapter 7 looks to the past, one can say that Chapter 13 looks to the future. Chapter 7, recall, takes a debtor's nonexempt assets on the filing date and distributes them pro rata to existing creditors. The debtor, however, receives a fresh start from and after the filing; section 541(a)(6), as you may remember, excludes postpetition service earnings from the estate, and thence from creditors.

Chapter 13 is different. It requires a debtor to commit to a three to five year payment plan for creditors, to be funded out of debtors' *future* income. Most importantly, it withholds the debtor's discharge—the most important reason for a debtor to file—until *after* that payment plan is complete. It also requires that the plan return to creditors at least as much as the creditors would have received in a Chapter 7 case, if not more. In return for agreeing to the payment plan, debtors can reinstate their car and home loans, and can receive a slightly better discharge (it used to be much better before 2005, but that's history now).

Chapter 13 filings account for about 30% of all bankruptcies. The alternative it presents also presents instructors with fodder for exams. Given the differences in treatment, chapter choice can be a key part of a final exam. So let's look at the Chapter 13 in detail.

B. Statutory Differences Between Chapter 7 and Chapter 13 Cases

We know Chapter 13 differs from Chapter 7 relief in its focus: forwards, rather than backwards. Let's now look at some of the major differences that cause 30% of all individuals to file under Chapter 13.

1. *Qualifying for Chapter 13: Individuals, Income and Debt*

Chapter 7, at least theoretically, is available to all debtors, be they humans or corporations. In Chapter 13, however, only individuals—that is, flesh and blood humans—qualify as debtors.[85]

Similarly, in Chapter 7, again at least theoretically,[86] there is no limit on the amount of income or debt that a debtor may have. In Chapter 13, however, there are income requirements and debt limitations. Chapter 13's income requirements are found in section 109(d). That section requires that only "an individual with regular income" may file for Chapter 13.

What's "regular income"? Section 101(30), in turn, defines "an individual with regular income" to be anyone "whose income is sufficiently stable and regular to enable such individual to make payments under a plan under chapter 13 of this title." Under this definition, individuals with only unemployment insurance or other government assistance payments have qualified, as have individuals with episodic and irregular income (such as real estate brokers). Individuals who derive their income from alimony, support or

---

[85]   Note that this does not exclude businesses. A debtor that is a sole proprietor is not disqualified from filed a Chapter 13 case simply because she is in business. If such an individual does file, however, all that person's assets and debts—business and personal—will be administered in the Chapter 13 case.

[86]   The limitation may be in the abuse provisions of section 707(b) and the means test, explored back in Unit 7.

investments have also qualified. They key is the stability of the income, regardless of source.

Chapter 13 also imposes debt limits. That is, you can't have too much debt in Chapter 13. In 1978, the limits were originally set as $250,000 in unsecured debt and $750,000 in secured debt. Through inflation, the corresponding numbers are now $383,175 in unsecured debt and $1,149,525 in secured debt. So when Ponoroff can't pay his $2 million mortgage on his palace in Tucson, he won't be able to file for Chapter 13 relief.

This debt must also be noncontingent and liquidated, but need not undisputed. So Ponoroff's pending defamation lawsuit against Markell for calling Ponoroff "a tawdry little zod with Napoleonic overtones" does not count against these limits—it is not liquidated. Neither would Markell's guaranty of Ponoroff's $2,000,000 mortgage if (hah!) Ponoroff was current on the mortgage—it is not noncontingent. These amounts and their characterization as noncontingent or liquidated are usually take from the debtor's schedules, so long as the debtor as estimated them in good faith.

2.   *The Co-Debtor Stay (§ 1301)*

Unlike any other chapter, Chapter 13 imposes a stay on collection activities against a *co*-debtor, even if the co-debtor does not file a bankruptcy case. The stated purpose of this stay is to prevent a creditor from indirectly coercing a debtor into paying debts in order to keep peace among those who helped him financially. Put another way, Thanksgiving dinner is a lot more pleasant if Ponoroff's mother has the benefit of a stay of her guaranty of Ponoroff's debts than if there were not co-debtor stay and if Mom were being pursued by Ponoroff's creditors.

This stay is as robust as the automatic stay of section 362(a), but has some limits. In particular, the debt must be a "consumer debt," defined in section 101(8) as any debt incurred for "personal, family or household" purposes. In this regard, courts generally consider alimony and mortgage debt as consumer debt.

So if Markell guaranteed Ponoroff's $1 million mortgage on his house, and Ponoroff files for Chapter 13, Markell gets a free pass on paying on his guaranty. Sweet.

But there are limits. First, Markell does not get the stay if Ponoroff's Chapter 13 plan does not provided for the guaranteed debt. Second, he also doesn't receive the benefit if Markell gave the guaranty as part of Markell's business activities—as when he had to guaranty Ponoroff's debts to ensure Ponoroff would come through with his promised parts of their joint publications. Third, if Markell, Inc. provides the guaranty, there is also no relief; the co-debtor stay only extends to individuals. Finally, Markell's protection ends when Ponoroff's case is closed, dismissed, or converted to another chapter. So when Ponoroff finishes his plan, gets his discharge, but hasn't paid the guaranteed debt in full, Markell is still on the hook for the balance. But all in all, it is a pretty good benefit for Chapter 13 debtors.

3. Discharge   Entered   After   Payments Completed (§ 1328)

Another significant difference between Chapter 7 and Chapter 13 is the timing of the discharge. In Chapter 7, recall, the discharge is issued 60 days after the date first set for the first meeting of creditors—so the discharge typically will issue in a Chapter 7 case within three months of the filing of the case.

In Chapter 13, however, debtors have to earn their discharge. The discharge is not granted until "after completion by the debtor of all payments under the plan." 11 U.S.C. § 1328(a). That means that if Ponoroff has a five-year Chapter 13 plan, he will not receive a discharge of any debt until after he makes his final payment in the fifth year. What about collection efforts in the meantime? Worry not. The automatic stay protects Chapter 13 debtors and is in place, recall, until the discharge is entered.

What if a sap like Markell can't finish his plan? Is all lost? No. Chapter 13 incorporates what is referred to as the "hardship discharge" in section 1328(b). A debtor can obtain a hardship discharge if three conditions are met: (i) if his or her plan has paid unsecured creditors at least as much as they would have received in a Chapter 7; (ii) if "the debtor's failure to complete such payments is due to circumstances for which the debtor should not justly be held accountable," 11 U.S.C. § 1328(b)(1); and (iii) if amendment of the plan is not practicable.

The hardship discharge isn't quite as broad as the regular Chapter 13 discharge; for one thing, all debts mentioned in section 523(a) will be non-dischargeable after a hardship discharge, even if some of those debts would have been discharged in the case of a regular Chapter 13 discharge.[87]

So say Markell, a Chapter 13 debtor, loses his job two years into his plan through no fault of his own. Assume a Chapter 7 case for him would have returned zero to creditors. He is thus a good candidate for a hardship discharge—if he has made one payment to creditors, they have received more than they would have received in Markell's Chapter 7. If the inability to complete the plan or amend the existing plan is because Markell has no income (because he lost his job through no fault of his own), then all three requirements are met.

What if Markell was fired for being drunk on the job?[88] Different result. Now, his inability to complete his plan payments are *not*

---

[87] This used to be a bigger deal before BAPCPA when many of the 523(a) categories of debt were dischargeable in Chapter 13 after completion of the plan—the so-called "superdischarge." See below in Section B.5.

[88] This raises the question as to whether anyone could tell the difference.

"due to circumstances for which the debtor should not justly be held accountable." So no hardship discharge.

4. Expanded Property of the Estate (§ 1306)

The time necessary to complete a plan and the delayed discharge could create problems if the property of the estate rules from Chapter 7 were incorporated without change. Recall that section 541(a)(6) excludes from property of the estate all income from services from and after the date of filing. Does that mean that all of Ponoroff's income during his five-year plan is his own, and not subject to creditor claims?

Of course not. If that were so, no debtor would have to contribute anything. So in Chapter 13, section 1306(a)(2) expands the definition of property of the estate to include "earnings from services performed by the debtor after the commencement of the case." Section 1306(b) then states that the debtor can retain possession of property of the estate. This only makes sense; if the debtor is to continue to earn a living, and make plan payments, he or she will have to have access to his or her assets that the debtor uses to earn that living.

5. Discharge Has Different Scope than Chapter 7

We saw that the Chapter 7 discharge covers all claims against individuals except those listed in section 523(a) (stuff like fraud, tax debts, domestic support obligations, and the like). Chapter 13's discharge, as originally envisioned, was called a "super discharge" in that it discharged many of the types of claims set forth in section 523(a); for example, fraud claims used to be dischargeable.

But that changed in 2005. Congress tightened up the scope of Chapter 13's discharge to make it much more like the Chapter 7 discharge.

There still are some exceptions. Debts dischargeable in a Chapter 13 case that aren't dischargeable in a Chapter 7 case include debts for some willful and malicious torts, some governmental fines and penalties (except for criminal fines and restitution included in a sentence on the debtor's conviction for a crime), or marital property settlement debts (not support debts— debts to pay money or property to equalize a division of assets).

As a consequence, if Ponoroff owes money to a former spouse from a property division (he got his prize Yugo in the settlement, and never bothered to pay the equalizing payment), and owes an administrative penalty to the state bar for nonpayment of his annual dues, he can discharge *both* in a Chapter 13. If he had filed a Chapter 7, *neither* would be dischargeable.

You have to be careful here. If a divorce-related payment is for alimony or child support, it would *not* be dischargeable in *either* Chapter 7 or Chapter 13. Same caution is also warranted with Ponoroff's fine; if it was imposed as part of a criminal sentence for the unauthorized practice of law, it would similarly not be discharged in either Chapter 7 or Chapter 13.

6. *Ability to Cure, Reinstate, and Modify Secured Debt*

One of the main reasons consumers file Chapter 13 is that they can deal with secured debt in ways not permitted under Chapter 7. And in today's world, secured debt touches on significant part of everyday life; one does not buy a car or a house with cash, and a bank will require a security interest or mortgage in any car or house bought with its loan funds.

Chapter 7 is pretty brittle on these points. All a consumer can do is redeem, reaffirm or surrender. But what if the consumer just got a little behind, and wants to make it up and continue on with the original payment scheme? Most modern contracts don't allow consumers to do that unless the bank agrees.

This is where Chapter 13 comes in. In ways we'll explore below regarding confirmation of Chapter 13 plans, Chapter 13 allows a consumer to reinstate most secured debts. All the consumer has to do is pay the back payments, with interest. But here's the kicker. Chapter 13 allows the debtor to make up these arrearages *over the life of the plan.*

So if Ponoroff has failed to make three months' worth of loan payments on his Mercedes Maybach auto (he spent the $2000 usually allocated to his monthly loan payment on paper and toner trying to get his chapters in this book right), he can reinstate the Maybach loan by resuming the payments, and by paying the missed $6,000 (with interest) over the life of the plan—usually three or five years.

7.   *The Chapter 13 Trustee*

Can an individual within these limits file a Chapter 13 and start paying creditors?[89] Not quite. We need to introduce a critical player in the Chapter 13 process first: the Chapter 13 trustee.

Every Chapter 13 case is overseen by a Chapter 13 trustee. Just like a Chapter 7 trustee, every judicial district has one (or more) appointed by the Office of the United States Trustee (usually called "standing trustees," although given the craziness they oversee, they mostly sit). Unlike a Chapter 7 trustee, however, the Chapter 13 trustee is active in each phase of the Chapter 13 case. He or she administers the case, collects the debtor's payments scheduled under the plan, reviews (and potentially objects to) the debtor's plan, monitors the debtor's compliance with the plan, and pay creditors as specified in the plan. For these pains, the Chapter 13

---

[89]   Actually, there is one more requirement. As in Chapter 7, the debtor must undergo prepetition debt counseling and file a certificate evidencing same. 11 U.S.C. § 109(h).

trustee is paid a percentage of all payments disbursed, which range from about 3.5% to 10% depending on where the debtor resides.

All this plan talk makes it look like the Chapter 13 plan is important. Well, it's more than that: it is critical. So let's look at what a plan is, and how it works.

C. The Centerpiece: The Chapter 13 Plan

The method by which Chapter 13 focuses on the future is the debtor's payment plan. A plan is essentially the debtor's budget; it proposes to pay creditors a monthly payment based on what the debtor has left of his or her income after paying living expenses. Or at least that's the theory.

1. What Is a Plan?

A plan is a document. It sets out the debtor's plan to pay his or her debts over the life of the plan. This means that the plan has to specify how unsecured debts will be treated and which secured creditors will get what treatment. Plans can be as simple, and expressed in one or two pages, or can be complicated and require 10 or 20 pages.

a. Who Proposes?

Why the variability? First and foremost, the only party who can file a plan is the debtor. No creditors. No trustees. At some point in the future, however, debtors will be required to use a standardized national form, but at least for the next several years, debtors will be the only source of Chapter 13 plans.

What's in a plan? Here we get to the down and dirty. A plan is the debtor's budget, combined with the debtor's commitment to make certain payments to creditors and to the Chapter 13 trustee. It is drafted so as to meet the confirmation requirements found in section 1325, a topic we'll look at starting in Section C below. Until then, we'll look at when the debtor has to start making payments, how long a plan lasts, and what it contains.

b.   When Must the Debtor Propose the Plan?

Chapter 13 moves fast. The debtor has to file his or her plan with the bankruptcy petition, or within 15 days thereafter. Moreover, under section 1326, he or she has to start making payments under the plan immediately, even before it is confirmed.

So a debtor starts paying immediately. When does he or she stop? In the lingo of the Code, how long is the "applicable commitment period"?

c.   How Long Does a Plan Last?—Of "Commitment Periods"

A Chapter 13 plan generally lasts three or five years. Whether it is three years or five years depends on the debtor's income. At a high level of generality, those debtors with high incomes have five year plans; those with lower incomes need only pay for three years.[90]

How do we distinguish between "high" and "low" income levels? Get ready for a bit of review. Remember the Chapter 7 "means test"? It rears its ugly head again here.

Recall that the "means test" calculates a debtor's "current monthly income." Section 101(10A), in turn, defines "current monthly income" to be the average of the debtor actual income for the six full calendar months before the debtor filed his case.

Well, Section 1322(d) calculates how long a plan is by multiplying the debtor's "current monthly income" by twelve, and comparing that to the "median family income" for the state in which the debtor resides. "Median family income," just to torture you, is

---

[90]   Obviously, if a plan pays all creditors in full in less time, the plan ends when all creditors are paid. 11 U.S.C. § 1325(b)(4)(B). If a plan does not pay all creditors in full, however, it is either three or five years in length.

also a defined term. Section 101(39A) defines it as "the median family income both calculated and reported by the Bureau of the Census in the then most recent year." Add to this the fact that the Census Bureau and the statute adjust the median for the size of the debtor's family, with the amount of the median increasing with the number of people in the debtor's household.

So if the debtor's "current monthly income" is above the applicable "median family income," the plan will last five years. If below, three years.

This can lead to some wild variances, given the different levels of income among the 50 states. The applicable median income, for example, of a single debtor in Mississippi is close to $36,000; for Hawai'i it is over $62,000. For a family of four, Arkansas is the lowest with its median being a little over $59,000, while Connecticut is the highest with its median being just over $109,000.[91]

d.   What Can a Plan Propose?

So now that we know how long a plan lasts, what does it contain? We'll start with the key provision: the debtor's obligation to pay to the Chapter 13 trustee all "projected disposable income."

i.   Payment of All Projected Disposable Income (§ 1325(b))

The projected disposable income test assists unsecured creditors; they get their payments from, and only from, the debtor's disposable income paid to the Chapter 13 trustee. As a consequence, any unsecured creditor or the Chapter 13 trustee can block confirmation of a plan by showing that the debtor has not committed all of his or her "projected disposable income" to the plan. Technically, section 1325(b)(1)(B) requires that "the plan

---

[91] If you're really bored, you can look at the current numbers at http://www.justice.gov/ust/means-testing.

provides that all of the debtor's projected disposable income . . . will be applied to make payments to unsecured creditors under the plan."

Why is disposable income so critical? As set forth above, the primary reason is that it is the only source of an unsecured creditor's recovery. In addition, and more importantly, most plans provide that if there is any unsecured debt left unpaid at the end of the plan period, the balance is discharged.

So if Ponoroff has $100,000 in credit card debt (those charges from dubious web sites do add up), but only has $100 a month of projected disposable income, a three-year plan will only pay $3600 of that debt (100 x 12 x 3). The rest of the debt—$96,400—will be discharged at the end of the plan payments.

As a consequence, if Ponoroff wants to confirm his Chapter 13 plan, he'd better draft it so that he is committed to pay all of his disposable income to the trustee. That requires us to look at what "projected disposable income" is.

ii. Calculation of Projected Disposable Income and the Means Test (Again)

As with many other things in Chapter 13, disposable income is a simple concept made excruciatingly complex by the Code. But the concept is easy to grasp: a debtor has to pay the Chapter 13 trustee whatever he or she has left at the end of the month after paying regular expenses. So if Markell has a monthly take-home income of $2000,[92] car payments of $400, a mortgage of $1,000, and regular expenses (for food, clothing, gas, etc.) of $500, he has $100 in disposable income. (Take the $2000 in income and deduct the car payment, the mortgage payment and the other expenses.) Under

---

[92] We assume here that any withholding taxes will be sufficient to pay the related tax or charge.

section 1325(b)(1)(B) he would have to pay that amount—$100—to the Chapter 13 trustee each month during the life of the plan.

But it's not that easy. Congress realized in 2005 that there is a lot of discretion packed into what someone "needs" to live each month. Does a consumer need a four-wheel drive car, and the payments associated with it? Does it matter if he or she lives in a mountainous area and needs something like that to go to work? Does a debtor who lives in a city with excellent public transport need a car at all? Does it matter if a debtor works the graveyard shift? Does a debtor need to send their child to private school? Does it matter if the public school system is a mess?

So, after defining "current monthly income," Congress focused on expenses. They created two categories of expenses: one for debtors who annualized current monthly income was below the applicable median, and another for debtors who were above that number.

For debtors whose incomes are below the applicable median, section 1325(b)(2)(A)(i) allows them to deduct "amounts reasonably necessary to be expended . . . for the maintenance or support of the debtor or a dependent of the debtor. . . ." At the beginning of a case, a Chapter 13 debtor files schedules indicating what his or her actual monthly income and expenses have been, so the Chapter 13 trustee has a baseline from which to examine the income and expenditures. But given the variability of debtors, the amounts and types of expenses will also be variable.

There's a different story for debtors whose income is above the applicable median. They have to use same expenses as section 707(b) calculates for Chapter 7 debtors under the Chapter 7 means test. So, after deducting actual costs of paying secured debt (car and mortgage payments, if any), they will use the IRS's estimate of rental housing costs in their county instead of actual rent; they will use the IRS's estimate of national costs for food and clothing expenses instead of their actual expenses; they will use the IRS' estimate of transportation costs for their region; and so on. In short, the government is telling above median debtors how much they can spend in order to live.

Take an extended example. Ponoroff lives a nice lifestyle. He rents a luxury condo for $3000 a month, drives a Jaguar XJ for which he has a $2000 a month car lease, and spends lavishly on food and drink, sometimes over $1000 a month for himself alone. He finances this lifestyle on his $6000 a month job tutoring nervous and desperate law students.

This all comes crashing down when Ponoroff loses a lawsuit to Markell in which Markell exposed Ponoroff for the fraud he is. Few students will take his classes now, and his income has fallen from $6000 a month to $500. What will happen to Ponoroff if he files now?

First, you need to calculate Ponoroff's current monthly income. If he files soon after he loses the lawsuit, that number will likely be close to $6,000—recall that current monthly income is an *average* of the six months' income *preceding* the filing. At that level, his annualized income will be $72,000 ($6000 x 12). That's higher than any state's median for a single person, so Ponoroff will be an above median debtor. That means any plan will have to be at least five years.

It also means that his projected disposable income will be calculated according to the national standards, rather than his actual expenses. So if housing in the area is $1000 a month according to IRS standards, and food and other expenses also $500, the amounts "reasonably necessary" for his support will only be $1500, regardless of what his actual expenses are. And there's more bad news: His current monthly income is $6000, not $500. So his projected disposable income—his mandatory plan payment—will be *$2500*!

How is that number calculated? First, take Ponoroff's current monthly income of $6000. Then deduct his car lease (recall that the means test allows deductions for secured debt or lease debt). Given his car lease of $2000, that leaves $4000. Then subtract his housing and other allowable expense under the means test of $1500. That leaves $2500.

But he doesn't have $2500 a month! He is only making $500 now. Although it is difficult to ever feel sorry for Ponoroff, this might be the time to do it.

Not surprisingly, these types of calculations have been challenged in the Supreme Court. In *Hamilton v. Lanning*,[93] the debtors won, at least somewhat. There, the Court held that "when a bankruptcy court calculates a debtor's projected disposable income, the court may account for changes in the debtor's income or expenses that are known or virtually certain at the time of confirmation."[94]

The Court cautioned, however, that Congress had imposed a presumptively mathematical standard. "It is only in unusual cases that a court may go further and take into account other known or virtually certain information about the debtor's future income or expenses."[95]

So how does this help Ponoroff? If his income-earning capacity has been permanently affected by Markell's lawsuit showing him to be a fraud (the power of the truth!), then Ponoroff has a good argument that it is "known or virtually certain" that he will not be able to earn $6000 a month in the future. Whether the $500 number is the right number, however, will depend on other circumstances (can Ponoroff earn more by memorizing "Do you want fries with that?").

---

[93]   560 U.S. 505 (2010).

[94]   *Id.* at 524.

[95]   *Id.* at 519.

That may help Ponoroff with the income side of the projected disposable income equation. What about the expense side? The possible silver lining of this cloud is that the means test allows debtors to deduct projected payments on secured debt, *without* adjustment for their reasonableness[96]—Section 707(b)(2)(A)(iii)(*I*) states that a debtor can deduct "the total of all amounts *scheduled* as contractually due to secured creditors" during the five-year plan period. (Emphasis added). So if Ponoroff can deduct his $2000 monthly car payment from the $500 he earns, then he will have *zero* projected disposal income before we ever get to the other expenses.

Can that be right? Ponoroff can't afford the payments, and won't be making them, so why should he get the deduction? The short answers is that he can't. If Ponoroff isn't going to pay the debt, he can't take the deduction. the Supreme Court has agreed. As stated in *Ransom v. FIA Card Servs., N.A.*[97] on a related issue, the Court stated: "[I]n short, [the Debtor] may not deduct loan or lease expenses when he does not have any."[98]

iii.   Other Terms (§ 1322)

Disposable income may be the focus of a Chapter 13 plan, but it is not the sole focus. A debtor may have all sorts of financial problems to deal with. Section 1322 recognizes this by giving the debtor the broad ability to sort out his or her financial affairs for all sorts of creditors.

Usually, this relief is targeted at different classes of claims— unsecured claims, car claims, mortgage claims, etc. So section 1322 requires the plan to classify his or her creditors and requires each

---

[96]   There may be an issue of good faith, but we'll address that later.

[97]   562 U.S. 61 (2011). This opinion ultimately affirmed a bankruptcy court decision issued by one of your co-authors.

[98]   *Id.* at 80. Circuit courts have agreed on the surrender issue. *See, e.g.,* In re Quigley, 673 F.3d 269, 273 (4th Cir. 2012)

creditor in a class to receive the same treatment as every other class member. It also requires that the plan not "discriminate unfairly" against certain claims of the same priority—a debtor can't propose to treat friends with unsecured debt differently than it treats enemies with unsecured debt.

With some exceptions, all classes of creditors may find their claims "adjusted." Section 1322(b) permits the plan to cure defaults, waive defaults, or to actually modify debt by changing its terms to do things like extend its maturity, change its interest rate or reduce its amount (sometimes called a "haircut").

The first major exception to this rule is the treatment that priority claims receive. Section 1322 requires that priority claims be paid in full over the life of the plan. This ability to extend the payment over the life of the plan is valuable to the debtor. Recall that priority claims include current tax claims, domestic support obligations and administrative claims. These types of claims can thus be paid over time (albeit with interest). This is, importantly, one of the only ways that a citizen can dictate to the government the terms of paying an unpaid tax debt. And, in a move that makes Chapter 13 viable, recall that attorney's fees are administrative expenses, and administrative expenses are priority claims. So Ponoroff's Chapter 13 practice can get full fees! Sweet!

Another limitation is the treatment that can be forced upon mortgage lenders. We take that up next.

e. What Can't a Plan Propose?

Chapter 13 very carefully protects mortgage lenders. We'll see how it protects secured lenders generally in Section C.2.d below when we look at cram down, but for now let's look at the restrictions section 1322 places on what a plan can do to a mortgage loan.

The key provision is section 1322(b)(2). That section states that a plan may *not* modify "a claim secured only by a security interest in real property that is the debtor's principal residence." Modification includes changing the interest rate, or the maturity, or the principal amount of the debt. So home mortgages are off limits.[99] Does that mean that a debtor who has missed a bunch of mortgage payments is completely out of luck?

Nope. What section 1322(b)(2) takes away, section 1322(b)(5) gives back (in part). Although a debtor cannot "modify" a home mortgage claim, his or her plan can "notwithstanding paragraph (2)" provide "for the curing of any default within a reasonable time and maintenance of payments while the case is pending on any unsecured claim or secured claim on which the last payment is due after the date on which the final payment under the plan is due."

In short, section 1322(b)(5) gives the Chapter 13 debtor the right to reinstate the mortgage loan. What that means is that so long as the debtor makes all scheduled payments post-petition, he or she can "make up" the missed payments over the life of the plan, albeit with interest. At the end of the plan, then, the mortgage will be current, and the debtor can go forward as if the missed payments never happened.

An example. Markell misses three payments of $1000 on his $200,000 home mortgage because he backed a cockamamie scheme of Ponoroff's, and as a result had a "cash flow" problem. Markell's lender has accelerated the maturity date of the loan and commenced foreclosure proceedings. If Markell files for Chapter 13,

---

[99] Well, most home mortgages. If a mortgage's final scheduled payment date falls before the plan ends, the debtor can cram down the mortgage. 11 U.S.C. § 1325(c)(2). This might look like a boon to a debtor with a "balloon" mortgage—one which payment schedules are set as if the mortgage were long term, but has the entire balance due in 5 or 7 years after the loan was made (the metaphor is that the principal balance "balloons" up at the end of the 5 or 7 year period). Although such a mortgage could be crammed down, the problem is that it would all have to be paid in full within the life of the plan; section 1325(a)(5)(B). And very few debtors have the financial wherewithal to carry and pay a five-year mortgage.

he can stop the foreclosure (section 362 and the automatic stay, remember?), and then propose a plan under which he will make all scheduled mortgage payments post-petition, and make up the $3000 in missed payments over the life of the plan, with interest. If Markell is a below median income debtor, that means he'll have 36 months (12 x 3) to make the $3000 in payments.

In addition to mortgage debt, a Chapter 13 plan cannot reduce the amount of any other long-term debt—defined as debt which has a scheduled final payment later than the last payment under the Chapter 13 plan. While the plan may cure defaults on such debt and provide for maintenance payments on it (that is, payment can be made to keep the long-term debt current), Chapter 13 provides that no such long-term debt will be discharged. *See* section 1328(c)(1).

But all this happens in a plan. And a court has to approve— confirm in bankruptcy lingo—all plans before they are effective. What does it take to obtain confirmation?

2. *Plan Confirmation Standards (§ 1325)*

Plan confirmation is the province of section 1325(a). In addition to the disposable income requirement, section 1325(a) contains nine conditions for confirmation, each of which occupies their own individual paragraph. But before we look at those paragraphs, let's look at what's *not* in section 1325.

a. No Voting in Chapter 13

There's *no* creditor voting in Chapter 13. If the debtor meets all of the requirements of section 1325, the plan is confirmed. Even if every creditor in the known universe opposes it. Put another way, section 1325 sets out Congress' conditions for what constitutes fair treatment of creditors' claims. Creditors' consent is just not one of those conditions.

b. Basic Requirements (Good Faith; Feasibility; Best Interests)

This turns the focus on section 1325(a) and its requirements for confirmation. Most of these requirements are fairly basic. There must be good faith, both in proposing the plan and in filing the case (§ 1325(a)(3) & (7)). The plan must pay creditors at least as much as they would have received had the debtor filed a Chapter 7 case instead, the so-called "best interests" test (§ 1325(a)(4)). The debtor has to be able to show that he or she can make the plan payments, sometimes called the "feasibility" standard (§ 1325(a)(6)). And, finally, secured creditors must either have consented to the plan or receive the treatment specified in § 1325(a)(5).[100] Let's look at these major requirements in a little more detail.

Good faith has been notoriously difficult to define concretely. It generally means that the debtor has filed his or her case, and his or her plan, with the intent to treat his or her creditors as the Code anticipates.

It is sometimes easier to say what the good faith requirement doesn't cover. It doesn't cover a filing in which the debtor has little or no disposable income to pay to unsecured creditors (so-called "zero percent plans"). A debtor can still do that. It doesn't cover a filing of a Chapter 13 after the debtor has received a discharge under Chapter 7; debtors can still file so-called "Chapter 20s."[101] It doesn't cover the debtor who files to keep a high-priced house (and

---

[100] These are other requirements which often do not excite much discussion. The debtor has to show: compliance with Chapter 13's other requirements (§ 1325(a)(1)); that all United States Trustee's fees have been paid (§ 1325(a)(2)); that he or she is current on all post-petition domestic support obligations (§ 1325(a)(8)); and that he or she has filed all tax returns for the four years preceding the filing of the case (§ 1325(a)(9)).

[101] Chapter 20 cases are sometimes used to avoid the debt limitations for Chapter 13. A debtor, for example, might file a Chapter 7 case with unsecured debt in excess of Chapter 13 limits, get a discharge of those debts, and then file a Chapter 13 to take care of any secured debt.

mortgage to boot) when a lesser house might serve the debtor's shelter needs; the incorporation of the means test means we don't alter payments on secured debt. It doesn't cover a debtor who declines to include his social security payments in the plan (since the Code excludes such receipts from the definition of "current monthly income"), even if creditors will not receive much, if anything, under the plan. Finally (and this is good news to you who want to go into the practice of representing consumer debtors), it doesn't cover plans under which the only payments made are to priority creditors, and the only priority creditors are . . . the debtor's lawyers.

The best interests test of section 1325(a)(4) is a standard way of measuring the merits of reorganization. Are creditors doing better? Here, be careful. In order to determine whether a plan pays more than a Chapter 7 case would, you have to do an analysis of what creditors might receive if the case had been filed under Chapter 7. That means you have to do an exemption analysis, a priorities analysis, and maybe an avoiding powers analysis. This is where evil instructors (such as those who are writing this book) get a "two-fer." By asking about a Chapter 13 scenario, you force the students to perform a Chapter 7 analysis. [Insert evil laugh here]

The feasibility standard of section 1325(a)(6) is a codification of common sense. A debtor has to show that he or she will be able to make all the payments the plan calls for—the payments to secured creditors, to priority creditors, and his or her disposable income payment. It is a low bar here; under general pleading rules, all the debtor has to show is that it is more likely than not that he or she can perform. But there still is a check on wild promises just to get Chapter 13 relief.

c.   Handling Unsecured Claims

A debtor will have unsecured claims and secured claims. Unsecured claims have, in one sense, already been covered. The whole disposable income inquiry tries to gauge what the debtor will pay to unsecured creditors over the life of the plan. Unsecured creditors look to their pro-rata share of these payments. They have no other source of repayment.

Secured claims are a different story. They are the province of section 1325(a). Since most debtors file Chapter 13 to deal with secured claims—car and mortgage loans—it is a provision deserving of its own section, and it is that provision we now turn.

d.   Handling Secured Claims (of Cars and Houses)

Each of the debtor's secured claims has to be dealt with in the Chapter 13 plan; each secured claim will normally be in its own class under the plan. Section 1325(a) provides that these secured claims can be dealt with in one of three ways: consent, surrender, or cram down. We'll look at each.

i.   Consent (§ 1325(b)(5)(A))

Consent is the easiest. Section 1325(a)(5)(A) states that, with respect to each secured claim, a plan can be confirmed if "the holder of such claim has accepted the plan." Many, although not all, courts have held that this consent can be implied if the secured creditor receives adequate notice yet declines to object; acquiescence can suffice.

But it will be the bold and reckless debtor who files a plan that just hopes the secured creditor will sleep on its rights. So we need to examine other forms of compliance with section 1325(a)(5).

ii.   Surrender (§ 1325(b)(5)(C))

Sometimes the debtor just doesn't want or need the creditor's collateral. Think of a car with a blown engine, or an over encumbered second home in a remote area the debtor doesn't visit often. In these cases section 1325(a)(5)(C) allows the debtor to "surrender[ ] the property securing such claim" to the secured creditor. That is, just give the creditor the keys.

While this might eliminate the secured debt, recall that section 506(a) still preserves an unsecured debt for any deficiency. So if the debtor walks away, he or she may have solved the secured claim, but will have simultaneously increased the pool of unsecured claims. The debtor may not care; he or she is going to pay his or her disposable income to take care of the unsecured claims, and that payment doesn't go up or down with the amount of claims to be paid.

iii.   Cramdown (§ 1325(b)(5)(B))

The final, and most common, method of handling secured claims is cram down. Although evocative and colorful in name, the concept again is relatively simple. A secured creditor has a property interest that has no more value than the value of the collateral; that's the teaching of section 506(a). If the debtor gives the secured creditor something worth what the collateral is worth, then the secured creditor is no worse off. That's what would happen if the creditor foreclosed outside of bankruptcy—it would get the value of the collateral from the foreclosure proceeds, and then be left with an unsecured claim.

So section 1325(a)(5) allows the debtor to replicate the economic effects of a foreclosure by giving the creditor property equal to the value of the collateral. The kicker is that the debtor is not limited to "property" that is cash; he or she can pay the debt with "other" types of property. Further, other types of property can include a promissory note or other obligation of the debtor!

If this sounds fishy to you, then join the ranks of all secured creditors. It means that if Ponoroff has an old car worth $2000 secured by a debt of $5000, he can cram down Markell, his secured creditor, by giving Markell his promise to pay $2000. Well, that and a little bit more. He also has to secure his promise with the old collateral, the car. Not too many problems there.

But there is another requirement: the value of his promise has to *really* equal $2000 in today's money. And herein is the problem. Ponoroff's plan will propose to pay the $2000 over the life of the plan, which at a minimum will be three years. Since Ponoroff's promise to pay $2000 over three years is not worth he same as his promise to pay $2000 today,[102] Ponoroff's promise has to be increased somehow. That "somehow" is by adding periodic interest to the obligation. (Think of a bank certificate of deposit—you wouldn't give the bank $100 today to get $100 in a year; you'd expect more in a year, and the more would be measured by "interest"). In economic terms, this process is called determining the "present value" of the debtor's promise.

Don't let the concept of present value scare you. As shown by the example, it is pretty common sense. Money tomorrow is worth less than money today. The difference can be expressed as an interest rate. End of story.

Well, almost. If you distill the above into its essentials, every cram down case revolves around two issues: what was the value of the collateral (which determines the amount of the secured claim) and what is the appropriate interest rate to apply the proposed deferred payments (which will determine the amount of the debtor's monthly payment). Not surprisingly, these two issues have

---

[102] If it has any value. That's why the old collateral has to be collateral for the new promise as well.

been the source to two Supreme Court cases, and it is to those that we now turn.

aa. Value—*Rash*

The amount of the secured claim is governed by section 506(a). It sets the secured claim for an underscored claim (one where the amount of the debt exceeds the value of the collateral) at the value of the collateral. But what value should be used? Retail? Wholesale? A mix?

The Supreme Court addressed this issue in *Associates Commercial Corp. v. Rash*.[103] There, the Court held that a bankruptcy court must value the collateral at the cost the debtor would incur to obtain a like asset for the same proposed use. This is a valuation measure usually called "replacement value." Although the Court left the determination of replacement value to the bankruptcy courts on a case by case basis, the Court made clear that it was not holding that replacement value was the retail value of the property.

In 2005, Congress codified and modified the Court's approach to valuation. Section 506(a)(2), added that year, provides that replacement value means the price a retail merchant would charge for property of that kind, considering the age and condition of the property.

bb. Interest Rates—*Till*

Once the collateral's value is set, then the applicable interest rate needs to be determined. Courts were all over the map on this one until *Till v. SCS Credit Corp*.[104] There, the Court held that the appropriate rate of interest would be a market rate of interest, determined by a formula that referred to some standard

---

[103] 520 U.S. 953 (1997).
[104] 541 U.S. 465 (2004).

measurement such as the prime rate would be appropriate if it was adjusted for risk. Since then, courts have taken the Court's lead and used the prime rate plus 1% to 3% as the appropriate rate of interest.

Another example will help illustrate. Assume again Ponoroff has an old car worth $2000 (valued in accordance with *Rash* and section 506(a)(2)). The car is collateral for a $5000 debt owed to Markell. Markell will have two claims, a secured claim of $2000 and an unsecured claim of $3000. The unsecured claim will be paid pro-rata from the Ponoroff's disposable income plan payments. But the secured claim will be treated differently.

In addition to his disposable income payment, Ponoroff will make a payment to the secured creditor. This payment will be based on the $2000 value, and will require interest to be paid under *Till's* formula of prime plus 1% to 3%. Since this is Ponoroff after all, let's use 3%. If the prime rate is 5%, then Ponoroff's effective interest rate—his market rate of interest—will be 8%.

With a value of $2000, and an interest rate of 8%, the only other item you need to know is the length of the loan. Section 1325(a)(5)(B)(i)(I)(bb)[105] limits the length of repayment to the life of the plan.[106] Since section 1325(a)(5)(B)(iii)(I) requires equal periodic payments, you can use readily available loan calculators to figure out the monthly payment.[107] Such a calculator will tell you that if the plan is for three years, Ponoroff's payments to Markell would be about $63 per month; if five years they would be about $41.

---

[105] Yes, that's a correct cite. For trivia buffs out there, the hierarchy of federal statutes is section, sub-section, paragraph, sub-paragraph, clause, sub-clause, item, and sub-item. So this citation is to item (bb) of sub-clause (I) of clause (i) of sub-paragraph (B) of paragraph (5) of sub-section (a) of Section 1325. Whew.

[106] Well, technically until the discharge is granted, but that's at the end of the plan.

[107] For the nerds out there who want to play around with these numbers, one such calculator can be found at http://www.bankrate.com/calculators/mortgages/loan-calculator.aspx.

If Ponoroff's contract with Markell had an interest rate of 10% (not unusual for cars), a loan of $5000 would require a monthly payment of about $161 if the term were three years, or $106 if the term were five. The difference between contractual payments and cram down payments provides a tremendous incentive to cram down secured loans if either the collateral is worth less than the loan (which will be almost every car loan) or where the contractual interest rate is more than the formula approved in *Till*.

cc. Special Rules for Homes (§ 1322(b)(2) & (5))

When cram down was being drafted, certain interest groups opposed extending it to their loans. We've already seen one such group—residential mortgage lenders. Section 1322(b)(2) provides that residential mortgage loans cannot be modified by cram down. So no cram down of homes.

There is a loophole here, however. Say Markell has a house that would sell for $100,000 if it was lien free. Assume also that Markell has taken out two mortgages on the house, the first mortgage for $150,000, and the second for $50,000. Is the second mortgage a secured claim? No! Under section 506(a), it is unsecured; there is no value for the second mortgage after taking care of the first mortgage. If the second mortgage is unsecured, do we assess how a plan treats it under Section 1325(a)(5)? No again; section 1325(b)(5) is for secured claims only. So debtors with mortgages that have no value often "strip off" these unsecured mortgages in Chapter 13 plans.

Note well that the mortgage has to be completely unsecured for this to work; if there is a $1 of value for the secured creditor, the "strip off" won't work. As we've seen before (recall *Dewsnup* and *Caulkett* in Section A.3.b. of Unit 3?), that you cannot "strip down" mortgage claims on residential mortgages if there is any value in the collateral.

dd. Special Rules for Cars (the So-Called "910 Provision")

Residential mortgages aren't the only sacred cows. In 2005, Congress added a new provision for relatively new car loans. This provision, which Congress forgot to give a place in the Code,[108] provides that Section 506(a) does not apply to purchase money car loans if the loan was made within 910 days before the debtor filed bankruptcy. What? Where did the 910 days come from? Your guess is as good as ours.

But the effect is significant. A debtor can no longer cram down a car's value if the he or she bought the car within 910 days of bankruptcy. Without section 506(a), the secured claim will be equal to the debt outstanding, *not* the collateral's value. Note that the debtor still might be able to cram down the loan if the *Till* formula produces a lower interest rate than the purchase contract does. But the primary benefit of cram down has been lost.

So when will you be able to use cram down? On older cars— ones for which the loan was made more than 910 days before bankruptcy. Also, for non-residential mortgages, as when the debtor has a rental house or a vacation house. Beyond that, there are pretty slim pickins.

3. *Effect of a Confirmed Plan*

The effect of confirmation is sweeping. Section 1327(a) states that "[t]he provisions of a confirmed plan bind the debtor and each creditor, whether or not the claim of such creditor is provided for by the plan, and whether or not such creditor has objected to, has accepted, or has rejected the plan."

So if Ponoroff has notice of confirmation and can't get it together to object to a plan—even if he has a valid objection (hah!)—

---

[108] Really! It is supposed to be somewhere in section 1325(a), but no one knows exactly where.

he is bound by a confirmed plan. Even if his debt is not specifically mentioned in the plan. So whatever treatment is in a confirmed plan binds creditors.

A confirmed plan also affects property of the estate. Section 1327(c) specifically states that property of the estate is free of pre-petition claims.

How long does property of the estate remain property of the estate? Section 1327(b) gives the debtor an election: he or she can provide in the plan that property of the estate will revest in the debtor upon confirmation (but before the plan is complete), or the plan can keep the property in the estate for the life of the plan. You might think that a debtor would want the property out of the estate, but if that happens, the property loses the protection of the automatic stay for certain post-petition claims. The Chapter 13 trustee also does not want the property to vest in the debtor, because post-petition earning are thus not part of the estate and the trustee cannot compel their payment as a matter of property law.

To assist the trustee with this control issue, section 1325(c) provides that the court may issue what is known as a "wage order" to the debtor's employer to pay over to the trustee a set amount each paycheck. That amount is usually equal to the debtor's monthly disposable income payment.

Recall from the discussion in Section B.5 above of this Unit, there is no discharge upon confirmation. That does not occur until completion of the plan (and possibly earlier if the debtor is eligible for a hardship discharge). *See* section 1328(a) & (b).

D. Post-Confirmation Issues

Lots can happen after the confirmation of a plan. Plans, recall, are three to five years in length, and lots can happen during that time period. Could you have predicted you'd be where you are today five years ago? Chapter 13 has provisions to address these future events.

1. Modification of Plan (§ 1329)

The plan, as we have seen, relies on the debtor to fund it with his or her disposable income. But what if the debtor loses his job and can't find another? Or gets a big raise? Can the plan be changed if the source of disposable income changes?

Sure. Section 1329 allows the debtor, the Chapter 13 trustee or any unsecured creditor (no secured creditors however) to seek modification of the plan. Any such modification has to go through all of the confirmation requirements; it has to be in good faith, pass the best interest test, be feasible, and commit all of the debtor's disposable income to the plan, etc.

If the debtor's income goes down, you can see why the debtor would seek modification to decrease plan payments. But what about modifications to increase plan payments. How would the trustee know if the debtor has a raise? Simple. The Code requires periodic reporting to the trustee (including tax returns) and many trustees request and obtain reporting requirements in the plan. So the trustee is watching the debtor, and his or her finances.

2. Revocation of Plan (§ 1330)

What if the debtor committed fraud in obtaining confirmation? Say Ponoroff intentionally and deceitfully understated his income in an effort to get a shorter plan with lower payments.

The somewhat surprising answer is that creditors have 180 days from confirmation to find out about the fraud. If they discover it during that period, they can seek revocation of confirmation and likely dismissal of the debtor's case (although section 1330 allows the debtor to seek to modify his or her plan).

After 180 days? Tough. No change. Congress wanted to bring an end to reorganizations and thus permits even fraudulent plans to be enforced if not caught in time.

So assume Ponoroff fraudulently understates his income (he gets an annual royalty payment from the *Short and Happy Guide* series that is really, really large—you are recommending this book to others, right?). No one discovers this payment until it is made some nine months (270 days) after confirmation. Are the creditors just stuck? Not really. Recall that the trustee and any unsecured creditor has standing to propose a modification of the plan. Even though they can't revoke confirmation, they can deprive Ponoroff of the benefit of his huge royalty check by seeking a modification. Poor Ponoroff (not).

E. Conversion and Dismissal (§ 1307)

As you've seen, Chapter 13 is fraught with many traps and pitfalls. Debtors who may be poor at financial management now have to propose and live with fairly tight budgets. They have to answer to the Chapter 13 trustee for all of their major financial choices. What happens if they fail? Indeed, even the rosiest of statistics indicate that only about 30-40% of Chapter 13 debtors ever complete their plan payments.

There are several possibilities. The case might be dismissed; that is, the debtor will be told that he or she cannot have the benefit or protection of the bankruptcy laws. Or the case might be changed to another chapter; this is called conversion.

Dismissal or conversion is typically achieved by a motion made by the creditors or the trustee. Section 1307(c) lists many grounds for dismissal or conversion. These include an unreasonable delay by the debtor that is prejudicial to creditors; failure to file a plan timely; failure to commence making timely payments under a plan; denial of confirmation of a plan; or a material default by the debtor with respect to a term of a confirmed plan. So if Markell is habitually late with his plan payments, the trustee can seek dismissal. If Ponoroff keeps proposing plans that can't be confirmed, he's toast.

The debtor can also seek relief via conversion or dismissal. Chapter 7 might be more conducive to the debtor's financial picture. The Code is very lenient here. Consistent with notions of good faith, a Chapter 13 debtor has the absolute right to dismiss his or her case, or to convert it to another chapter. Contrast this with Chapter 7, which typically requires court permission to dismiss or convert a case.

F. Review of Chapter 13—What to Look for on Exams

Chapter 13 issues can be messy. But you can sort through them if you just take the issues one at a time.

First, you need to focus on whether the debtor is eligible, and if so, whether he or she can confirm a plan. As to eligibility, look to whether the debtor has regular income. Then look at the amount of debts, and whether they are disputed or contingent. If disputed or contingent, the debts don't count against the debt limits. It is easy for professors to test these matters since they are somewhat mechanical.

Next, after eligibility issues are dealt with, look to whether the debtor can confirm a plan. To determine this issue, first determine what types of creditors the debtor has: unsecured, secured, lessors, or what have you. Then determine what type of treatment Chapter 13 permits the debtor to provide for these classes.

The easiest are unsecured creditors; they have the protection of the projected disposable income test. If you need to go into this test, keep in mind that the professor will have to provide you a lot of information—the applicable median income, for example—and the presence of such information should be a giveaway that disposable income is be an issue.

Next up are the secured creditors and lessors; they have to deal with cram down and the various exceptions to cram down. Remember the special treatment given residential mortgages, and car loans made with 910 days. Here your instructor will have to give you some information that will give away the issues. Look for facts that mention different types of value (remember *Rash* and replacement value) and applicable interest rates (remember *Till* and formulas involving the prime rate).

Once the creditors are sorted out, you can then focus on the general confirmation requirements. Key here will be to show that any Chapter 13 plan will pay creditors more than they would receive in Chapter 7 dividends. This test will require you to compare the Chapter 7 treatment with the Chapter 13 treatment, something your instructor is probably looking for.

Keep in mind that the Chapter 13 discharge is only granted after the payment plan is complete, and that, for the most part, Chapter 13 has the same nondischargeability rules as Chapter 7 (with the exception of some intentional torts, non-criminal fines and marital property settlements). This similarity actually makes any comparisons with Chapter 7 easier, since the analysis will be the same for both chapters.

Special Problems in Chapter 11

Chapter 11 is the residual reorganization Chapter in the Code. It is complicated, expensive, and currently the subject of intensive review and various calls for reform.[109] Although initially designed for business, it is now used by individuals as well.

One thing to keep in mind. Although Chapter 11 looms large in bankruptcy lore, it is small in terms of its footprint. Less than 1% of all bankruptcy filings (actually, about .8%) are Chapter 11 cases. Of course, if the amount of assets affected is looked at instead of the number of cases, Chapter 11 regains its prominence. The Lehman Brothers Chapter 11 case, for example, dealt with over $639 billion in assets, while the Washington Mutual cases dealt with almost $330 billion. That's a trillion dollars of assets in just two cases.[110]

The good news is that if you know Chapter 7 and Chapter 13, you'll be familiar with many of the concepts in Chapter 11. Just as

---

[109] The main investigation has been done by the American Bankruptcy Institute. Its 396-page, 1255-footnote report can be found at https://abiworld.app.box.com/s/vvircv5xv83aavl4dp4h.

[110] Against this list, General Motors and Chrysler look relatively small, with assets of $82 billion and $39 billion, respectively.

in Chapter 13, Chapter 11 achieves its aims through a court-approved plan of reorganization; just as in Chapter 13, this plan can be only confirmed if creditors will receive at least as much as they would under Chapter 7. But before we look at the ways in which Chapter 11 is different from these familiar concepts, we first we have to look at the different players and procedures in Chapter 11.

A. Eligibility, Players and Procedure in a Chapter 11

Many aspects of Chapter 11 are different than in other chapters. In particular, the statute defines different players and provides for vastly different procedures. We turn to those now.

1. Eligibility

Section 109(d) makes determining eligibility for Chapter 11 relatively easy. Any entity that is eligible for Chapter 7 is eligible to file for Chapter 11 relief.[111] For a while after Congress passed the 1978 Code, it was thought that individual consumer debtors were not eligible for Chapter 11 reorganization relief (that's what Chapter 13 was for, after all), but the Supreme Court held otherwise in *Toibb v. Radloff*[112] in 1991. Since then individuals have been eligible for Chapter 11, regardless of whether they have a business. Recently, almost 30% of all Chapter 11 filings have been by such individuals.

2. Players

The Code populates Chapter 11 cases with a diverse and unusual cast of characters—so unusual, that many countries initially

---

[111] In addition, railroads, which are not eligible for Chapter 7 relief, are eligible for Chapter 11. They are subject to highly specialized statutes which are almost never covered in any detail in an introductory bankruptcy course.

[112] 501 U.S. 157 (1991).

would not recognize United States Chapter 11 cases due to their assignment of roles. Let's look at these players.

3. *The Debtor in Possession*

The most distinctive aspect of Chapter 11 practice is that the Code allows the *prepetition* debtor to run the *postpetition* case. When this happens, the "debtor" is called the "debtor in possession."

The debtor in possession is a fiduciary to the estate, which means that it can be viewed as a distinctive and different entity from the prepetition debtor. It is also the "representative of the estate," so that in the typical Chapter 11 case, the debtor in possession manages the estate and works towards the confirmation of a plan of reorganization. Indeed, section 1107(a) specifically gives a debtor in possession most of the powers of a regular trustee, including the ability to commence avoiding power actions such as preferences and fraudulent transfers.[113]

This ability for the prepetition debtor (actually, in corporations, for the debtor's prepetition management) to continue in control is what the rest of world thought was crazy. For a while, for example, Canadian courts would not recognize a debtor in possession as the estate representative in a Chapter 11 case. Congress' choice here, however, was the result of experience. From 1934 to 1978, reorganization cases of any size had to have a trustee. Against this background, Congress found that the loss of control to a trustee caused many debtors to wait too long to commence bankruptcy proceedings—with a resultant loss of the ability to reorganize. In addition, Congress believed that most reorganization cases did not involve fraud (just bad luck), and thus the need to

---

[113] So when analyzing a Chapter 11 problem, and you encounter a statute that gives a power to a "trustee," you can read that grant of power to include a debtor in possession.

retain the knowledge and experience of existing management in any reorganization outweighed the possibility of a continued fraud on creditors. So the 1978 Code allowed the debtor in any Chapter 11 case to continue on as the debtor in possession.

In current practice, however, many debtors in possession appoint "chief restructuring officers" (CROs) to run the debtor during the Chapter 11 proceedings. CROs differ from trustees in that they are appointed by the debtor, albeit usually in conjunction with the consent or at the instance of significant secured creditors.

Does this mean that all Chapter 11 cases are run by the prepetition debtor? Of course not.

4. *Chapter 11 Trustees and Examiners*

While Chapter 11 defaults to the debtor in possession model, it is quite possible for a Chapter 11 trustee to be appointed. Section 1104(a)(1) permits the court to order the appointment of a trustee "for cause, including fraud, dishonesty, incompetence, or gross mismanagement of the affairs of the debtor by current management, either before or after the commencement of the case. . . ."

So if Ponoroff was stealing from Ponoroff, Inc. before a Chapter 11 filing, the court can appoint a trustee to run Ponoroff, Inc.'s Chapter 11 case. Heck, it can appoint a trustee if it is shown that Ponoroff was just "incompetent," which, if you know Ponoroff, couldn't be that difficult.

The Code also has provisions that allow for a remedy short of a trustee. If the court does not wish to completely supplant management, it has the option of appointing an official called an "examiner." An examiner's powers are set by the court, but section 1104(c) indicates that an examiner, once appointed, can "conduct such an investigation of the debtor as is appropriate, including an investigation of any allegations of fraud, dishonesty, incompetence, misconduct, mismanagement, or irregularity in the management of the affairs of the debtor of or by current or former management of the debtor. . . ."

So if the court thinks Ponoroff is okay at running the business, and isn't quite convinced that he is incompetent or a thief, it can order the appointment of an examiner to look into the way in which Ponoroff ran, and is running, the business. This remedy has recently been used in leveraged buyouts to allow current management to remain in place, while the propriety of the prepetition transactions are investigated.

5. The Creditors Committee

Chapter 11 can often be viewed as a class action by a debtor against a class consisting of the debtor's creditors. How is that class organized? Well, we'll split off secured creditors—they can usually take care of themselves from the proceeds of their collateral. That leaves unsecured creditors (which of course will include undersecured creditors to the extent of the difference between what is owed to them and the amount of their secured claim under section 506(a)(1)). Understanding that the cost of organizing effectively in such circumstances is high, the Code provides for a committee of unsecured creditors, which can hire its own experts (and lawyers) and have the estate pay for them.

Section 1102 allows for the appointment of an unsecured creditors' committee,[114] and membership is usually extended to the seven unsecured creditors holding the largest claims. Section 1103 gives the committee the power to appear in the debtor's case, to consult with the debtor in possession, as well as the power to

---

[114] It also allows for the appointment of an equity securities holders committee, but such an appointment is rare, and often is denied if the debtor is insolvent (since in such cases there is no value for the equity security holders).

investigate the debtor and to propose a Chapter 11 plan. To complete the circle, committees also have the power to seek the appointment of an examiner or a Chapter 11 trustee.

Committees are fiduciaries to their constituencies (just as debtors in possession are fiduciaries to the estate), and often act as information clearing houses to creditors. They are important in the plan process, and their endorsement can often make a critical difference in the approval of any Chapter 11 plan.

6. The Office of the United States Trustee

Congress believed that the size and complexity of a Chapter 11 case required oversight. For this purpose, Congress created the Office of the United States Trustee ("OUST"). The OUST is part of the Department of Justice.[115] We've seen the OUST before; it is the agency responsible for keeping and compiling the data for the means test in Chapter 7, and for calculating the applicable commitment period and disposable income in Chapter 13.

In Chapter 11, however, the OUST has direct supervisory responsibility. They are the agency responsible for selecting and appointing unsecured creditor committees, and for the selection and appointment of Chapter 11 trustees. They supervise the administrative side of Chapter 11 cases, making sure, for example, that the debtor in possession has adequate insurance and sets up the appropriate bank accounts. More importantly, the OUST has standing to appear and object to confirmation of plans and the award of professional fees. All of this, however, is secondary to the primary thrust of Chapter 11: the plan of reorganization. And it is to that we now turn.

---

[115] For purely political reasons, there is no OUST in each of the judicial districts of North Carolina and Alabama. Those districts have a different but similar official called the bankruptcy administrator.

7. Procedure and Timelines

The statutory goal in Chapter 11 is the confirmation of a plan. Unlike Chapter 13, creditors in Chapter 11 vote on all plans of reorganization. The general structure of this process is provided in the statute, although in practice there can be significant variances.

To understand plans, start with the proposition that plans of reorganization are the goal of most Chapter 11 cases. We'll see inroads on this notion later in Section C, but confirmation of a Chapter 11 plan is a big deal. The creditors have to vote. In order to cast their votes intelligently, they have to be informed about the debtor and the changes anticipated in the plan. To accomplish this, there are four basic stages of the plan process.

The first stage is plan formulation. This can be short, or it can be extended. As we see later, the Code privileges debtors at this stage, giving them 120 days in which they are the only entities who can file a plan. This initially forces all plan negotiations through the debtor. (During this stage, and all stages but the last, the debtor is also trying to keep the business afloat and keep it operating so that there is something to reorganize.)

Once a plan is formulated, the second stage commences. The plan proponent[116] solicits votes on the plan from creditors. The Code highly regulates this process. Votes can only be solicited if the creditors have been provided an adequate disclosure statement. Both disclosure statements and plans are heard as regular motions, and normally courts require about four weeks' notice before they will consider approving them. Thus, taken together, once the plan is formulated, the second stage will take a minimum of two months in order to inform and solicit creditors.

---

[116] The person soliciting the votes is called the "plan proponent," since it is not necessarily the debtor.

That leads to the third stage: plan confirmation. At this stage, the court reviews the creditor votes to see if sufficient creditor support exists. The court also will check the plan against the other requirements set forth in section 1129(a). These requirements include the best interest of creditors test and feasibility, as well as whether sufficient creditor support exists.

The fourth and final stage is the implementation of the confirmed plan, which can take whatever form specified in the plan.

So, if Markell waltzes into court with a plan he penned on the back of an envelope, and wants immediate confirmation, he will politely be told to try again. Although the time frames can be reduced, they are rarely shortened unless there is some business reason to shorten the time. Markell is, at a minimum, at least two month away from confirmation. The take away here is that the plan process is long at best, and frustratingly long at worst.

B. Operating the Business During the Case

Plans of reorganization are just legal documents. What is being reorganized is the debtor's business. If the business is neglected, the whole reason for reorganization crumbles. So significant attention needs to be paid to keeping the business running.

1. Critical Vendors, Priorities, and Administrative Expenses

The first concern, as stated, is keeping the business operating. This requires most business to buy goods and services they need to produce the goods or services that is their business.

The Code assists the debtor by making a clean division between prepetition debts and postpetition expenses. Prepetition debts, as we have seen, get paid in bankruptcy dollars; that is, they get paid (generally) a fraction of their amount. Section 503 categorizes postpetition expenses, however, as having administrative priority, and they are paid in, 100%, dollars. This encourages people who sell goods and services to the debtor to extend new credit to the debtor on the strength of being paid first out of the estate's assets.

But what about the debtor's regular vendors? They may get assurances that future goods and services will be paid, but what about debts existing on the date of the filing? This is especially important if the vendor supplies a critical good or service: nothing requires a creditor to continue to do business with a debtor, and if the debtor isn't paying its bills, the creditor can choose to not deal with debtor postpetition. In response to this, Congress enacted section 503(b)(9) in 2005, which, as we have seen, gives administrative priority to "the value of any goods received by the debtor within 20 days before the date of commencement of a case under this title in which the goods have been sold to the debtor in the ordinary course of such debtor's business."

So some creditors will get their prepetition debts paid in full. Assume that Ponoroff is an attorney for Markell, Inc. Ten days before Markell, Inc. files for Chapter 11, Ponoroff does some crackerjack work for Markell, Inc., and bills them $15,000. When Markell, Inc. files a Chapter 11 case, it thanks Ponoroff for his work, but tells him that he is unsecured and will be lucky to get 10% of his claim. May Ponoroff use section 503(b)(9)?

No. Note that section 503(b)(9) only applies to "the value of any *goods* received" so that services such as Ponoroff are excluded. Poor Ponoroff.

Before 2005, many courts allowed some debtors in possession to pay so called "critical vendors" if it was shown that these vendors were critical to the success of the reorganization. Since 2005, and the enactment of section 503(b)(9), the issue has not been raised in any significant case, especially since employees already have a priority for their unpaid wages.

2. Hiring Professionals

Debtors in possession need help to navigate the waters of Chapter 11. The Code allows debtors in possession (and creditors' committees) to hire lawyers and other professionals (such as accountants, auctioneers, investment bankers, etc.) and have their fees and expenses paid from the estate. Under section 327, however, these professionals have to be "disinterested"—a defined term in section 101(14)—which means, among other things, that they can't be owed any money on the petition date, and also cannot "an interest materially adverse to the interest of the estate or of any class of creditors."

Under section 330, these professionals can be paid after the bankruptcy court approves their fees and expenses as reasonable which, under the recent case of *Baker Botts L.L.P. v. ASARCO LLC*,[117] does not include fees expended in defending the reasonableness of fees. Once approved, however, the attorney's bill becomes an administrative expense.

3. Secured Creditors: Stay Relief and Cash Collateral Issues (§§ 362 and 363)

There is one class of creditors that require special care: secured creditors. At this point, it would be good to review the material in Section C of Unit 3 about relief from the automatic stay. In particular, recall that section 362(d)(2)(B) allows a creditor to obtain relief from stay as to certain collateral if the debtor does not have an equity in the collateral (that is, the debt exceeds the collateral's value) and the collateral "is not necessary to an effective reorganization."

What's "necessary to an effective reorganization"? To answer that, you have to know a lot about what it takes to confirm a plan.

---

[117] 135 S. Ct. 2158, 61 Bankr. Ct. Dec. (CRR) 41 (2015).

Indeed, many opinions on plan requirements are relief from stay cases in which the issue is really whether there can be an effective reorganization. The Supreme Court has weighed in here, indicating that an "effective" reorganization "requires . . . not merely a showing that if there is conceivably to be an effective reorganization, this property will be needed for it; but that the property is essential for an effective reorganization that is in prospect. This means . . . that there must be "a reasonable possibility of a successful reorganization within a reasonable time."[118]

As a result, many relief from stay motions focus on whether the debtor in possession can successfully reorganize in a reasonable time. Since a debtor's reorganization prospects are often cloudy or contingent at the beginning of a case, bankruptcy courts are likely to give somewhat more leeway early on in a case for the debtor to prove[119] that a successful reorganization is likely soon.[120]

Even if a relief from stay request is not successful, secured creditors have another way to press their claims. Section 363 gives special protection to "cash collateral." "Cash collateral" is defined in section 363(a) as "cash, negotiable instruments, documents of title, securities, deposit accounts, or other cash equivalents" in which the estate and the creditor both have an interest (which would be the case if the creditor had a security interest in the property.) Although it will not be common for the debtor to have cash that itself is collateral, section 363(a) extends the notion of

---

[118] United Sav. Ass'n of Texas v. Timbers of Inwood Forest Associates, Ltd., 484 U.S. 365, 375-76 (1988).

[119] And it is the debtor in possession's burden to prove the property is necessary for an effective reorganization. 11 U.S.C. § 362(g)(2).

[120] Even the Supreme Court acknowledges a more lenient standard early on in a case. "Bankruptcy courts demand less detailed showings during the four months in which the debtor is given the exclusive right to put together a plan . . ." United Sav. Ass'n of Texas v. Timbers of Inwood Forest Associates, Ltd., 484 U.S. 365, 376 (1988).

cash collateral to "the proceeds, products, offspring, rents, or profits of property" that is collateral.

So all proceeds, that is sales proceeds, are cash collateral if the goods that produced the proceeds were a secured lender's collateral. That means if a lender has a security interest in inventory, the sales proceeds of that inventory, whether they be cash or checks, will be cash collateral. If the lender has a security interest in the debtor's accounts receivable, then the payments by the debtor's customers are also cash collateral.

What is the big deal about cash collateral? Section 363(c)(2) states that "[t]he trustee[121] may not use, sell, or lease cash collateral . . . unless—[¶] (A) each entity that has an interest in such cash collateral consents; or [¶] (B) the court, after notice and a hearing, authorizes such use, sale, or lease in accordance with the provisions of this section."

So the debtor can sell its inventory and collect its receivables, but it can't use the cash if a secured party has a security interest in it? That's right—unless the creditor consents, or the court orders otherwise.

Consent is usually obtained through an agreed cash collateral order. In it, the debtor in possession usually gives back to the secured creditor a security interest in assets acquired postpetition, such as receivables and new inventory (an interest that was taken away from lenders by section 552(a), which provides that, once the debtor has filed, a security interest does not attach to after-acquired property). So the estate gets to use the cash in return for giving a replacement lien on the newly-created accounts or inventory.

What if the creditor doesn't consent? That's where the court can authorize the use, "in accordance with the provisions of this

---

[121] This includes the debtor in possession, remember?

section." That's a reference to section 363(e), which requires the court to grant adequate protection for any nonconsensual use of another's property.

What would that be? The same thing that the lender might have asked for: the debtor in possession usually gives back to the secured creditor a security interest in assets acquired postpetition, such as receivables and new inventory.

So assume that Ponoroff Points, Inc. (PPI) is a knife maker. It buys steel and turns it into dull knives (that's one of the reasons why it is in Chapter 11). Its main lender is Markell's Marvel's, Inc. (MMI), which has a security interest in PPI's accounts and inventory.

When PPI files, MMI can move for relief from stay so that it can repossess PPI's steel and collect the receivables from PPI's customers? Under section 362(d)(1), PPI has to provide adequate protection of MMI's interest or it will lose—as shown before, it can do this by showing that there is equity in the collateral, or by paying adequate protection payments equal to any decline in value of the collateral during the case.

But PPI is not out of the woods yet. MMI can also seek relief from stay under section 362(d)(2) by showing that its debt is more than the collateral's value and that the collateral is not necessary for an effective reorganization. If the collateral is worth less than the amount of the debt (and so MMI is undersecured), then the issue will be whether PPI can effectively reorganize. That, as we have said, will turn on whether PPI can satisfy all the confirmation requirements of section 1129, a subject we'll get to shortly.

But even if PPI squeaks by section 362(d)(2), there is the cash collateral issue. When Ponoroff sells inventory for cash, or collects cash from its customers, cash collateral is created. Ponoroff can't use this cash without MMI's permission or a court order. If PPI can't get MMI to consent (the principal of MMI is an SOB)[122], then PPI will have to seek a court order. To obtain that order it will have to give MMI adequate protection of the cash collateral. If its sales are steady or increasing, it can probably give this adequate protection through granting MMI a replacement lien in its accounts and inventory acquired postpetition.

Whew. Given all this, can't the parties just agree ahead of time as to how PPI will manage its cash? Sure. That's what postpetition financing is all about, and we turn to that next.

4.   *Postpetition Financing (§ 364)*

Chapter 11 anticipates on-going operations by the debtor in possession. For most businesses, continuing operations means that they need continued access to credit—it is a simple fact that most business entities need to be able to borrow to conduct business.

This need for credit presents a potential problem. Start first with the proposition that administrative expense creditors obtain first priority on the estate's assets. Add to that the fact that prepetition creditors only get paid from the estate. So if the estate's value decreases after the filing, prepetition creditors are hurt; there's less to pay them with. Put another way, if an operating bankruptcy estate loses money—its receipts from sales don't cover its expenses—prepetition creditors stand to receive a smaller bankruptcy dividend.

Imagine that Ponoroff Points, Inc. (PPI) files for Chapter 11 with $6 million in assets and $10 in liabilities. In Chapter 7, creditors could expect a 60% dividend. But if PPI's operations are losing money without outside financing, and if it keeps operating, that dividend will go down. If PPI is losing $2 million a year (its revenues are $4 million and its expenses $6 million, for example), a year in

---

[122] *S*ophisticated and *O*pulent *B*usinessperson. [Yeah, right! /s/ Ponoroff]

bankruptcy will increase its debts to $12 million, while keeping assets at $6 million. Unsecured creditors expected dividend of 60% is now 50%, and heading south.

Enter section 364. It has a hierarchy of priorities for postpetition credit. For regular unsecured credit extended in the ordinary course of business, section 364(a) allows an administrative priority without court approval. Although there has been some kerfuffle over whether a court determines "ordinary course" with reference to the debtor's prepetition actions ("vertical" ordinariness), or with reference to others in the debtor's trade or business ("horizontal" ordinariness), this type of credit is thought not to present much concern; it's just continuing what had already been done, and if the debtor is losing money hand over fist, there are other methods to address the loss. [123]

If the unsecured credit is not in the ordinary course of business, then section 364(b) requires court approval on notice to creditors. Makes sense; if Ponoroff wants to borrow $1 million unsecured from Markell, with plans to take it to Vegas and put it all on "00," someone ought to stop him.

What a postpetition creditor really wants, however, is security or collateral for the new credit extended. This topic is the province of section 364(c). Not only is court approval necessary, but the debtor in possession will have to show that it could not obtain similar credit on an unsecured basis. Approval under section 364(c) includes not only approval of secured credit on previously unencumbered assets, but also approval of priority status and of secured credit in a junior position on previously encumbered property.

---

[123] As we will see in Section E below, "substantial or continuing loss to or diminution of the estate and the absence of a reasonable likelihood of rehabilitation" is grounds for conversion of a Chapter 11 case to another Chapter, or for outright dismissal. See 11 U.S.C. § 1112(b)(4)(A).

Section 364(c) is the source of debtor in possession financing— so called "DIP Financing." Often, a debtor will have a secured loan with a creditor prepetition. That loan may be a continuing loan or a revolving loan—one which the debtor can use like a credit card, borrowing this month, paying back next, and then re-borrowing later. In this cases, the lender will sometime support, or at least acquiesce in, the debtor's bankruptcy filing.

This support (or more likely, this effort to protect its position), will take the form of DIP Financing. The debtor and the lender will enter into an agreement before the debtor files to continue or expand the financing after the filing, all subject to court approval. These agreements are quite complex and extensive. Lenders will want a security interest in everything they can get, and priority for all of their debt.

DIP Financing is quite common, and given debtors' constant craving for credit, usually requested and approved within the first month of a Chapter 11 case. Capitalizing on this need, lenders often attempt to improve their position in these financing arrangements. That is, they will sometimes attempt to cross-collateralize their debts—they will try and obtain a security interest in property not part of their prepetition collateral to secure not only their postpetition loan, but also their prepetition deficiencies. This move is typically denied, and with good reason: it is essentially creating a preference by securing postpetition debt that was unsecured prepetition collateral.

Another form of typically prohibited deal is the "roll-up"— lenders will require the first advance under the DIP Financing to pay off the prepetition debt, thereby converting a prepetition claim into a postpetition administrative claim.[124]

---

[124] We'll see why this is nefarious when we look at the role of administrative claims in the plan process in Section D. below.

One last variation. What if lender wants a security interest that is *senior* in priority to an existing lien or security interest? This is sometimes call "priming" a lien. While section 364(d) permits priming, it does so with a condition that typically kills the deal: the new lender has to give adequate protection to the old lender for its loss of priority. This is the same "adequate protection" that we talked about when looking at relief from stay. The crux of the condition is that the old lender will not lose its expected interest as a result of the priming lien.

That will rarely happen. A lender will request priming only when a junior lien will not be sufficient protection. But if you attempt to reduce the priority—subordinate in technical terms—of an existing lien, you are offering that existing lender the same priority that the new lender has rejected as insufficiently protective!

The rare circumstance where section 364(d) might makes sense is where, with the new loan, the debtor in possession will be able to create more value than the amount of the loan. This often occurs in a construction project. If construction is stopped by the filing, the debtor might have a hole in the ground and maybe some improvements. If the existing lender refuses to lend more, a new lender might see more promise and lend money to finish the project which, when done, will be worth enough to cover both loans.

Another PPI example. Say that PPI was in the process of constructing a new manufacturing plant when it filed. Markell Meany, Inc. (MMI) has lent $5 million towards construction, secured by a mortgage on the land. Due to cost overruns, the project will take another $2 million to finish. But as is, PPI's hole in the ground has an "as-is" value of $4 million. So MMI is undersecured, and presently has an unsecured deficiency of $1 million. No one would lend new money to PPI with MMI's lien in place. But say that Epstein

Exceptional Lenders (EEL) thinks that the project, when finished, will be worth $8 million. But EEL only lends in a first lien position.

Under section 364(d), EEL could propose to lend PPI the $2 million necessary to finish the project. It would try to convince the court of a finished value of $8 million; if accurate, then EEL would have a first lien on an $8 million asset for its $2 million loan—sweet! And MMI won't do so badly either. At an $8 million value, MMI will have $6 million in collateral covering its $5 million loan. Everybody's a winner—if it works out, that is.

So why wouldn't MMI just lend the extra $2 million? There could be many reasons. MMI may just want to be rid of PPI. Also, valuation of unbuilt buildings is not a science. MMI may disagree with the finished value, or the sufficiency of the $2 million to get there—MMI got into trouble when PPI went over budget initially, remember? MMI may also argue that if EEL is so convinced that the building will be worth $8 million when finished, EEL can just lend $7 million to PPI, taking out MMI (or can buy MMI's loan at par, that is, at 100% on the dollar). In either of these later cases, EEL would have the same protection it is claiming that will adequate protect MMI.

C. Section 363 Sales

Often, the debtor in possession will not attempt a reorganization plan, even though confirming a plan is the legislative model for Chapter 11. Instead, and usually in concert with their secured lenders, debtors in possession often attempt to sell all or substantially all of their assets to a third party rather than reorganize. Section 363 has some features that makes this feasible and desirable in many cases.

1. General Requirements: Ordinary Course and the Business Judgment Rule

Section 363 of the Code allows the estate representative to sell property of the estate.[125] This permission comes in two forms: without court permission if the sale is within the ordinary course of the debtor's business; with court permission if it is any other type of sale.

As we saw with cash collateral, a court determines "ordinary course" under one of two tests. Section 363(c)(1) states that the debtor in possession "may enter into transactions, including the sale or lease of property of the estate, in the ordinary course of business, without notice or a hearing, and may use property of the estate in the ordinary course of business without notice or a hearing." The court either looks at the debtor's prepetition actions ("vertical" ordinariness), or at similar actions by others in the debtor's trade or business ("horizontal" ordinariness).

So, under the vertical test, if Ponoroff Points, Inc. sold knives at retail before it filed under Chapter 11, it can sell its inventory of knives to retail customers after it files, without obtaining court permission. Under the horizontal test, if PPI's competitors or others in the industry of producing knives sold knives at retail, then PPI can sell without obtaining court permission. The rationale behind this provision is that the debtor's practices, or the practices of the industry or trade the debtor is in, set reasonable expectations among creditors as to what will be sold, and thus no separate court approval is necessary.

Any sale not in the ordinary course must obtain court approval. Section 363(b)(1) states that "The trustee, after notice and a hearing, may use, sell, or lease, other than in the ordinary course

---

[125] You'll remember section 363 from our discussion above on cash collateral. Same section; different application. But the concepts are quite similar.

of business, property of the estate." What happens if the debtor in possession guesses wrong and sells something outside the ordinary course of business? The transfer is then an unauthorized postpetition sale, and the estate representative may use section 549 to avoid it. Because of the threat of section 549, transactions that present close questions as to whether they are in the ordinary course are almost always brought before the court for approval.

If the transaction is brought before the court, what standard does the court use in deciding whether to approve it? Although the Code is silent on this point, most courts adopt a "good faith business judgment" test. If the estate representative, usually the debtor in possession in a Chapter 11, believes the sale to be in the estate's best interests after exercising its good faith business judgment, then the court will defer to that judgment and approve the sale. This is a standard that is heavily weighted in favor of debtors in possession, and often results in a court approving a sale if it is otherwise permissible.

2. *All or Just Some of the Assets?*

Some transactions out of the ordinary course of business raise special concerns. What if a Chapter 11 debtor proposes to sell all of its assets? If such a sale is only subject to the good faith business judgment test, it would seem to short-circuit many of the protections and restrictions found in regular reorganizations. When the Code was first adopted in 1978, some courts took this view, and held that, absent a show of emergency circumstances, a debtor in possession could not sell all of its assets under section 363. Such sales were referred to as "sub rosa" plans that could not be approved under section 363.

As time passed, however, sales of all or substantially all of an estate's assets came to be an accepted use of Chapter 11. Often, these sales are made by debtors in possession who have granted prepetition security interests in all or most of their assets, and thus are somewhat at the mercy of their secured creditors—and the secured creditors prefer the quick sale that section 363 permits, rather than the more lengthy (and costly) reorganization process. As a consequence, a Chapter 11 often results in a relatively quick sale (or sale process) for the estate's assets.

You might asked why the parties could not just have sold the assets outside of bankruptcy. A good question, and one that is answered in part by the Code's authorizations of sales free and clear of interests, an authorization found in section 363(f).

3. *The Power of Selling Free and Clear (§ 363(f))*

The Code gives the estate representative the power to sell property of the estate "free and clear of any interest in such property" if one of five conditions are met (assuming, as well, that the estate representative can meet the good faith business test). These conditions are:

(1)   applicable nonbankruptcy law permits sale of such property free and clear of such interest;

(2)   such entity consents;

(3)   such interest is a lien and the price at which such property is to be sold is greater than the aggregate value of all liens on such property;

(4)   such interest is in bona fide dispute; or

(5)   such entity could be compelled, in a legal or equitable proceeding, to accept a money satisfaction of such interest.

Paragraph (1) requires non bankruptcy law to allow a sale free and clear. This most often happens with respect to sales of inventory by a debtor. Under Article 9 of the Uniform Commercial

Code, for example, a sale of inventory by a debtor to a buyer in the ordinary course of business is a sale free of any inventory lender's security interest. *See* U.C.C. § 9-320. So if Ponoroff Points, Inc. sells its knives in a section 363 sale to an ordinary course buyer, then any security interest the lender had in that inventory is lost (although under state law the lender will obtain a lien in whatever PPI receives as the purchase price).

Paragraph (2) is the subject of negotiation in many cases. Especially with lenders that wish to see a debtor's assets sold (so that they can take the proceeds and pay the debts owed to them), consent is frequently obtained. The consent can, and often is, conditional. Usually, the non-debtor will bargain for its lien to transfer to the proceeds of sale as a condition of its consent.

Paragraph (3) is the subject of some controversy. The dispute arises as follows. In many cases, the debtor will wish to sell assets which are subject to a lien or security interest, but the creditor holding such interest will not consent. Outside of bankruptcy, this lack of consent would kill the sale; any transfer to a buyer would be a transfer of the asset as encumbered, and thus the buyer would essentially have to pay all liens in order to retain or keep the property.

All agree that paragraph (3) can be used to sell the asset if the price to be paid exceeds the value of all liens on the property—the lender will be paid in full from the proceeds of sale. Where the controversy arises is in cases in which the assets are over-encumbered; that is, when the debt secured by the lien or security interest is greater than the purchase price.

Some courts look at the wording of paragraph (3) and hold that, because of the way liens are determined in bankruptcy, paragraph (3) applies. They reason that the "aggregate value of all liens" is equal to the value of the asset securing such liens (recall how section 506(a)(1) works) and thus the sales price covers the lender's lien, and paragraph (3) applies. This interpretation equates the definition of "secured claim" with the phrase "aggregate value of all liens" in paragraph (3).

Other courts, however, reason that the use of the word "liens" suggest a different valuation than that used in section 506(a), and so read "aggregate value of all liens" to mean the "aggregate value of *all debts secured by* liens." In any event, these courts also point out that paragraph (3) requires that the price by "greater than" the aggregate value; under the first interpretation, however, the aggregate value is equal to, not greater than, the purchase price.

Paragraph (4) is often used when the estate disputes the claim held by the holder of the interest. The estate may claim, for example, that the amount of debt claimed by a bank is not what is really owed under the loan documents, or that any mortgage or secured interest is flawed in some way. Since claims can be easily raised, the statute requires a "bona fide" dispute, which most courts hold to be a dispute that could not be resolved by summary judgment.

Finally, paragraph (5) is a puzzle. There has been no standard interpretation of what it means. Some courts look to nonbankruptcy proceedings, such as partition, which allows a sale free of one the interest holder's rights. If that is all paragraph (5) covers, it is exceedingly narrow. Another interpretation is that since any debt or claim can be satisfied with money, paragraph (5) can justify any sale. If that is what paragraph (5) covers, it is exceedingly broad, and would swallow up the other exceptions.

Courts in the middle tend to look to specific types of actions that allow liens to be severed from property upon the payment of money. In this vein, some courts reason that since the lien of junior claimants under nonbankruptcy law is often eliminated by a foreclosure proceeding, then paragraph (5) allows a sale free of junior interests if there is consent or another exception available for a senior lienholder (since action by that senior lienholder would sever the junior lienholder's claim upon payment of any proceeds). Still other courts look to the Bankruptcy Code itself and reason that if the interests of a lienholder could be detached upon the payment of money under section 1129 (of which more later), then section 1129 could be the statute to which paragraph (5) refers. At this point, there is no consensus as to paragraph (5)'s scope, and most courts look for other exceptions they can apply.

An extend example can illustrate how these exceptions work. Say that Ponoroff Points, Inc. (PPI) is a Chapter 11 debtor in possession. It owes $10 million to MarkellBanc (MB), secured by an uncontested and incontestable lien on all of PPI's assets. PPI also stupidly allowed, before the bankruptcy filing, one of its creditors (Epstein) to obtain a judgment lien on its real property to secure a $2 million debt. The assets, however, are not worth more than $8 million, but there is a buyer, Lake, who would gladly pay $8 million to obtain the assets free and clear of any adverse claim. In this situation, outside of bankruptcy, Lake would not pay anything for the assets unless it had some understanding with each of MB and Epstein. Given Epstein's crotchety nature and animus towards PPI, that's not gonna happen.

In bankruptcy, however, there might be a different result. If PPI can get MB to consent to a sale to Lake, then the sale can be free of MB's interests under paragraph (2)—as a price for this consent, however, MB will have some understanding with Lake as to how to pay MB's debt, or will agree to take all consideration Lake pays. But that still leaves Epstein.

If PPI can legitimately contest Epstein's claim, then PPI can use paragraph (4) to sell free of Epstein's interest; this might be the case if PPI were appealing's Epstein's actions in state court. Epstein's lien would attach to whatever proceeds Lake would pay.

But if Epstein's claim is golden and untouchable, PPI would then have to resort to paragraph (3)—which is not likely to provide a good result since the "aggregate value" of Epstein's liens would have to be $0 in order for the sale to comply with paragraph (3)'s terms, as MB's interest would suck up all value until MB is paid $10 million.

Finally, paragraph (5) might be used if the court analogizes the sale to a foreclosure by MB, which, if it were a real foreclosure under nonbankruptcy law, would eliminate Epstein's interest. That option, however, requires the court to adopt one of the contested interpretations of paragraph (5), as would a claim that PPI could force Epstein to take $0 under section 1129. Many courts in these circumstances will not authorize a sale free and clear, and will require the parties to file and confirm a reorganization plan that would convey property free and clear to a third party.

4. *Structured Dismissals*

If there is a sale, then what? At this point, two things can happen. Historically, the case was converted to a Chapter 7 case and the new trustee would wind up whatever was left, and then close and dismiss the case. In some cases, however, the parties wish to avoid the necessity of a trustee—in the views of some, it simply adds time and money to a foregone conclusion.

As a result, many Chapter 11 cases that involve a sale of all or substantially all of the estate's assets now present the court with what is known as a "structured dismissal." This is essentially no different than a dismissal with conditions—conditions the parties, rather than the court or the Code—impose. It is not, for example, unusual for the dismissal to require funds to be paid to lawyers or even some parties from the sale proceeds before the dismissal is complete.

Courts have split on the propriety of such a dismissal, some favoring the flexibility it offers and others favoring traditional simple, one-page, dismissals. The trend, however is to approve such dismissals, thus giving more options and flexibility to the structure and flexibility of sales under section 363.

A contentious example of a structured dismissal can be found in *Official Creditors Committee v. CIT Group/Business Credit Inc. (In re Jevic Holding Corp.)*.[126] There, the structured dismissal favored creditors not favored in the Code's distribution section, and arguably violated absolute priority (more on that later in Section D.7 below, but trust us, that's a big thing). Despite these objections, the Third Circuit approved the dismissal, finding "that there was no prospect of a confirmable plan in this case and that conversion to Chapter 7 was a bridge to nowhere. . . . For present purposes, it suffices to say that absent a showing that a structured dismissal has been contrived to evade the procedural protections and safeguards of the plan confirmation or conversion processes, a bankruptcy court has discretion to order such a disposition."[127]

D. Plans (§ 1129)

As we've said before, the goal of a Chapter 11 cases is the confirmation—court approval—of a plan of reorganization. Even though sales under section 363 may dominate distribution of a debtor's assets in a large percentage of current Chapter 11 cases, the Code's structure still anticipates a plan. To understand Chapter 11, you thus have to understand three things: what a plan is; how a plan is proposed and voted on; and the standards used to confirm the plan. We'll look at each in order.

---

[126] 787 F.3d 173 (3d Cir. 2015).
[127] 787 F.3d at 181–82.

1. What Is a Chapter 11 Plan?

A Chapter 11 plan is a document that affects all contractual and other relationships of the debtor. It affects debts; it also affects ownership (in the case of a non-human debtor). Many liken it to a novation (substitution) of all relationships the debtor has with its creditors and owners.

How does it do this? By words. A Chapter 11 plan is usually a long document. You can see what a form plan of reorganization looks like by going to Official Form B 25A[128]—it is the official form plan for small businesses.

What does a plan contain, and what does it do? Read on.

2. Classes and Classification (§ 1122)

The contents of a plan are governed by section 1123. The first thing section 1123(a)(1) requires is that claims and interests[129] be *classified*. What does that mean? Each class of claims must contain only those claims and interests which are "substantially similar" to every other claim or interest in the class. That's the test required by section 1122(a). No secured claims with equity interests; no unsecured claims with secured claims.

Note the structure of section 1122(a). It does *not* require all claims that are substantially similar to be in one class; it only requires that a class only contain substantially similar claims. What's the difference? The Code permits separate classification of claims that might be deemed substantially similar. An example: unsecured trade debt that is, debt incurred through the purchase of goods or use of services—might be classified separately from unsecured bank debt. Even though these types of claims are

---

[128] After December 1, 2016, the form will be called Official Form B 425A.

[129] Interests, recall, is the Code's way of referring to equity interests such as shares of stock in a corporation or membership in limited liability companies.

substantially similar—both are unsecured and would have access outside of bankruptcy to the same assets to satisfy the claims—they may have different motives with respect to the reorganization of the debtor. Trade debt traditionally likes to keep a customer (even a defaulting one if it looks like more business will be forthcoming), while bank debt is not so wed to a relationship.

Especially if the unsecured bank debt is a deficiency claim tied to an undersecured secured claim, courts are suspicious of separate classification. Accordingly, most cases impose a judicially-created limitation on classification, and require that any separation of legally similar claims be supported by a good faith business justification.

Why the fuss about classification? Classification bears on two very important points: plan voting and dividend distribution. As we will see, voting in chapter 11 is by class; the confirmation requirement looks to whether all *classes* have accepted the plan, not if a majority of all claims have. Similarly, distribution of assets and value under a plan is by class. Each class member gets their pro rate share of the value or assets allocated to that class under the plan. So classification can be used to combine favorable creditors into one class (or segregate enemies), or to favor (or disfavor) distributions to that class.

There is one exception to this. The Code recognizes that small claims can present administrative costs which exceed their value. In acknowledgement of this, section 1122(b) allows for the creation of "convenience" classes in which a relatively low number is set, and allows plans to create a convenience class for all claims at or under that number (or which elect to be reduced to that number).

3. *Substantive Content (§ 1123)*

What else must a plan contain? Aside from procedural requirement, the Code is very flexible. Although section 1123(a)(5) requires "adequate means for the plan's implementation," the Code gives the plan proponent many tools. Among other things, a plan may: cure or waive defaults; extend maturities of debt; reduce or eliminate debt; reduce or eliminate interest; swap one debt instrument for another; swap equity or equity interests for debt; sell any or all of the estate's assets; merge or consolidate the debtor into another entity. Section 1123(b) allows a plan to: leave untouched certain classes of claims; assume or reject executory contract; modify secured creditor claims; and retain any avoiding powers actions. Finally, section 1123(b)(6) allows the plan "to include any other appropriate provision not inconsistent with the applicable provisions of" title 11.

Whew. That's lot. So if Ponoroff Points, Inc.'s (PPI) plan extends all maturities of all debts for ten years, and the plan otherwise complies with title 11, the plan may so provide. If PPI's plan gives each creditor a note equal to 25 percent of the creditor's claim, and discharges the balance, and the plan otherwise complies with title 11, the plan may so provide. If PPI instead wanted to convert all outstanding debt to stock, and the plan otherwise complies with title 11, the plan may so provide.

4. Impairment and Effect (§ 1124)

Must the plan affect all debt? No. The plan may be as flexible and responsive to the debtor's financial situation as it needs to be. In some cases, an entire class of claims may be untouched—this could happen when, for example, the debtor only needs to restructure its bank debt and not its trade debt. In the latter case, the plan could leave the trade debt "unimpaired," a classification that has important consequences. Section 1124(1) says that impairment occurs when the plan purports to alter the "legal, equitable or contractual" rights of a creditor or interest holder.

Why is impairment important? Only impaired classes may vote on a plan, so unimpaired classes simply sit on the sideline, since, after all, their claims are not affected. If a class is not impaired, then, and the plan is confirmed, the creditors in that class have to accept the plan's treatment without being allowed to vote on the plan. They (to use a Ponoroffism) "have no dog in that hunt." Their protection comes from the "good faith" and "feasibility" requirements discussed in Section D.6 below.

Sometimes a plan proponent can "unimpair" a claim in default. Much like the template for executory contracts, section 1124(2) allows a plan to treat an impaired claim as unimpaired (and thus not solicit the claim holder's vote) if the plan cures any default, reinstates the maturity, compensates the holder of the claims for any damages incurred in reasonable reliance on the default, and leaves all other rights unimpaired.

When would a plan proponent "unimpair" a claim under section 1124(2)? If the claim is for borrowed money, and the interest rate on the debt is less than the prevailing market rate of interest, it is in the estate's interests to preserve the low interest rate. This interest rate difference gives the plan proponent the incentive to use section 1124(2) to keep the low-rate loan (and gives the claim holder the incentive to contest the plan proponent's proposed cure and reinstatement).

5. Plan Process

To confirm a plan, creditors must vote on it. To vote on it, creditors must know about it. That's what the plan process is about. There are three basic components to this process: who can propose a plan (the plan proponent); what must the plan proponent tell creditors and interest holders about the plan (the disclosure statement); and who gets a say in whether the court adopts the plan (plan voting).

a.   Exclusivity and Who May Propose a Plan (§ 1121)

Congress tried to be realistic about debtors in financial trouble. When a debtor files for bankruptcy, it is likely that there is financial chaos, caused by the myriad demands of angry and weary creditors. The first tool Congress gave debtors to calm the chaos was the automatic stay. It stops creditor collection efforts, as we have seen in Unit 3.

But there has to be a way forward. Angry and weary creditors may disagree over what the best path is, or they may just want to liquidate the debtor and be done with it. That's where Congress gave debtors a second tool: exclusivity.

Exclusivity is found in section 1121. It provides that for the first 120 days of a case, the debtor is the *only* entity that can propose a plan. And if the debtor files a plan within this time period, it gets an extra 60 days—for a total of 180 days—of exclusivity. The thought here is that centralizing the plan process in the debtor for this period is more likely to produce a viable plan than allowing everyone to put forward their plans all at once.

Exclusivity can be extended, for cause (but not beyond 18 months after the filing). How does this work? Assume that Ponoroff Points, Inc. (PPI) has a sprawling empire of 2000 stores selling crappy knives. It may need more time than 120 days to get its financial plan together because it may need that time (and more) to get its landlords together and know how many stores locations will be viable. A court could thus find financial complexity constitutes "cause" for termination of exclusivity.

Exclusivity can also be shortened for cause. Say PPI has but one landlord, and one other creditor, a bank. The bank and the landlord agreed to cut short PPI's existence, and they are each owed more than PPI is worth lien free. If one of these creditors requests it, the court may very well cut off PPI's time, and allow a creditor to file a plan.

Incidentally, the ability of someone other than the debtor to file a plan is why the person proposing the plan, even if it is the debtor, is called the "plan proponent." Use of that term recognizes the possibility that someone other than the debtor may sometimes file a plan.

What if a possible plan proponent files during the exclusive period? Say Markell Bank (MB) files a liquidation plan the day after PPI files. Courts don't like this, and will not only strike MB's plan, but may sanction MB for its filing as well.

b.   Disclosure Statement (§ 1125)

We know that creditors vote in a Chapter 11. How do they know which way to cast their ballot? Chapter 11 has an answer to that: the plan proponent must first prepare and obtain approval of a disclosure statement, and send it to creditors with the Chapter 11 plan ballot. Under section 1125(b), this document is supposed to contain "adequate information." Section 1125(a) states that adequate information "means information of a kind, and in sufficient detail, as far as is reasonably practicable in light of the nature and history of the debtor and the condition of the debtor's books and records, . . . that would enable . . . a hypothetical investor of the relevant class to make an informed judgment about the plan . . ."

The Code is fairly clear that adequate information does not necessarily include a discussion of other plans, nor does it require the plan proponent to conduct an appraisal of the estate's assets. Against this background, most disclosure statements give a history of the debtor's financial problems, a description of how the plan is supposed to work, along with an estimate of the return or recovery for each class of claims or interests. For reasons explored below with respect to confirmation, the disclosure statement will also usually contain a cash flow estimate for the near future (three to five years, and sometimes more), a liquidation analysis, and a valuation of the debtor as a going concern.

Sometimes creditors raise confirmation issues at the disclosure statement hearing. If the issue requires any consideration of facts, the court will usually defer it to the confirmation hearing. If the objection raises a pure issue of law, however, the court may take the issue into consideration at the disclosure statement hearing—no sense in approving a disclosure statement for a plan that will be dead on arrival regardless of what the plan proponent can demonstrate.

Disclosure statements must be approved by the court after notice and a hearing. When the court approves the disclosure statement, it often sets the date for the confirmation hearing. In small cases, or when time is critical, the court has the power under section 105(d)(2)(B)(vi) to combine the disclosure statement and the confirmation hearings.

c.   **Pre-Packaged Plans**

In many circumstances, the debtor and its creditor body are in general agreement about what should be done without the need for extensive court proceedings. However, there may be holdouts or minority interests that could block a plan outside of bankruptcy, but could be outvoted in bankruptcy. In such cases, the debtor can prepare, circulate and solicit votes before ever filing a case. If the debtor does this, it files what is known as a "pre-packaged plan," one in which all the requirements for confirmation can be summarily shown.

In such cases, section 1125(g) permits approval of a disclosure statement "if such solicitation complies with applicable nonbankruptcy law and if such holder was solicited before the commencement of the case in a manner complying with applicable nonbankruptcy law."[130] To expedite matters, the court will often combine the disclosure statement hearing on a pre-packaged plan with the hearing on confirmation. If the court does combine the hearing, the debtor's counsel has to be prepared to show that the debtor's prebankruptcy solicitations were in accord with, among other laws, state and federal securities laws.

d.   Voting (§§ 1126 and 1129(a)(8))

Once the court approves a disclosure statement, the plan and disclosure statement are circulated to creditors, and they vote to accept or reject the plan. Voting is by class; the confirmation requirement is not that a majority of creditors approve, but that each class accept the plan.

Under section 1126, a class accepts a plan if (i) more than half the creditors voting in a class accept the plan; and (ii) those creditor voting to accept the plan hold at least two-thirds of the amount of claims voting. Note those two requirements are connected by the word "and" not "or."

Note also what this test requires. It only counts the claims of creditors actually voting. There is no quorum requirement—if only one claim in a class of 50 claims votes, and votes in favor of the plan, then that class has accepted the plan. If no creditor votes, however, then the class rejects the plan.

There are other wrinkles. If a class is unimpaired, it is deemed to have accepted the plan without any solicitation; if the class is eliminated, it is deemed to have rejected the plan.

Now let's see how this works in practice. Assume our old friend, Ponoroff Points, Inc. (PPI) somehow managed to get a plan

---

[130] In such cases, the first meeting of creditors is eliminated "if the debtor has filed a plan as to which the debtor solicited acceptances prior to the commencement of the case." 11 U.S.C. § 341(e).

drafted and circulated to creditors. PPI's creditor body consists of one secured creditor, Markell Bank (MB), and an unsecured class of creditors containing 10 creditors with claims of $100 each. Accordingly, PPI's plan has two classes: one secured creditor class, and one unsecured creditor class.

PPI solicits votes, and MB votes against the plan while the unsecured class unanimously votes in favor. The secured creditor's class rejects the plan; the unsecured creditor class accepts it. That's easy.

What if MB is too damn lazy to cast a ballot, and all the unsecured creditors vote in favor of the plan. Same result. Without any ballots the secured creditor class has nothing to count, and thus is deemed to have rejected the plan.

What if MB votes in favor, and six unsecured creditors vote in favor while four vote against. Here, the secured class obviously accepts. The unsecured class, however, does not. While more than 50 percent of the claims voting accepted, those voting only held 60% of the amount of claims ($600 out of $1000). Two-thirds is 67-2/3 percent and thus has not been met.

Same facts accept this time MB votes in favor, and only six unsecured creditors vote: four in favor, and two against. Different result here. More than a majority approved, and *those voting* held exactly two-thirds of the claims voting ($400 out of $600).

Final example. This time assume that there are ten unsecured creditors, but that one of them holds a $910 claim, while the remaining nine hold claims of $10 each. When the ballots are tabulated, there are only six unsecured creditors voting: three (including the holder of the $910 claim) vote in favor; the remaining three reject.

No approval. While there is approval from way more than two-thirds of the voting creditors, the vote is split evenly at 50-50. The requirement, however, is that *more than one-half* in number must accept. Here there is just one-half, not *more than* one-half.

6. *Consensual Confirmation Standards (§ 1129(a))*

To confirm a plan, a plan proponent must meet all of the requirements of section 1129(a). There are sixteen of them, although not all of them apply in every case. Of these sixteen, six are of critical importance: voting; good faith; best interests; feasibility; payment in full of administrative claims; and the affirmative vote of at least one noninsider class. We'll look at each of these, and then summarize the rest.

a.   Voting (§§ 1126 and 1129(a)(8) with a Little Bit of § 1124)

Voting is the requirement we've focused on thus far. It is found in section 1129(a)(8), requires that every class of claims and interests must accept the plan. Note that this does *not* mean that every *creditor* must accept—only that every *class* must accept. Given the hybrid rules of section 1126, the vote is calculated on a class by class basis. This means that a creditor rejecting plan that his or her class accepts has no recourse; he or she is part of an accepting class.

Note also that if the plan eliminates any class of claims or interest, then you cannot confirm a plan under section 1129(a). In that case, the only way to confirm a plan is through cram down, which is described in Section D.7 below.

b.   Good Faith (§ 1129(a)(3))

Section 1129(a)(3) requires that a plan "has been proposed in good faith and not by any means forbidden by law." This requirement has been interpreted to mean that the plan must be designed to achieve results consistent with the Code. Courts have used this open-ended formulation to validate plans that seek to stop and undo state court foreclosures (using the Code's tools) or to reinstate accelerated maturity dates under state law.

A lack of good faith, however, has been found when a competitor/creditor files a liquidation plan, or when a debtor uses Chapter 11 to evade taxes or to unduly delay creditors.

A plan is not proposed by "any means forbidden by law" if the plan issues interest in accordance with the Code but contrary to state law, as might happen if stock or other equity interests are issued without being fully paid for. Courts have found that if section 1123 authorizes the means of implementation, then it is not a violation of good faith to propose it.

c.   Best Interests Test (§ 1129(a)(7))

Contrary to voting, which is focused on classes of claims and interests, the best interest test of section 1129(a)(7) looks at *individual* creditors and equity holders. Often called the "best interest of creditors" test, it requires that the plan distribute to each creditor, unless they are unimpaired, at least as much under the plan as they would if the debtor were liquidated. Apply this test requires the creation of a distribution in a hypothetical chapter 7 liquidation. The plan proponent usually provides this analysis in the disclosure statement.

Why does the test not included unimpaired creditors? Congress took the position that if a plan gives a creditor what they bargained for—the essence of non-impairment—then that is all they are entitled to. Their protection is the next requirement examined: feasibility

d.   Feasibility (§ 1129(a)(11))

Section 1129(a)(11) is called the feasibility requirement. It requires the plan proponent to prove that the plan is not likely to be followed by the need for further financial reorganization. In other words, the plan should take care of the known financial problems, and not leave anything to be dealt with later on.

As with all other confirmation requirements, the civil preponderance of evidence test applies. So a plan proponent only has to show feasibility is more likely than it is not. This allows many cases to be confirmed that will ultimately fail—if the standard is only more likely than not, almost half of the cases confirmed could fail.

Nonetheless, there has to be a showing that the financial obligation in the plan can be met. This usually requires a cash flow statement for a reasonable period, which ordinarily will be three to five years, but with some cases projecting out over ten years. Because of this requirement, the disclosure statement will contain cash flow projections similar if not identical to those the plan proponent will introduce at the confirmation hearing.

e.   Full Payment of All Administrative Claims (§ 1129(a)(9))

We've seen that the Bankruptcy Code marks a sharp dividing line between prepetition and postpetition debts. From and after the filing, debts incurred need to be paid in full. Section 1129(a)(9) carries this forward in Chapter 11. It requires that all administrative expenses to be paid in full as of confirmation.

Several consequence flow from this requirement. First, the Chapter 11 discharge occurs as of confirmation—so administrative claims unpaid by the plan would be discharged unless the requirement were enforced.

This requirement gives creditors incentives to have their debts classified as administrative. This is particularly important with debtor in possession financing. If a prepetition lender succeeds in having its first postpetition advances pay off its prepetition debt, then it has succeeded in elevating non-priority unsecured debt into priority administrative claims payable upon confirmation. This gives debtor in possession lenders who obtain such payments greater control over the Chapter 11 case, and thus courts tend to disapprove this type of "roll-up" of prepetition debt into postpetition administrative claims.

f.   At Least Once Consenting Class (§ 1129(a)(10))

Section 1129(a)(10) seems odd—it requires that at least one noninsider class approve the plan. But if section 1129(a)(8) requires all classes to approve, what role does paragraph (10) play? Well, none in purely consensual confirmation. Its role is seen because non-consensual confirmation—cram down—requires satisfaction of all requirements, except voting. So section 1129(a)(10) really has a role in confirmations under section 1129(b)—non-consensual confirmation—and prohibits plan in which there are no assenting classes (something that was actually permitted in certain real estate bankruptcies before 1978).

g.   Other Confirmation Standards

The other confirmation standards are important in bankruptcy cases, but tend not to be heavily tested in bankruptcy classes. Paragraphs (1) and (2) of section 1129(a) require that the plan and the plan proponent comply with title 11. This essentially means that the plan process be complied with, that the plan proponent has obtained court approval of its disclosure statement, and that the cash collateral provisions of section 363 have been followed.

Sections 1129(a)(4) and (5) require the approval of the management of the reorganized debtor, as well as the compensation paid to such management.

Section 1129(a)(6) requires regulatory approval if the debtor is subject to regulation—the approval of a utilities commission if the debtor is, say, an electrical utility, or of a gaming commission if the debtor is a casino.

Section 1129(b)(12) requires the debtor pay all fees imposed by the Office of the United States Trustee and section 1129(b)(13) requires compliance with provisions regarding unions and pensioners.

The remaining three paragraphs—(14), (15), and (16)—relate to plans filed by individuals, and we'll handle those in Section F.1 below.

7. Non-Consensual Confirmation Standards (§ 1129(b))

What happens if a plan proponent cannot obtain the acceptance of all classes? This will happen automatically if the plan eliminates any class (as it might with respect to equity interests if the debtor is insolvent). Or a class might just vote "no." Is all lost?

No. A plan may be confirmed "non-consensually" under Section 1129(b). But non-consensual confirmation is not easy.

a. All Consensual Requirements Except Voting

Section 1129(b)(1) has three basic requirements for nonconsensual confirmation: (i) the plan proponent must satisfy all the applicable requirements of section 1129(a) except voting (so the plan proponent still has to show that the best interests test is met with respect to all impaired creditors and that the plan is feasible and proposed in good faith, among other things); (ii) the plan must not discriminate unfairly; and (iii) the plan has to be fair and equitable.

Compliance with the requirements of section 1129(a) is complex, but can be followed. The unfair discrimination and fair and equitable requirements, however, are a little more squishy[131].

---

[131] That is definitely a "Markellism."

b. No Unfair Discrimination (§ 1129(b)(1))

Unfair discrimination can be looked at as "horizontal" equity. That is, it mediates between classes of claims or interests of roughly the same priority. The requirement is that the plan, otherwise confirmable, does not discriminate unfairly against a dissenting class.

Not the odd phrasing. You can discriminate, but apparently not unfairly. The means you can have "fair" discrimination. When would that occur? It often comes up in two situations. First, in mass tort cases, the tort victims typically represent a class that is numerous, and the aggregate claims are huge. The only way to compensate these claimants is to either give them an ownership interest in the business going forward, or guaranty payments from future operations; an insolvent debtor doesn't have the cash to pay their claims.

But to sustain the business going forward (either to support the value of the new equity interests or to generate the cash to make guaranteed payments), the cooperation and support of existing trade and other consensual creditors may be needed. Thus, even though contract claims and tort claims have the same non bankruptcy priority—they are both unsecured claims—plans often pay the tort claims a different amount of cash (or in equity interests instead of cash) over a longer period of time.

This treatment is discrimination; the plan is treating similar unsecured claims differently. But is it unfair discrimination? Courts have struggled with tests to distinguish fair from unfair discrimination. In essence, a materiality standard seems to have emerged. If an accepting class is receiving a materially better recovery or materially better property as consideration (cash instead of notes or equity interests, for example) than a dissenting class, then the discrimination is unfair.

What is material? As with any law school question, the answer is that it depends. As a consequence, courts examine the reasons the plan makes the discrimination. If necessary or desirable to comply with feasibility, or to secure the cooperation and consent of necessary future trading partners, courts have been far more willing to approve the discrimination as "fair."

The problem cases have arisen with secured creditor deficiencies. Recall that section 506(a) splits undersecured claims into two claims: a secured claim equal to the collateral's value, and an unsecured claim for the balance (if any). If the deficiency claim can be separately classified (a controversial proposition, as stated above, although there may be a good faith business reason for the classification if that test applies), then can it be treated differently? As with tort claims, the size of the deficiency may present feasibility problems if all unsecured creditors are treated similarly. So there may be business reasons for different payment terms (although perhaps not for different percentage recoveries). Mileage may differ depending on the district and the reasoning for the discrimination offered by the plan proponent.

c. Fair and Equitable—Cram Down of Secured Claims (§ 1129(b)(2)(A)(i)–(iii))

If the plan proponent can get by the unfair discrimination requirement, it then faces the "fair and equitable" requirement.[132] Whereas unfair discrimination protects horizontal equity, the fair and equitable rule protects vertical equity, that is, the relationships between claims and classes of different priority.

The most senior claims are those secured by estate property. Under nonbankruptcy law, those claims have the ability to take and sell the collateral after a debtor's default. And since a creditor's

---

[132] The statute really says "fair and equitable." Congress just took these works from early 20th Century equity receivership cases, and with those words incorporated that jurisprudence.

claims to a particular item or type of collateral is bound up in the unique aspects of that collateral, secured creditors must usually be classified in their own class—there simply is no substantially similar claim to the lender's secured claim.

What if that lender rejects the plan? Is it doomed? No. Section 1129(b)(2)(A) gives three examples of fair and equitable treatment of a secured creditor's claim.

Section 1129(b)(2)(A)(i) is the most commonly used example. It states that a plan is fair and equitable as to a dissenting secured creditor if, after confirmation, the creditor retains its lien in the collateral, and the plan distributes to the creditor property equal in value to the value of the secured creditor's collateral.

This last locution is tricky. What is "property" for this purpose? The key is that while it can be cash, or goods or land, it most often is a note. That is, an obligation or promise of the debtor that bears interest. What interest rate? We'll spare you the economics, but a note payable over time has a present value equal to its face amount if it bears a "market" rate of interest.

An example. Assume Ponoroff Points, Inc. (PPI) has a secured creditor, Markell's Sharp Iron, Inc. (MSI) which has a lien on PPI's plant and equipment. PPI owes MSI $100,000; the plant and equipment securing the lien are worth $75,000. Note that MSI will have two claims: a secured claim for $75,000 and an unsecured claim for $25,000. The unsecured claim will either be placed in its own class or with the general unsecured creditors; we'll put that aside for now.

PPI can confirm its plan over the dissent of MSI under section 1129(b)(2)(A)(i) if the plan gives MSI a note for $75,000, and if that note bears a market rate of interest and is secured by the same collateral as before confirmation.[133] This treatment complies with each requirement of section 1129(b)(2)(A)(i) because MSI is receiving property that has a value equal to its collateral and is retaining its lien. How does the court know what a market rate of interest is? That's up to PPI to prove by the civil law standard of a preponderance of the evidence (but courts often start with the *Till* standard developed in Chapter 13 cases, and discussed in Unit 7 above).

A second way PPI could confirm its plan is by a sale of the collateral. Here, section 1129(b)(2)(A)(ii) is met if the plan provides that either: (i) the creditor receives the proceeds of the collateral's sale, or (ii) the creditor receives property equal to the value of the collateral (calculated in the same way was under subparagraph (i)), and the lender retains a lien on the sale proceeds. In either case the purchaser obtains lien-free title to the assets bought.

If pressed, this means that the debtor can sell its over-encumbered property to a purchaser, free of the lender's lien (compare this to the disputed ability of an estate to sell over encumbered property under section 363(f)).

What can the secured creditor do if it doesn't like the price being offered? Sales under section 1129(b)(2)(A) are subject to credit bidding as allowed by section 363(k). This means that if the secured creditor believes that the sale price is too low, it can bid in all or some of its claim, and wind up with ownership of the collateral.

The final way is oddly named. Under section 1129(b)(2)(A)(iii), a court will confirm a plan over the dissent of a secured creditor if the creditor receives the "indubitable equivalent" of its claim. These weird words are sort of an in joke. They were originally used

---

[133] How far out can the maturity date be? As far out as the plan proponent can prove is consistent with the feasibility requirement of section 1129(a)(11). This is often limited to ten years, although some plans have been confirmed with 15 or 20 year notes.

in an opinion by Judge Learned Hand in the 1930s.[134] What do they mean? An accepted understanding is that if the plan returns the collateral to the secured creditor, the creditor receives an indubitable equivalent of its secured claim. After all, it gets its collateral to do with what it pleases. So if PPI just hands over its plant and equipment to MSI, MSI has received the indubitable equivalent of its secured claim, and must accept the plan's treatment.

Some debtors have tried to combine the indubitable equivalent and the sales option. Their plans called for the sale of the property and the immediate transfer of the proceeds to the secured creditor. Since the claim was that the sale simply provided a market-based valuation of the collateral, it was contended that the secured creditor was receiving the indubitable equivalent of its claim. The benefit of this argument was that sub-paragraph (iii) does not mention credit bidding, and the sale could thus proceed without the brooding over presence of an undersecured secured creditor.

The Supreme Court put the kibosh on that. In *RadLAX Gateway Hotel, LLC v. Amalgamated Bank*[135], the Supreme Court resolved an important circuit split concerning the right of secured creditors to credit bid in cases under Chapter 11 of the Bankruptcy Code. It held that secured creditors may not be denied the right to credit bid at a sale of their collateral pursuant to a Chapter 11 plan of reorganization, even if the plan proposed to deliver the indubitable equivalent sales proceeds to the creditor.

Apart from the consensus that surrender of collateral is the indubitable equivalent of a secured claim, however, there is not much agreement. Some plans have tried "dirt for debt" plans in which only a part of the collateral is returned in satisfaction of part of the secured creditor's claim. Courts have nixed this, in large part

---

[134] The case was In re Murel Holding Corp., 75 F.2d 941 (2d Cir. 1935).
[135] 132 S. Ct. 2065 (2012).

because valuation of property without an arm's length sale rarely returns the "indubitable" equivalent of a sales price.

d. Fair and Equitable—The Effect of the Dreaded § 1111(b) Election

There is a complicating factor in any analysis of secured creditor cram down. It is the dreaded section 1111(b) election. What is that? First, some basics. We know from section 506(a) that if the value of collateral is less than the amount of debt it secures, the creditor has a right to a deficiency; that is, after it realizes on its collateral, it can file a claim against the debtor, as an unsecured creditor, for any debt left over.

Sometimes, however, a lender may make a loan which contains terms stating that the lender will not to pursue the debtor for a deficiency; that is, it will agree to look only to the collateral to satisfy its claim. This is called "non-recourse financing" from the fact that after foreclosure the lender has no recourse to the debtor for any deficiency. Not surprisingly, this type of financing occurs only when the lender believes that the collateral is worth more than the debt amount. But collateral values fall, and so lender's fortunes.

One thing that non-recourse lenders take into account is their ability to time a foreclosure. After all, it that is their sole source of recovery, so they should be able to orchestrate when the hammer falls. Bankruptcy and its sale rules upset this balance. The choices are reversed. In bankruptcy, the debtor determines when to sell, not the lender. If it chooses to sell at the bottom of the market, that harms the lender.

Congress had this mind when drafting the rules regarding secured creditors. It thus added section 1111(b)(1)(A) to the Code. This section gives non-recourse creditors a deficiency claim in bankruptcy when they would have none under nonbankruptcy law.

The only exception is if the lender elects otherwise (more soon), or if the property is sold under section 363 or under the plan. In the latter cases, the lender can protect itself by credit-bidding its claim, and taking title to the property, and selling it when the market turns.

So if Bank Ponoroff (BP) lends $1 million Markell's Messes (MM) on a non-recourse basis, BP will get a deficiency claim in MM's bankruptcy if the collateral is worth less than $1 million when MM files. Thus, without more, MM will have to contend with BP's unsecured deficiency claim as well as its secured claim.

But BP (as well as any secured creditor, not just non-recourse creditors) can elect to be treated differently. Under section 1111(b)(2), it can elect to opt out of section 506(a), and have its entire claim treated as secured, even if the collateral is worth less than the total amount of its claim. To take the above example, if the collateral securing BP's $1 million claim is worth only $800,000, and BP makes the election,[136] it will have a secured claim of $1 million, not $800,000.

This election is tempered somewhat by how section 1129(b)(2)(A) treats such claims. If BP makes the section 1111(b) election, then a plan proponent must give the lender property (which, recall, can be a secured note) equal in value to $800,000, the same as if the lender had not made the election and kept its deficiency. The difference the election makes is that the statute now requires that the post-confirmation lien on the property be for the full amount of the debt ($1 million in the example) and that the total payments under the crammed down loan equal the amount of the debt (again, $1 million).

---

[136] If lien is held by a class of secured creditors, as would be the case if the loan were syndicated and various lenders all contributed to the lion and each took a lien commensurate with its debt, the election is made only when two-thirds of the holders of the claims vote in favor of making the election.

How can that be? How can a note have a present value of $800,000 yet still require payments of $1 million? Courts have adopted two approaches. The first, and the one that is not the best, counts the interest paid along with the principal. So plan proponents stretch out the note's maturity so that at least $200,000 of interest is paid.

The second, and better, interpretation is that the debtor can give the creditor a note with a face amount of $1 million, but which only has a present value of $800,000—and the way to do that is to use a below-market rate of interest on the note. If the market rate of interest is, say, 10 percent, the plan proponent might propose that the $1 million note bear an interest rate of 4.9 percent. In a market in which the prevailing rate is 10 percent, such a note would have a present value of less than $1 million (which makes sense, since if you had a million, you'd invest at the market rate and get more money each month which would make the market-rate note more valuable). Actually, if you take a ten-year payout, the monthly payment would be the *same* under each note (the $800,000 note bearing 10% interest and the $1,000,000 note bearing 4.9% interest) —about $10,570. So structured, the plan proponent's projected cash flow is the same regardless of whether the note is for $800,000 at 10%, or $1 million at 4.9 percent. Sweet; well, except for the post-confirmation consequences outlined below.

So, by way of summary, what was the effect of the section 1111(b) election? Well, MM gets basically the same payment options as if BP's secured claim were equal to the collateral's value. BP loses its unsecured deficiency claim. But it gains a larger lien on the property post confirmation. That means if MM sells the property at any time after confirmation, BP will recover the full amount of its lien.

Take the above example. If market rates of interest are 10%, and if MM proposes a 10-year payout, the monthly payments for an

$800,000 claim would be about $10,500. If BP did not make the section 1111(b) election, BP would receive these payments along with whatever it is paid under the plan for its deficiency claim. If MM sells the property two years after confirmation, and the sales price is $1 million, MM pays off what remains of the $800,000 loan, and keeps the rest. Sweet.

If BP makes the section 1111(b) election, however, MM still gets to make mostly payments of $10,500—payments under 1129(b)(2)(A)(i) are keyed to the value of the collateral. BP gets nothing on its deficiency. But now when the property is sold in two years, BP will have a claim and lien equal to whatever is left on its original $1 million secured claim—the post confirmation increase in value in property will go to BP, not MM. Lenders like BP thus have to make a choice as to what is more valuable: a dividend on their deficiency, or the likely appreciation of the property before the debtor makes a sale. This approximates, so Congress thought, the bargain struck by a non-recourse lend outside of bankruptcy.

There are two exceptions to a creditor's right to make an election. First, if the lien is of inconsequential value, then the election cannot be made. If the value of the collateral is $1, and BP's claim is $1 million, then the collateral is of inconsequential value. Second, if the creditor has recourse, and the property is to be sold under section 363 or the plan, then the election cannot be made.

As a result, secured creditors tend to make the section 1111(b)(2) election when it looks like property values are appreciating and the likely appreciation will exceed the dividend on an unsecured claim.

e. Fair and Equitable—Cram Down of Unsecured Claims and the "Absolute Priority Rule" (§ 1129(b)(2)(B)(ii))

Embedded within the fair and equitable requirement is a rule some would say is the fundamental rule in Chapter 11: the absolute priority rule. Stating the rule is simple: no junior class may participate in a plan unless all senior classes consent or are paid in full. This extends to equity classes, and means that equity owners of an insolvent debtor cannot participate in any plan—because the debtor is insolvent, it will not have enough property to pay all creditors in full.

Cram down can be avoided if the senior class consents by voting to accept the plan. But if they do not, junior classes must be eliminated.

Recall that elimination of a class means that it is deemed to have rejected the plan. In that case, the debtor usually has to be valued to ensure that senior creditors are not being paid (in property or equity interests in the reorganized debtor) more than they are owed. That is why in most cram down plans the disclosure statement will also contain a valuation of the reorganized debtor—it is part of the showing that there is insufficient value to flow to junior classes.

Plans for insolvent debtors thus typically cancel existing equity interests and issue new equity interests (common stock in corporations, membership interests in limited liability companies) to the last class entitled to receive any value, typically the unsecured creditors.

Assume that PPI is worth $5 million on a going concern basis. PPI has a senior secured lender owed $4 million, and also has $3 million in unsecured debt. On these facts, no plan can be confirmed that keeps existing equity holders and which does not receive the vote of the unsecured creditor class. Instead, the senior secured creditor would agree to a deal (or be crammed down), and the creditors in the unsecured class would likely exchange their debt claims for all of the equity interests in the reorganized debtor.

There may be some hope for equity holders in insolvent companies. A corollary to the absolute priority rule indicates that if the equity holders contribute necessary new value (in money or money's worth) to the reorganized debtor, they can receive any interest equal in value to their contribution. For the other creditors, this leaves them in the same position as if a third party bought the assets; equity holders' cash is as green as a third-party purchaser's.

But there remains a suspicion of debtors. They control the debtor and initially control the plan process through exclusivity. There is concern that these equity holders could use this control to manipulate the reorganization process to their selfish ends. In *Bank of America National Trust & Savings Ass'n v. 203 North LaSalle Street Partnership*,[137] the Supreme Court held that if equity holders were to propose to bid on the equity in a new, reorganized debtor, they either had to relinquish the control of the plan process (through termination of exclusivity), or open up the process by which investors can contribute (allowing third parties to buy into the reorganized debtor on the same basis as existing equity).

f. Fair and Equitable—Cram Down of Equity Interests (§ 1129(b)(2)(C))

Debtors sometimes have complicated equity structures, with preferred stock and common stock. Section 1129(b)(2)(C) extends the fair and equitable rule to these pre bankruptcy priorities, and requires plans to respect those priorities.

---

[137] 526 U.S. 434 (1999).

E. Dismissal and Conversion (§ 1112)

All good things must come to an end. All bad things too. Chapter 11 cases are supposed to end by confirmation of a plan, but many don't. They end by conversion to a Chapter 7, or by dismissal. Both conversion and dismissal are governed by section 1112.

Section 1112 was revised in 2005 to be almost unintelligible. It essentially requires conversion or dismissal if one of sixteen types of cause, found in section 1112(b)(4), are present. These types of cause range from the obvious—continuing losses and the inability to confirm a plan—to the picayune—unexcused failure to meet a reporting requirement. Other important grounds for cause include the failure to follow a court order, the failure to follow cash collateral requirements that injure at least one creditor, failure to pay postpetition taxes, and failure to have insurance.

If cause is found, then the court must dismiss or convert the case, whichever is in the best interests of the creditors and the estate—UNLESS. Here's where it gets messy. The 'unless' kicks in if, after cause is shown, the debtor (or anyone else opposing conversion or dismissal) shows that: (i) "unusual circumstances" led to the "cause;" (ii) dismissal or conversion is not in the best interest of the creditors or the estate; (iii) the debtor is likely to confirm a plan within a reasonable time; and (iv) the debtor can offer a reasonable explanation for the existence of the cause (unless "cause" consists of continuing losses) and can offer to cure the "cause" within a reasonable time. All-in-all, a high standard, so best not to allow cause to exist in the first place.

Congress also required bankruptcy courts to hear such motions within 30 days of their filing, and to decide them within 15 days of the hearing on the motion. Whew.

F. Exotic Forms of Chapter 11

Chapter 11 has different rules for special types of debtors. Aside from railroads (which are not covered in basic bankruptcy courses), these include individuals (that is, flesh and blood humans), small businesses, and single asset real estate debtors.

1. *Individuals and Chapter 11*

Chapter 11 changed radically for individuals after the 2005 amendments. Congress did not want Chapter 11 to be a convenient escape hatch to the means test. So it changed some assumptions, and changed the confirmation requirements.

The most basic change is that Congress made was in Section 1115. Before 2005, Chapter 11 had the same rule as Chapter 7: postpetition wages were not property of the estate. Section 1115 changes this rule. Now, an individual debtor's postpetition earnings from services are property of the estate, just as they are in Chapter 13. This allows the wages to form the basis of a plan and to receive protection from the automatic stay.[138]

Confirmation requirements were also changed. To confirm a plan, an individual Chapter 11 debtor must be current on alimony and child support, as well as taxes.

But the biggest change was the importation into Chapter 11 of Chapter 13's disposable income test. Under section 1129(a)(15), upon the objection of an unsecured creditor, an individual Chapter 11 debtor has to commit his or her projected disposable income for the five years following confirmation to the plan. Paragraph (15) applies on a creditor-by-creditor basis, just as the best interest test

---

[138] It also raises interesting issues if the debtor converts to Chapter 7—the estate will lose all of the individual debtor's postpetition wages and they will revert to the debtor.

of section 1129(a)(7) does, so it matters little that the complaining unsecured creditor is a member of a class that accepts the plan.

To back this up, Congress also added section 1123(a)(8) to the Code to require individual debtors to commit their future earnings to the execution of the plan.

Finally, Congress also changed the date the discharge applies. Recall that in Chapter 11, the default rule is that the discharge is coextensive with plan confirmation. For individuals, however, Congress adopted the Chapter 13 rule in section 1141(d)(5) making discharge applicable only upon completion of plan payments. There are hardship rules as in Chapter 13, and a possibility of an earlier discharge "for cause" (which is unhelpfully left undefined), but for the most part individuals in Chapter 11 will not receive a discharge until the completion of the plan.

2. *Small Business Debtors*

The 2005 legislation also changed the rules for small businesses. Defined in section 101(51D), a small business debtor is a debtor which has less than (currently) $2,490,925 in noncontingent liquidated debts owing to noninsiders.

Small business debtors need to work harder that most debtors. They have enhanced reporting requirements in section 1116, and have different deadlines for exclusivity and plan confirmation.

Under section 1121(e), a small business debtor has 180 days of exclusivity, rather than the normal 120 days. Moreover, the plan and disclosure statement must be filed within 300 days of the filing date. Once filed, section 1129(e) requires confirmation to be within 45 days of the filing of any plan.

The consequences of failure to meet these deadlines is the creation of cause under section 1112(b), and the resultant likelihood of a motion to dismiss the case by a creditor or by the Office of the United States Trustee.

3.   *Single Asset Real Estate Debtors*

The 2005 legislation also affected single asset real estate. Section 101(51B) defines single asset real estate as a single property or project which generates all or substantially all of the debtor's gross income. There cannot be any substantial business being conducted on the property other than the operation of the real property.

As a result, owners of commercial buildings own single asset real estate if they act as landlords. Owners of golf courses, marinas, hotels and other businesses do *not,* so long as the debtor is providing services that such businesses typically provide clients of such establishments—such as restaurants at golf courses, boat cleaning services at marinas, room service in hotels.

The only provision in the Code that applies to single asset real estate is section 362(d)(3), relating to relief from stay. Section 362(d)(3) provides that, with respect to single asset real estate, the court must grant relief from stay unless the debtor files a reorganization plan that has a reasonable possibility of being confirmed within a reasonable time within the later of: (i) 90 days after the order for relief; (ii) such longer period as the court determines during the initial 90-day period; or (iii) 30 days after the court determines that the debtor is subject to the single asset real estate provisions.

Alternatively, the debtor can avoid relief from stay if it has commenced monthly payments equal to interest on the secured debt at the then-applicable non-default contract rate of interest on the value of a consensual lien creditor's interest in the property. The monthly payments can be made from rents or other cash collateral.

G. Discharge and Dischargeability (§ 1141)

Discharge in Chapter 11 occurs upon confirmation, unless the debtor is an individual. As with all other discharge provisions, the discharge affects all creditors, even if they voted against the plan or did not vote at all.

Discharge occurs in all cases, except in liquidation cases in which a nonindividual ceases to engage in business after confirmation.

Confirmation revests all property in the debtor, such that after confirmation the debtor is sometimes referred to as the "revested" debtor. Such property revests free of all liens and encumbrances, except as may be provided by the plan itself.

For individuals, all of the nondischargeability provisions of section 523 apply, with the deadline for filing such nondischargeable claims being the same as in Chapter 7 cases.

H. Post-Confirmation Issues

After confirmation, the revested debtor is free to conduct its business as it sees fit (or as specified in the plan). A confirmation order is a final order and can be appealed, and can be set aside, although special rules apply in each case.

1. Equitable Mootness

A plan proponent who successfully confirms a plan will want it to stick. No one wants to wait around to see if an appellate court will affirm or reverse; business must go on. To this end, some, but not all, courts have developed a doctrine of "equitable mootness." Under this doctrine, a court will not disturb a confirmation order, even if it is not moot under traditional measures, if consummation of the plan has caused third parties to rely on its provisions to their detriment, and reversing the transactions would be unduly complicated.

As a result, plan sponsors often rush to make all the transfers contemplated by the plan so that any appeal will be deemed equitably moot—sort of like scrambling the eggs so that no one can make the cook put the yolks back in shell.

2. Revocation of Confirmation

Finally, section 1144 allows a court to revoke confirmation, but only if it was obtained by fraud, and then only if the request is made within 180 days of the entry of the confirmation order. Congress shorted the time frames and reduced the grounds for attacking a confirmation order because it believe that it best that reorganization be final.

I. Review of Chapter 11

Chapter 11 exam questions tend to be fact intensive, and can be quite intimidating. But you can use the dense facts to your advantage.

First, identify what stage of the proceeding you are at. Is it the beginning of the case? If so, you will likely have cash collateral issues. You might also have debtor in possession financing issues as well.

Relief from stay issues are also a favorite here because section 362(d)(2) requires that the property subject to the relief from stay motion not be necessary for an effective reorganization. That requirement, in turn, will lead you discuss whether the debtor is a good (or bad) candidate for a successful reorganization. Even if the debtor has a good chance of reorganizing, you may also have to consider adequate protection issues here as well under section 362(d)(1).

In terms of the debtor's prospects for successful reorganization, you will need to examine the many confirmation requirements. With respect to these, focus first on the best interests of creditors test—your instructor will likely have given you enough financial information to determine if a creditor is receiving at least as much as they would receive in a Chapter 7 case (and is a sneaky way for an instructor to combine issues since you have to figure out not only if confirmation is possible, but also what would happen in a Chapter 7).

On the other confirmation issues, create a checklist to see if there is good faith, if administrative claims are being paid in full, if the plan is feasible, and so on.

If your fact pattern has numerous creditors, you are likely being asked to compute votes. Recall that you need more than half of the creditors actually voting, and those voting creditors must hold at least two-thirds of the claims voting in that class.

If your instructor is cruel, you will get cram down issues as well. Be stout of heart. You can get through these. Simply focus on the value of what is being offered to the dissenting creditor.

If the dissenting creditor is a secured creditor, compare what is being offered to the value of the collateral (and always recall that deficiency claims are unsecured claims, and that an undersecured creditor will have two claims under section 506(a): a secured claim equal to the collateral's value, and a deficiency unsecured claim). If the value of what is being offered is less than the collateral's value, and equity is retaining its interest, there cannot be a cram down.

If your instructor gives you numbers, focus on the interest rate being offered. If it is below market, then the secured creditor is likely receiving property less than the value of its claim. It it's above market, there may be a violation of the fair and equitable rule as to equity, in that the creditor will be paid more than what it is owed. And remember always to mention absolute priority somewhere in your answer; ideally, in a relevant place, but at least somewhere.

Always indicate that the consequence of a denial of a confirmation is likely to be conversion or dismissal.

Well, that's all folks; good luck!

Table of Cases